Europe and the Politics of Language

Palgrave Studies in Minority Languages and Communities

Titles include:

Máiréad Nic Craith
EUROPE AND THE POLITICS OF LANGUAGE
Citizens, migrants and outsiders

Glyn Williams
SUSTAINING LANGUAGE DIVERSITY IN EUROPE
Evidence from the Euromosaic project

Forthcoming titles:

Anne Judge
LANGUAGE POLICIES IN FRANCE AND BRITAIN

Vanessa Pupavac
LANGUAGE RIGHTS IN CONFLICT

Palgrave Studies in Minority Languages and Communities
Series Standing Order ISBN 1–4039–3732–X
(*outside North America only*)

You can receive future titles in this series as they are published by placing a standing order. Please contact your bookseller or, in case of difficulty, write to us at the address below with your name and address, the title of the series and the ISBN quoted above.

Customer Services Department, Macmillan Distribution Ltd, Houndmills, Basingstoke, Hampshire RG21 6XS, England

Europe and the Politics of Language

Citizens, Migrants and Outsiders

Máiréad Nic Craith

Academy for Irish Cultural Heritages
University of Ulster

palgrave
macmillan

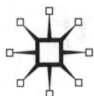

First published 2006 by
PALGRAVE MACMILLAN
Houndmills, Basingstoke, Hampshire RG21 6XS and
175 Fifth Avenue, New York, N.Y. 10010
Companies and representatives throughout the world

PALGRAVE MACMILLAN is the global academic imprint of the Palgrave
Macmillan division of St. Martin's Press, LLC and of Palgrave Macmillan Ltd.
Macmillan® is a registered trademark in the United States, United Kingdom
and other countries. Palgrave is a registered trademark in the European
Union and other countries.

ISBN-13: 978-1-4039-1833-8 hardback
ISBN-10: 1-4039-1833-3 hardback

This book is printed on paper suitable for recycling and made from fully
managed and sustained forest sources.

A catalogue record for this book is available from the British Library.

Library of Congress Cataloging-in-Publication Data
Nic Craith, Máiréad.
      Europe and the politics of language / Máiréad
      p.   cm. — (Palgrave studies in minority language and communities)
      Includes bibliographical references and index.
      ISBN 1-4039-1833-3 (cloth)
      1. Language policy—Europe.   2. Linguistic minorities—Europe.
      3. Europe—Languages—Political aspects.   I. Title.   II. Series.
      P119.32.E85N53 2005
      306.44'94—dc22   2005049300

10   9   8   7   6   5   4   3   2   1
15   14   13   12   11   10   09   08   07   06

Printed and bound in Great Britain by
Antony Rowe Ltd, Chippenham and Eastbourne

Contents

List of Tables

List of Maps

List of Abbreviations

AEBR	Assembly of European Border Regions
AERT	Autonomous European Region Tyrol
BSL	British Sign Language
CoE	Council of Europe
EBLUL	European Bureau for Lesser Used Languages
ECRML	European Charter for Regional or Minority Languages
EEA	European Economic Area
EEC	European Economic Community
ETA	Euskadi ta Askatasuna (The Basque Country and Freedom)
EU	European Union
GIDS	Graded Intergenerational Disruption Scale
MEP	Member of the European Parliament
NATO	North Atlantic Treaty Organisation
NGO	Non-Governmental Organisations
OSCE	Organisation for Security and Co-operation in Europe
UK	United Kingdom
UN	United Nations
UNESCO	United Nations Educational, Scientific and Cultural Organisation
USSR	Union of Soviet Socialist Republics

Acknowledgements

There are many individuals at the University of Ulster whom I should thank for their involvement in the preparation of this book. First I would like to thank Robert Welch, Dean of the Faculty of Arts at the University of Ulster for his continuing support for my research. Mary Delargy from the Academy for Irish Cultural Heritages and Koldo Iarrea from the School of Languages and Literature offered invaluable research assistance while Killian McDaid from the School of Environmental Sciences prepared the maps. Antony Alcock read the entire manuscript from beginning to end and sparked many an interesting discussion on different political points on Europe. The help of colleagues from other universities in reading individual chapters should also be noted: Helmut Daller, Gabrielle Hogan-Brun, Dónall Ó Riagáin, Colin Williams and Mark Wise.

Palgrave Macmillan has been entirely supportive of this project from the beginning. Jill Lake, the Commissioning Editor was particularly helpful in refining the focus of the book in the initial stages while the process of peer review identified many useful pointers for the final presentation. Gabrielle Hogan-Brun, the series editor has consistently supported interdisciplinary research in the field of language planning. I would also like to acknowledge the assistance of Satishna Gokuldas in preparing this text for publication.

Research in this book draws on visits and field work over a number of years to places such as Bozen/Bolzano, Galicia, Kashubia, Lusatia, Schleswig-Holstein and Trentino-Süd-Tyrol. In the past 2 years I have been in contact with many cultural and linguistic organisations with queries on aspects of their respective language communities. I would like to acknowledge the help of the following in particular: Markus Warasin, University of Innsbrück; Miquel Strubell Trueta, Universitat Oberta de Catalunya and Marina Solís, Directorate General for Language Policy, Government of Catalonia; Deirdre Davitt, Seosamh Mac Donncha and Leachlain Ó Catháin from Foras na Gaeilge, Dublin; Neasa Ní Chinnéide and Peadar Ó Flatharta, EBLUL; Tom Moring, University of Helsinki; Domino Kal, Roma Cultural Centre, Sweden; Rolf Olsen, Sámi Parliament, Norway; Sigrid Stångberg and Kjell Herberts on Sámi languages; Teresa Condeco, Language Policy Unit, DG for Education and Culture, European Commission; Ilmars Mezs, International Organization for Migration,

Riga; Mark Rannut, Tallinn Pedagogical University on Baltic languages; Karen Scriven, Sai Pak Community Centre, Northern Ireland and Daniel Holder, Multicultural Resource Centre, Northern Ireland.

On a personal level, I would like to thank those individuals who encouraged my interest in languages and more importantly in the people who speak them. These include my parents Thomas and Máiréad who encouraged bilingualism in our home and Seán Ó Coileáin, National University of Ireland, Cork, who supervised my PhD thesis on Anglicisation and cultural change. My husband Ullrich Kockel furthered my interest in language status and bilingual contexts – although in this instance the focus was on German rather than Irish.

This is a book about language communities and the politics they engage in and very often this occurs at a subconscious rather than an overt level. The primary aim of the work is to call for a much more intensive commitment on the part of universities to the study of language planning at an academic level. All languages are equal. Yet some have very privileged positions in contemporary society while others are in rapid decline. Such hierarchies are a consequence of intensive policies and planning rather than any inherent quality in the languages themselves. In understanding the process of language politics we may be able to reverse many inequalities and generate greater respect for the potential of all rather than a limited number of languages. Ultimately the aim is to improve the linguistic context particularly in minority and immigrant language situations for the people who speak and wish to live in such languages.

Series Editor's Preface

Worldwide migration and unprecedented economic, political and social integration in Europe present serious challenges to the nature and position of language minorities. Some communities enjoy protective legislation and active support from states through policies that promote and sustain cultural and linguistic diversity; others succumb to global homogenisation and assimilation. At the same time, discourses on diversity and emancipation have produced greater demands for the management of difference.

This book series has been designed to bring together different strands of work on minority languages in regions with immigrant or traditional minorities or with shifting borders. We give prominence to case studies of particular language groups or varieties, focusing on their vitality, status and prospects within and beyond their communities. Considering this insider picture from a broader perspective, the series explores the effectiveness, desirability and viability of worldwide initiatives at various levels of policy and planning to promote cultural and linguistic pluralism. Thus it touches on cross-theme issues of citizenship, social inclusion and exclusion, empowerment and mutual tolerance.

Work in the above areas is drawn together in this series to provide books that are interdisciplinary and international in scope, considering a wide range of minority contexts. Furthermore, by combining single and comparative case studies that provide in-depth analyses of particular aspects of the socio-political and cultural contexts in which languages are used, we intend to take significant steps towards the fusing of theoretical and practical discourses on linguistic and cultural heterogeneity.

Gabrielle Hogan-Brun
University of Bristol

1
Europe: Discourses of Inclusion/ Exclusion

The concept of Europe typically generates a geographical response. The central continental core has peninsulas in all directions – Spain to the west, Italy to the south, the Balkans to the east and Scandinavia to the north. Geographically Europe also extends to the islands of Ireland, Britain, Corsica, Sardinia and Sicily. Surrounding seas form part of geographical Europe. The Mediterranean Basin along with its subsidiary seas lies to the south of Europe, while the Adriatic, the Aegean and the Black Sea are in the east. The Baltic Seas form part of Northern Europe and the Atlantic Ocean marks its Western boundary.

One difficulty in examining the geographical concept of Europe rests in the matter of borders. Does one include Russia to the east or Iceland, which is a member of the European Free Trade Association (EFTA)? A particularly pertinent question in the context of a currently expanding European Union (EU) is the matter of Turkey. Although its land mass is overwhelmingly in Asia, Turkey is a long-standing member of the North Atlantic Treaty Organisation (NATO) which has been a crucial component of Europe's defences. It is also a member of the Council of Europe (CoE) and has adapted many Western European legal practices. Moreover, it has long aspired to membership of the EU. In December 2004, the EU agreed to begin accession talks with Turkey.

The lack of clarity in Europe's geography is not confined to its boundaries but extends to conceptual divisions within the continent. The decline of communism has served as the catalyst for the fragmentation of Eastern Europe in particular and that concept has become increasingly blurred. It now appears that there could be a threefold division between East Central, the Balkans and Eastern Europe 'proper' (i.e. Belarus, Ukraine and Russia) (Burgess 1997: 23). Perhaps the Balkans should be regarded as the 'Real East' as they are east of Poland which is sometimes located in Central and sometimes in Eastern Europe. According to the logic of their own joke, the Poles no longer exist as they are in a country that is 'East of the West' and 'West of the East' – although in common with many of their Eastern neighbours, they wish to be perceived as an integral part of Western Europe. And what about Armenia and Georgia – Christian states once part of the Byzantine Empire?

The chapter explores changing definitions of Europe in a historical and contemporary setting. Regardless of its spatial limits, changing concepts of Europe inevitably impact upon European discourses of inclusion although some groups such as non-European migrants and Muslims have generally been excluded from the terms of reference of a 'European culture' or 'identity'. Even those regarded as 'insiders' have hardly been treated in an equal manner and the languages and cultures of those deemed to belong in and to Europe are ranged in a hierarchical manner in various European institutions. This first chapter explores the social and political European context for such categorisations, which underpin the remainder of the book.

Conceptions of Europe

It has always been difficult to determine precisely where Europe is and perhaps this is because Europe is more a conceptual than a spatial entity. Long before the emergence of Benedict Anderson's notion of 'imagined community' (1983), it had become fashionable to conceive of Europe in terms of an 'imagined space' (Said 1978). In spatial terms Europe has frequently been defined in terms of one's own position on the continent and perceptions of Europe have varied considerably from one geographical location to another (Malmborg and Stråth 2002).

From the traditional Danish perspective, for example, Europe was located between their Southern border and the Dolomites, whereas the English viewed it 'as the mystical, mythical frontier of civilisation beyond the trans-Channel homeland of their one-time colonisers' (Kockel 2003: 53). As both England and Denmark are located on the periphery they often refer to Europe as though it were foreign territory (cf. Ludlow 2002). Russians have always been aware of Europe on their doorstep 'over one of their cultural shoulders'. The German and French perspective on Europe has been tempered by centuries of bloody conflict. For them 'Europe could be just about anywhere they could live peacefully alongside one another' (Kockel 2003: 53).

Generally speaking, the concept of Europe is assumed to have historical as well as current relevance and contemporary European values appear to 'draw on centuries of tradition and shared heritage among the peoples of Europe, or at least their dynastic rulers, scholars, ecclesiastics, artists and traders' (Phillipson 2003: 29). The historiography of the EU, in particular, represents European history in a progressive linear fashion in which contemporary European identity 'is portrayed as a kind of moral success story: the end product of a progressive ascent through history' (Shore 2000: 57).

The origins of Europe are usually located in Greek mythology (Tsoukalas 2002). The original Europa was the daughter of Agenor who was King of Tyre. The God Zeus fell in love with her. Transformed into the shape of a bull, he abducted her and swam with her on his back to the island of Crete. This image has been termed both 'resonant and ambiguous'. On the one hand it locates the origins of Europe in an act of molestation 'hinting at a dark and barbaric energy that has been at play in this territory ever since'. On the other hand it serves to remind us that Europe derives from elsewhere in the East, 'that its vigour has always lain in its ability to adopt and adapt, to pour into its deep pool of resources an endless stream of elements borrowed from elsewhere' (O'Toole 2004: 1).

In common with many other theories of ethnogenesis, this tradition is an invention from the nineteenth century when George Grote, a banker and historian, proposed that European civilisation had its roots in Greek democracy. 'Laying claim to a democratic tradition rooted in the past is often unlikely to be the product of new historical evidence' (Burgess 1997: 66). Instead it served as an endorsement or reinforcement of the concept of democracy.

Europe's history is usually presented as a series of stages from Greek civilisation to the present day and the emergence of the Roman Empire is regarded as a crucial element of that historical narrative. Roman culture contrasted strongly with that of the Greeks. While the latter enjoyed elegant theatrical athletics, Roman entertainment was more bloodthirsty. Following the conquest of Greece, Romans learnt the Greek language. The first poets to record their work in Latin 'wrote in the Greek epic genre about Roman history and heroes and translated Greek plays for the Roman stage' (Crawley Quinn 2002: 72).

Between the first century BC and the middle of the fourth century AD, the Roman Empire expanded rapidly and at one stage included all territories around the Mediterranean (Map 1.1). The reign of Marcus Aurelius is traditionally regarded as the high point of the Roman Empire. At the zenith of its power the boundaries of the Roman Empire stretched from Scotland in the north to the Sahara in the south and from Gibraltar in the west to the Euphrates in the east. Many major

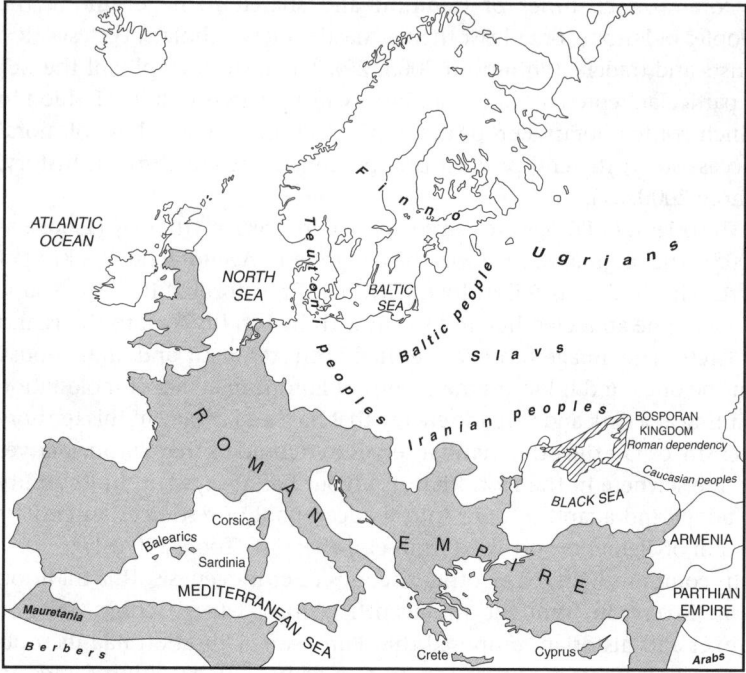

Map 1.1 Roman Empire. *Source*: Adapted from Cussans *et al.* (1998).

modern cities had already emerged as centres of Roman administration – Londinium (London), Lutetia (Paris), Vindobona (Vienna) and Serdica (Sofia). Peoples in these territories worked as slaves or soldiers in Roman legions and their citizenship was categorised as Roman – a notion that was based upon the city itself but applied to the Empire as a whole. Citizenship provided equality for all individuals but Jews, Armenians, Gauls and others were still seen as Jews, Armenians, Gauls and others.

By the fourth century AD, the Roman Empire had begun to decline and the struggle to exclude the peoples to the North and East became impossible. 'Barbarian' tribes, primarily of Germanic origin, were gradually admitted to the territories of the Empire where they proved their worth as mercenaries or allies against other groups. As these barbarians gradually adopted the administrative system and the Christian religion of their host society, the distinction between Roman and non-Roman began to diminish.

At the end of the fourth century AD, the Empire split into separate Eastern and Western parts, each with their respective emperor. By AD 565, the Western Empire had disintegrated and strong bases were established by the Franks and Visigoths in lands that would subsequently become France and Spain. Many of the Roman customs persisted in these territories and Latin continued to function as the language of religion, eventually evolving into the individual Romance vernaculars with which we are familiar today – French, Italian, Spanish and Portuguese.

The Eastern or Byzantine civilisation differed from the Western in many important dimensions. Of great significance in the Eastern division was the tendency towards fusion of Church and State, where the emperor and patriarch were regarded as two partner elements of divine authority. 'In the East the Emperor was considered the living image of Christ and he was head of the Church.' Constantine was regarded as God's chosen deputy. 'The imperial power was seen as the earthly reflection of God's heavenly power' (Alcock 1998: 43). (This relationship is not unlike contemporary Britain where the monarch is also head of the established religion.)

The most significant moment in the development of concepts of separate Western and Eastern divisions occurred on Christmas Day AD 800, when Charlemagne was crowned emperor in the West by Pope Leo III in Rome. This action was perceived in Constantinople as a usurpation of the imperial power which belonged solely to the Byzantine Emperor and relations between the West and East declined dramatically. On his death in AD 814, the Frankish rule Charlemagne left his descendants a vast territory, comprising most of Western Europe with the exception of the Iberian Peninsula (Map 1.2).

The significance of religion in early East–West relations generated an association between Europe's history and Christianity. A subsequent challenge from the Ottoman Empire confirmed Europe's Christian character (Burgess 1997: 69). However, Europe's Christian space which already had been shattered by conflicts between Eastern and Western Churches was further devastated by the Wars of Religion in the second half of the sixteenth century. This was an age which brought 'a new and murderous intensity' to religious conflicts within Europe. In particular the rise of Calvinism and the emergence of a Catholic counter-reformation 'brought two strong and mutually incompatible faiths into conflict' (Pettegree 2002: 219). For the next 40 years, Northern and Western Europe was plunged into turmoil which culminated in the massacres of Paris and Amsterdam before peace was restored. The Edict of Nantes in 1598 heralded the conclusion of French civil wars but religious conflict

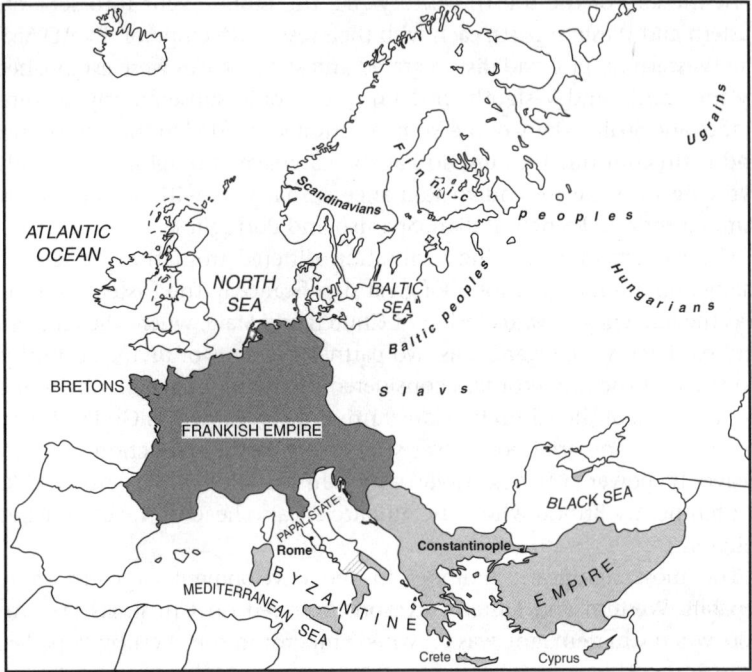

Map 1.2   Frankish Empire. *Source*: Adapted from Cussans *et al.* (1998).

in Europe was hardly at an end. The Thirty Years War (1618–48) between Catholics and Protestants involved almost every European power and was prolonged by conflicts between the Dutch Republic and Spain, France and Spain and between the Baltic powers. The Peace of West-phalia in 1648 marked a major point because it 'signified a concerted attempt to create conditions for long-term peace in Central Europe' (Stevenson 2002: 243).

An Age of Absolutism and Enlightenment followed the national and international conflicts of the sixteenth and seventeenth centuries and a more secular bias emerged in post-Revolution France (Frank 2002). The slogan 'Liberty, Equality, Fraternity' which dominated the French Revolution of 1789 continued to be an inspiration in the decades that followed. The *Declaration of the Rights of Man* pronounced the personal worth of each individual citizen and implied justice and equality for all. The notion of a shared European civility became acceptable 'as a standard of demeanour from London to Prague' and upper echelons of societies across Europe believed themselves to participate in a common European civility (Hale 1993: 54). Secular norms were deemed more appropriate for a progressive society than traditional Christian values and the concept of Europe became increasingly material rather than spiritual and associated with power and superiority.

By the end of the eighteenth century, Europe's boundaries were no longer coterminous with Christendom although Christianity was still a significant characteristic for many Europeans (Burgess 1997: 70). While one can hardly speak of a single Christian tradition when examining the concept of Europe, it became strongly associated with Roman Catholicism – a fact which may explain the contemporary pro-European stance in a Catholic Italy (Malmborg 2002). In the case of Germany, visions of Europe in the nineteenth century were often contradictory and state boundaries incorporated divisions between a Protestant North and a Catholic South (Spohn 2002). The negativity associated with Roman Catholicism gained a new relevance in the twentieth century with the rise of dictators such as Hitler and Stalin. In Sweden, Europe was equated with Catholicism and both were perceived as a threat (Stråth 2002).

At the turn of the twenty-first century the concept of Europe has frequently become confused with that of the EU and the term 'Europe' is often used as shorthand in the media when journalists make references to EU administrative and political decision-making bodies (Phillipson 2003: 29). This is despite the fact that the two are not coterminous and many states such as Switzerland and Norway form part of historical, geographical Europe but have no representation in the 'European Parliament'.

Divergence and divisions

In common with other identities, the notion 'European' is a social organisation of cultural difference and the essence of 'European identity' emphasises the boundary between insiders and outsiders which is a major theme of this book. Throughout the history of the continent, one can identify discourses of exclusion which were applied to those who were deemed not quite to belong to the European Club although they lived within its geographical boundaries.

The ancient Greeks, for example, identified the migrant *Keltoi* or Celts as barbarian neighbours in Europe and did not really perceive of them as part of civilised European society. 'Greece passed on to the Romans its view of the shape of the world, which like that of other civilizations saw itself as the ordered centre of the universe, while others were seen as peripheral, strange and inferior' (James 1999: 52). In a sense the notion of Celticity was an early strategy of exclusion of those who were not considered part of the Greek heartland.

A binary division emerged in the Middle Ages with the split between Western and Eastern Empires in Europe. This 'otherness' derived as much from religion as from location. While the Eastern Empire was associated with Orthodox religion, the Western Empire was strongly dominated by Roman Catholicism. A significant moment in this development occurred when Christianity received its first major boost at the hands of the Emperor Constantine. In AD 313 Constantine promulgated the Edict of Milan which prohibited the persecution of any form of monotheism. In AD 330 the Emperor inaugurated Constantinople (formerly Byzantium) as his imperial capital. However, it is important to note that Constantine himself did not actually declare Christianity as the official religion of the Roman Empire. Instead 'he wanted to rule his Empire in peace and if Christians were now very numerous, there was no reason to offend those, still in the majority, who were not' (Alcock 1998: 40).

Although Constantine succeeded in reuniting a fragmenting Roman Empire, his establishment of a new capital in the east consolidated an already existing tendency for the Empire to split into Eastern and Western divisions which subsequently developed as separate entities. This cleft had an inevitable impact on Christianity in Europe and over time the Western division became known as the Roman Catholic Church, deriving its legitimacy from the Pope. The Eastern part evolved into the Orthodox Church under the rule of its patriarchs, of whom the Patriarch of Constantinople was the most important (Shaw 1998: 125).

Although the Southern states of Baltic were colonised by the Teutonic Knights who owed their loyalty to Rome rather than Constantinople, the final split between Eastern and Western Churches came in AD 1054. This division consolidated the division between Latin and Orthodox Europe and introduced an East–West cultural boundary from the Baltic to the Eastern Mediterranean (Map 1.3).

However, both Eastern and Western Empires were aware of the challenge from Islam. In the early seventh century, the Arabs had been engaged in a hugely successful campaign to spread the new religion of Islam. As well as occupying Palestine, Mesopotamia, Syria and Egypt, the combined military force drove right across North Africa and moved northwards up into Spain. In AD 711 a small Moorish group crossed the Strait of Gibraltar. By AD 716 virtually all the Iberian Peninsula was in Muslim

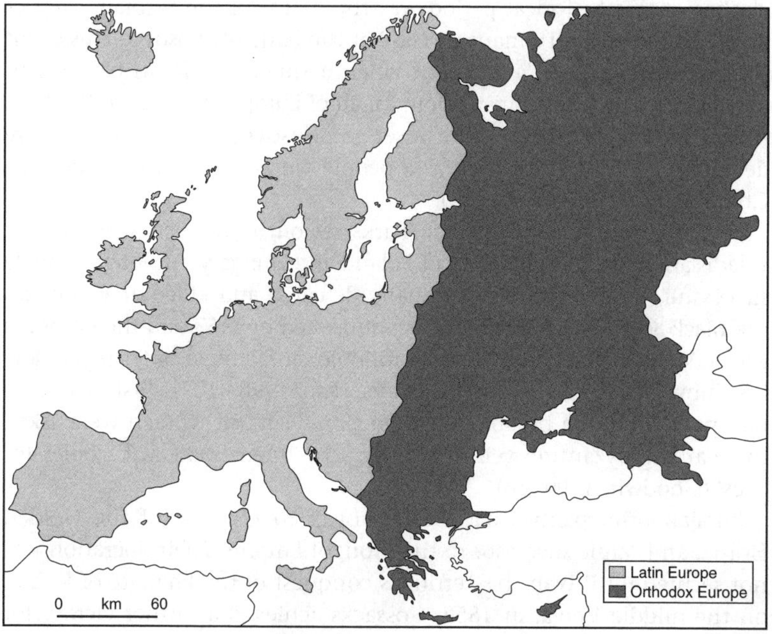

Map 1.3 Latin/Orthodox Europe. *Source*: Adapted from Kockel (1999).

hands. The Arabs were also asserting themselves into a maritime power in the Mediterranean, though by the early ninth century, the beginning of a Christian re-conquest in Northern Spain and Portugal was evident.

The impact of Islam was also felt in the East where it was resisted in several locations. In Russia, for example, the tsar Volodymyr came to the throne in AD 980. He chose Christianity rather than Islam for his people. With this action 'Volodymyr cast Russia's ambitions for ever in Europe rather than Asia, and by taking Christianity from Byzantium rather than Rome he bound the future Russians, Ukrainians and Belorussians together in Orthodoxy, fatally dividing them from their Catholic neighbours, the Poles' (Reid 1997: 8).

For a time the Ottoman Empire was the strongest military power in Europe, Western Asia and North Africa. In 1354 the Muslim Turkish State had captured Gallipoli. Expansion continued into Thrace and South towards the Mediterranean. The Ottomans continued their push forwards into the Balkans. In 1385 they captured Sofia. Three years later, Bulgaria was obliged to accept Ottoman overlordship. One of the most renowned clashes of this historical period was the defeat of the Serbian army of King Lazar by the Ottomans in 1389 at the battle of Kosovo. This event is commemorated as 'a moment when a small people, in battle with mortal foes, defended Christendom for all of Europe' (Ignatieff 1994: 169). Although the Serbs were the losers at Kosovo, the Serbian culture developed a concept of itself as a people who heroically defended the Christian faith (Ignatieff 1994).

In 1443 a crusade against the Turks set out under the leadership of Wladislaw 1, the Catholic King of Poland and Hungary. Although initially successful, Wladislaw was eventually defeated and killed at Venice on the Black Sea. Turkish advances recommenced in 1453 and the Ottoman leader Mehmet II captured Constantinople, 'inflicting a bitter psychological blow on Christendom' (Cussans *et al.* 1998: 107). 'Asia came to Europe, the church became a mosque; and Turkish women were asked to wear the Byzantine veil in place of the linen hood, with holes for eyes' (Goodwin 1999: 46).

Russian principalities had been subject to the rule of the Golden Horde, an Islamic successor to the Mongol Empire. Their liberation was not secured until Ivan the Terrible's conquest of the khanate of Kazan, on the middle Volga, in 1552. Cossacks achieved a further victory for Russia and for Christendom when they routed an Ottoman garrison on the Don delta in 1637. In this instance horsemen from the steppes of Russia defeated the non-Christian enemy within the city walls. A siege of three days was necessary before the Islamic enemy was finally defeated.

Turkish influence in Central and Western Europe gradually declined. Although Muslims had controlled Spain for most of 800 years, their power had been restricted to the region of Granada in the south of the country by the time of the accession of the Catholic Queen Isabella to the throne of Castille in 1474. Following her expulsion of the Jewish population during the Spanish inquisition, Isabella turned her attention to the Muslims in the South. After a 10-year war, the city of Granada surrendered in 1492 to Isabella's army. An unknown number of Muslims were subsequently expelled from the country. Those who chose to remain rather than emigrate lived for the most part in agricultural areas in the south of Granada or in Valencia and Aragon. 'Persecuted by the Inquisition, in 1521 the Moriscos, "little Moors" as they were then called, were forced to convert en masses to Christianity and banned from reading or writing Arabic' (Webster 2005: 85).

However, Muslim influence in Europe was hardly at an end. The Turks reached Vienna in 1529. (This was the high point of their advance into Europe.) Although they were later to return with reinforcements, the

Cossacks had gained an initial victory against them and basked in the glory of Christian success. Later in the century in 1683 the Catholic Polish King John Sobieski relieved the city of Vienna from the onslaught of Turks in 1683, 'although Poles ended up looking so oriental' that Sobieski ordered his troops 'to wear straw cockades so as to distinguish them from the enemy Turks' (Reid 1997: 28). His actions curtailed the threatened Muslim expansion into Central Europe and contributed to the Polish self-image as the 'eastward bastion (*przedmurze*) of Christendom' (Ascherson 1996: 168).

Following the decline of Turkish influence in Europe, and the emergence of the Enlightenment, nationalist thinking came to the fore. Many nation states established their political boundaries in the period 1849–1914. Pressure from the nationalist movement in the Italian peninsula helped to shape the march towards a nation state and the aspirations of Italian nationalists focused on one liberal Italian monarchy which was achieved in 1859. Subsequently Bismark transformed a German confederation of loose states into the German Empire. Following the Revolution of 1848 in France, Napoleon galvanised support to become elected president of the Second Republic. He embarked on a mission to make his own authority absolute.

Victorian Britain became one of Europe's leading industrial nations at this time and was one of the first modern industrial societies. Imperial Germany also underwent a period of phenomenal industrial expansion. When Alexander III became the tsar in 1881, Russia initially enjoyed some impressive state-driven economic expansion, but following a period of strife and revolution, Russia was falling behind its rivals. Eastern Europe came to be regarded as a barbarian region where manners were hardly as civilised as the West although still considerably better that those of Asia. It 'emerges as a kind of halfway house on the ascent to civilization with Western Europe basking in sunlight at the peak...and Asia and other parts of the world in the gloom of the valley' (Shaw 1998: 124–5).

One of the more decisive events of twentieth-century Europe was the Second World War which divided Europe into democracy versus communism – between Western Europe and those countries whose economies were centrally planned on a Soviet model. However, one can not be entirely simplistic about this as Czechoslovakia, Hungary and two-thirds of Poland 'belonged' to Western Europe in the eighteenth and nineteenth centuries and up until 1939 since they were either integral parts of the German and/or Austro-Hungarian empires or independent after 1918. They certainly saw themselves as part of the 'Western' polity of nations, being Catholic rather than Orthodox, which was the previous 'Iron Curtain' distinction. Slovenia and Croatia were also part of the (Western) Austrian empire. One might also add that Hungary was seen as a bastion of Western civilisation – and Catholicism – until its destruction by the Turks at the battle of Mohács in 1526!

The map of Europe following the Second World War did not superficially look very different to that of interwar Europe. The Baltic States, Estonia, Latvia and Lithuania were now incorporated into Soviet territory but the Central European States remained, with Poland winning territories in the west from Germany in compensation for those it lost in the east, to the Union of Soviet Socialist Republics (USSR). The separate existence of Poland, Czechoslovakia and Hungary did not, however, involve any real independence. Britain and the US had agreed at Yalta and Potsdam conferences that Central and Eastern Europe should be in the Soviet 'sphere of influence' which included the seven European members of the Soviet bloc – namely Bulgaria, Czechoslovakia, the German Democratic Republic, Hungary, Poland and Romania as well as the USSR itself. It also included Yugoslavia and Albania, which had adopted Communist systems. As Greece did not become communist it was generally not associated with these communist countries although it was located in the same region (Shaw 1998: 122–4).

This opposition between Western and communist Europe was reinforced with the establishment of the European Coal and Steel Community in 1951 involving six Western countries namely Belgium, France, Germany, Italy, Luxemburg and the Netherlands. Six years later the Treaties of Rome established the European Economic Community (the EEC or Common Market). Many of the prominent figures in the drive towards post-war European integration were Catholic. Konrad Adenaur, Jacques Delors, Alcide de Gasperi and Robert Schuman had strong convictions of religious and cultural ties between their fellow Europeans. The EEC has undergone several periods of expansion in the decades that followed. Britain, Denmark and Ireland joined in 1973 and Greece became a member in 1981. Five years later, Spain and Portugal signalled their rejection of a dictatorship past with their entry into the Community. In 1995 Austria, Finland and Sweden joined.

During the decades that followed there was a notion that the further East in Europe one ventured, the more 'backward' society became (Burgess 1997: 47). Gregory Campbell (1975: 247) points to the example of a British Minister in Prague who asked whether we could

> get back to the state of affairs in which the Slovaks return to their natural job of scrubbing windows, the Romanians are confined to

the exercise of their only national industry . . . the Poles are restricted to piano playing and the white slave traffic, and the Serbs are controlled in their great national activity – organising political murders on foreign territory.

Since the fall of Communism, former members of the Soviet Bloc have endeavoured to escape from this categorisation of 'Eastern European', thereby achieving greater inclusion within the broader European context and there has been some recognition of diversity. One consequence of this has been vague subdivisions of the region into three: the Balkans, East-Central Europe (the Czech Republic, Poland, Hungary and Slovakia) and the states of the former Soviet Union, but such categorisations are not without difficulties (Shaw 1998: 124). Ultimately the concept of 'Eastern' like that of 'Europe' itself has hardly a precise geographical meaning. Instead it has been used 'to refer to sections of Europe not considered 100 per cent European' (Burgess 1997: 63).

Inclusion/exclusion and citizenship

Many former communist countries applied for membership of the EU in the final decade of the twentieth century and the way for enlargement was paved in 2000 with the passing of the Nice Treaty. The year 2004 became a year of tremendous significance in the story of EU enlargement when 10 new countries joined the Union. These included the three Baltic States – Estonia, Latvia and Lithuania (which will feature strongly in the next chapter) – and other countries which have emerged from the former Iron Curtain such as the Czech Republic, Hungary, Poland and Slovakia (Map 1.4). The islands of Cyprus and Malta also entered the Union at this time along with Slovenia, a member of the Former Federation of Yugoslavia. (The impact of this phase of enlargement on language policy in Europe will be investigated in Chapter 3).

With the accession of many of these countries to the EU, they feel that they can no longer be perceived as outsiders. This sentiment is reflected in the statement in 2004 by Miklós Dérer, a national security expert in Budapest concerning Hungary's membership of both NATO and the EU: 'Our yes vote means that we've made a choice to be Europeans, not Eastern Europeans. It means the end of ambiguity' (Belt 2004: 63).

Nationals in these Eastern European countries automatically acquired EU citizenship with entry to the Union. The origins of the modern conception of citizenship in Europe are usually located in the French

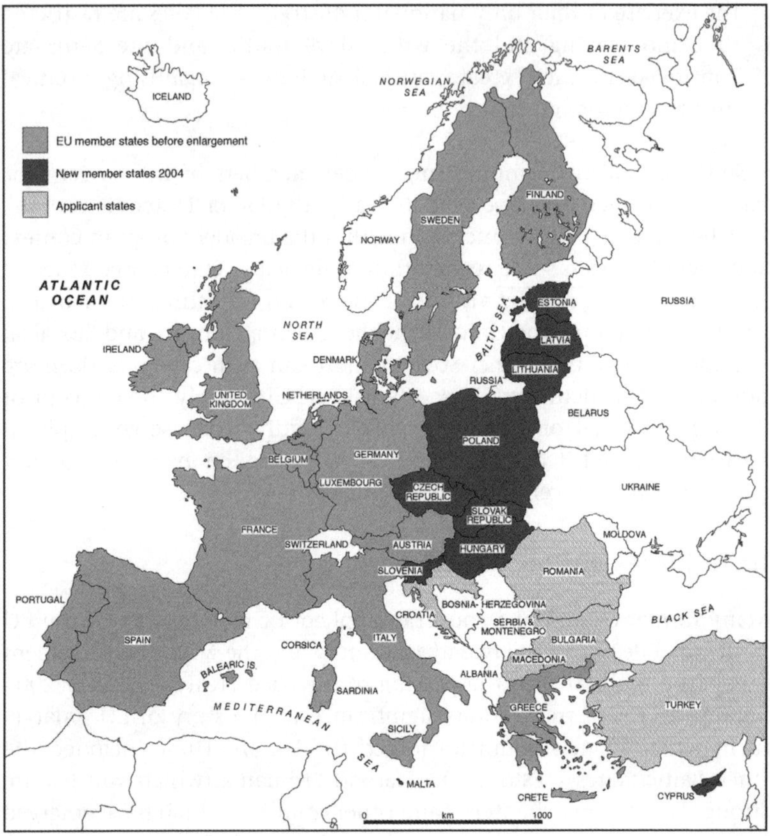

Map 1.4   European Union.

Revolution in 1789. At the heart of this movement was a new conception of citizenship as an active and radical process – one which emphasised the universal and egalitarian potential of each person. Emphasis was placed on the individual and rights would reside in citizens rather than in minorities or specific groups. The French Revolution in 1789 is often viewed as an event in a process which asserted the primacy of citizenship over culture and of universalism over specificity. France is regarded as a prime illustration of an approach to social membership, which is political more than cultural.

However, within the Union, there are different citizenship laws. Germany embraced the notion of ethnicity when it established the ethnic basis of citizenship in 1913. For decades to come, the acquisition of German citizenship was solely dependent on genetic factors rather than on German culture which was actually of limited importance in defining members of the imagined community. Although there were some millions of Turks living in Germany, these were effectively prevented from acquiring German citizenship. Second- and third-generation Turks who adapted to German cultures and spoke perfectly fluent German and lived in Germany were still considered *Ausländer* (Outsiders). In the case of Germany and many other countries in Europe there was an expectation that migrants would return home after satisfying their needs in the labour market. Hence there was little need for them to acquire citizenship and 'it used to be extremely difficult for Turkish migrants to obtain the status of citizenship even after living there for two or more generations' (Dunkerley *et al.* 2002: 18).

But recent events have indicated some changes in the emphasis on bloodline. In May 1999 the German Parliament opted to revise their traditional citizenship policies and the new law offers automatic citizenship rights to immigrant children born on German soil. These individuals are permitted to retain two passports until the age of 23, when they must choose their preferred option (Kivisto 2002: 169). However, this concession applies only to the children of immigrants and does not alter the non-citizenship status of their parents. Overall it appears that there are millions of legal residents in Germany and throughout the EU as a whole without citizenship status. This has implications at both national and international levels.

Transnational citizenship of the EU is a relatively recent phenomenon and is only available to those who have already acquired citizenship at national levels. The process was possibly sparked by a report in 1975 by the Belgian Prime Minister Leo Tindemans which suggested that Europe should become closer to its citizens. In the decade that followed two further reports of an *ad hoc* committee chaired by Pietro Adonnino suggested a series of practical measures for greater freedom of movement and citizens' rights within the EEC (Shore and Black 1994: 285). At the 1990 inter-governmental conference, Felipe Gonzales proposed to introduce the notion of 'European citizenship' in the new European treaty.

The EU citizenship was formally introduced with the revised Treaty on European Union, which was signed in Maastricht on 7 February 1992 and replaced the old European Community with the EU. Article 8 inserted the notion of 'Citizenship of the Union' into the Treaty and proposed that a citizen of any member state automatically became a citizen of the EU. It conferred obligatory freedoms of goods, persons, services and capital on these citizens. Article 8a granted citizens 'the right to move and reside freely within the territory of any Member State'.

The emergence of an EU citizenship might appear to herald the development of a post-national form of citizenship, but this is not the case as nationality of an EU member state is a precondition of EU citizenship. Article 8 of the Treaty of Amsterdam also affirms that 'Every person holding the nationality of a Member State shall be a citizen of the Union'. It also asserts that 'Citizenship of the Union shall complement and not replace national citizenship.'

This effectively reinforces the traditional construction of citizenship which was centred on principles of nationality and statehood and assumes a dominant, majority culture in a national context which prevails in many of Europe's political and social structures. It has also led to the creation of a group of second-class citizens and non-citizens who were automatically excluded from certain basic rights. 'European citizenship, within the limits of the currently existing union, is not conceived of as a recognition of the rights and contributions of *all* the communities present upon European soil, but as a postcolonial isolation of "native" and "non-native population"' (Balibar 2004: 170, italics in original).

Balibar (2004: 171) takes this argument further and argues that EU citizenship with its basis on national citizenship transforms and damages the status of the non-citizen. '*In each particular country*, the foreigner is only the national of another member state, enjoying equivalent "belonging" which is the object of reciprocal recognition.' In contrast 'at the level of the *newly instituted union*, he or she becomes an object of an internal exclusion' (italics original).

From his perspective, citizenship of the EU which was designed as a process of inclusion has become one of damaging exclusion. It becomes the mechanism which 'includes some of the populations historically present in the space of the community while rejecting others, most of which are long established and contribute equally to the development of the civil society of the organism' (Balibar 2004: 171).

Overall, European citizenship makes no concessions to migrants (Islamic or Christian) who are not already citizens of member states and the question of integrating rather than assimilating immigrant communities has relatively low priority (Shore and Black 1994: 297). Moreover, as immigration and asylum policy becomes more and more stringent, there is a growing number of foreigners and legal residents who are excluded from citizenship of the EU – a situation which is somewhat ironic when one considers the significance accorded by various treaties to the right of freedom of movement within Europe.

This emphasis on freedom of movement was designed to encourage economic potential within the EU and Articles dealing with citizenship in the Treaty signed at Maastricht placed the focus firmly on economic rather than cultural issues. From this and subsequent treaties it would appear that the EU citizen is primarily perceived as a worker, rather than a cultural being, which ultimately limits the scope of citizenship rights at a European level. This narrow perspective reflects the emergence of the EU from an economic context and the primary focus of European integration on the economic sphere. EU citizenship is rooted in market rather than cultural forces.

Nevertheless, there is some recognition given to the importance of languages and their political context. Article 8d of the Amsterdam Treaty reinforced the EU's commitment to official, nation-state languages and reiterated the right of citizens to petition the European Parliament, to apply to the European Ombudsman and to write to the institutions and advisory bodies of the Union in any of the latter's languages and to obtain a reply in the same language.

Apart from languages, the only other aspect of European culture that seems obvious is its exclusion of Muslim cultures. The logo of the CoE (12 stars set against a blue background) was adopted among other reasons because of its resonance with the 12 apostles (cf. Shore 2000: 47). Bainbridge and Teasdale (1995: 189) postulate an association with the Virgin Mary's halo. This idea has been reinforced with comments from Arsene Heitz who designed the logo in 1955. He suggested that his inspiration had been a reference in the Book of Revelations to 'a woman clothed with the sun...and a crown of twelve stars on her head' (Anonymous 2004a: 52).

The role of Christianity within the EU was an important focus of debate throughout the process of EU enlargement and the development of a constitution for Europe. During the 2-year long effort to draft a constitution, one of the more controversial issues that emerged was whether the text should contain a reference to Europe's Christian roots. The debate that followed such questions was evidence of tensions between religious and secular opinions on European values. Although the Vatican in Rome lobbied vigorously for the inclusion of a reference to Christianity in the preamble to the EU Constitution, it failed in its efforts.

Yet much of Europe's history has been associated in a vague sense with Christendom and this has been reinforced through images such as banner-waving Christian knights on horseback representing Christendom defending itself against Islam. Here one could cite the example of the statue of St James in the Cathedral of Compostela, which it has been suggested should be moved from the cathedral because of potential offence to Muslims.

The Christian/Muslim debate has raised the question of what the notion of European really means as 'Europeanness'. This has generally been constructed in opposition with the non-European, and in particular with Islam (Delanty 1995). Some scholars have called for the evolution of a 'European Islam' – a hybrid form that will take account of Europe's culture and politics (Anonymous 2002b: 9). Arguments in favour of such a proposal point to the foreign training of imams in many of Europe's mosques. This dependence on non-European imams perpetuates the link with non-European countries of origin and encourages 'long-distance nationalism' (Schiller and Fouron 2002). Ultimately it is argued that this hinders the development of loyalties to new European homelands. The ever-increasing numbers of Muslim immigrants within the EU have been perceived as major threat to European integration at this time and the issue of non-European languages will be explored in Chapter 8.

There is also the question of Turkey which wishes to become a full member of the EU. In earlier centuries, Turkey was a core part of the Ottoman Empire that occupied the Balkans and Hungary for centuries but in recent decades it has sought accession to the EU. Until December 2004 it was deemed ineligible because of human rights violations and many were less than enthusiastic about Turkey's potential membership. A former French president, Valéry Giscard d'Estaing objected to Turkish membership on the basis that Turkey has 'a different culture, a different approach, a different way of life' (Anonymous 2004b: 3). This argument suggests that cultural homogeneity is the basis of membership of the EU – a principle which utterly contradicts the slogan 'unity in diversity'.

The accession of Turkey would vastly increase the proportion of Muslims in 'Europe' which could be problematic for those who view the continent as essentially Christian space. 'Few people now insist that the EU is a Christian club, but the feeling that it should be is widespread.' This view is held in particular by Christian democratic parties. 'September 11th, Iraq and the war on terror have all focused renewed attention on whether the EU is right to consider admitting a Muslim country' (Anonymous 2004b: 34). However, this debate has not been entirely resolved.

Conclusion

While Europe as a concept can be vague, there is no doubt that it serves as a social space in which there are clear boundaries between insiders and outsiders. Social status within Europe can bring significant benefits for specific and in particular for national languages. Such benefits are not readily available to languages spoken by minorities, migrants and outsiders. This book will focus on languages spoken in Europe by Europeans and non-Europeans alike. It will not necessarily confine itself to Indo-European language families – namely Albanian, Armenian, Baltic, Celtic, Germanic, Greek, Romance and Slavonic. Finno-Ugric languages such as Estonian will be dealt with in the next chapter while the Basque language (particularly on the Spanish side of the border) will feature strongly in Chapter 4. Chapter 7 will examine the Indo-Aryan languages of the Roma and the Sinti with special focus on the implications of a nomadic lifestyle for the acquisition of language recognition. The intention throughout this book is not to explore the linguistic features of any of these languages. Instead the work adopts an interdisciplinary approach from a social science perspective examining the impact of European politics on languages spoken within the continent.

2
Statehood, Citizenship and Language

Language as a concept appears perfectly obvious. We all identify with a mother tongue and recognise, and perhaps even speak several other languages. Like Europe, languages give the impression of having existed from time immemorial. Whether in fact this is the case is another matter. Political scientists and theorists are increasingly of the view that language, like any tradition, is a constructed concept. 'The concept of "a language" – at least in the sense which appears so banally obvious to "us" – may itself be an invented permanency, developed during the age of the nation-state' (Billig 1995: 30).

If this is the case all national languages are in some sense artificial and allied with the construction of nation state. We are accustomed to thinking of Spanish or Portuguese as two separate languages. This may simply be a consequence of the former geopolitical dominance of these nation states rather than the result of any linguistic factors. If the political boundaries had been drawn differently, we might consider both forms of communication as dialects of the 'Iberian' language instead of separate speech forms (McWhorter 2002).

The concept of nationalism has been criticised for transforming languages from a means of communication into 'a political issue for which men are ready to kill and exterminate each other' (Kedourie 1966: 70). Eric Hobsbawm (1990: 102–3) cites the examples of Germany and Italy to explain the intensity of the primordial association between language and nation. He argues that 'for Germans and Italians, their national language was not merely an administrative convenience or a means of unifying state-wide communication'. In fact 'it was *only* thing that made them Germans and Italians, and consequently carried a far heavier charge of national identity than say, English did for those who wrote or read that language' (italics original).

This chapter begins with a very brief resumé of historical instances of strong links between language and nationhood. However, its primary focus is on the contemporary significance of language for statehood and citizenship for newly independent states in Eastern Europe. To that end this chapter shall explore the politics of language in the Balkans – with special emphasis on the case study of Croatian, before proceeding to examine the extraordinary significance of language for citizenship in the Baltic States.

Community, language and citizenship

Linguistic groups, such as the Catalans, frequently think in terms of their 'own' language (Conversi 1990: 59). Fishman (1980: 87) calls this role of language a 'peculiarly sensitive web of intimacy and mutuality'. In Northern Ireland, the expression 'our own language' is often used in relation to Irish (Maguire 1991). To belong is to be with a people who understand your codes and 'speak your language' (Ignatieff 1994: 7). Language can be as important, if not more important than territory or history for the generation of a sense of belonging.

> One can, of course, be understood in languages and in countries other than one's own; one can find belonging even in exile. But the nationalist claim is that full belonging, the warm sensation that people understand not merely what you say but what you mean, can only come when you are among your own people in your native land. (Ignatieff 1994: 7)

Many nations have sought to cultivate a sense of belonging precisely through the promotion of a common language. 'Language is the medium which makes the nation as an "imagined community" imaginable. It connects the individuals in social time and social space to fellow nationals whom he or she will never hear of, meet or know' (Suleiman 2003: 30). In the case of the Basque country, for example, some 600,000 people speak Euskarra or the Basque language, which is the only non-Indo-European indigenous tongue in Western Europe. The *Euzkadi ta Askatasuna* (Basque Homeland and Freedom) group have included this language as part of their nationalist demands for independence from Spain. Its founder Jose Luis Alvarez Enparanza has argued that Basque was one of the primary valid definitions of the nation (see Chapter 4). While the Basque people were defined as unique by their ethnicity, this was a product of their language. If

Euskera were endangered, the Basque nation would disappear (Kockel 1999).

A language community is situated in two spaces – symbolic and communicative – which are in constant interaction with one another (Edwards 1985: 17). Both of these spaces operate at synchronic as well as diachronic levels and constantly exert influence on members of the linguistic group. The symbolic and communicative spaces do not necessarily correspond. In the case of the former, language operates as a symbol of cohesion and unity within certain territorial boundaries. In contrast, a language can operate as a communicative instrument far beyond such territories.

This chapter focuses primarily on language as a symbol of national or state unity. In many instances of state-building, a particular language was deemed to 'fulfil all the necessary conditions to be an excellent national symbol: it had a "natural" appearance, its own history and a determined territory' (Škiljan 2000: 9). Because of these natural assets, specific languages were 'borrowed' from linguistic communities to serve as symbols of clearly defined national boundaries. A separate medium of communication identified a distinct nation that was entitled to self-government.

Germany is the classic example offered of the historical significance between language and nationhood since this country has traditionally stressed ethnic origins rather than political commitment when defining legitimate membership of the nation. The division of the German people into 39 states after Waterloo in the early nineteenth century was not very satisfactory for the Romanticists who dominated the German intellectual class and who feared the long-term consequences of German disunity. Friedrich Schlegel (1772–1829) argued forcefully that a nation was a closely knit family unit held together by ties of blood and history as well as language (Kohn 1967).

Heinrich Luden (1778–1847), a Professor at the University of Jena, believed in the uniqueness of each nation. He proposed that true fatherlands should be built on the principle of ethnicity and that nations and states should be coterminus. 'Language, the symbol of the spiritual and intellectual independence of the nation was the only bond linking the past to the present, and the only bond linking Germans, wherever they were after the dissolution of the Holy Roman Empire, the first reich, uniting them for a common effect' (Alcock 2000: 25).

National consciousness in nineteenth-century Germany was derived from the ideology of Herder and the Grimm brothers who emphasised the importance of the German *volk* and their culture. Of primary significance was the German language and its peasant literature, but even then, there were some complications with this line of reasoning. During Herder's lifetime, there was hardly a single recognisable 'German' language. Instead there were several mutually unintelligible ways of talking, none of which had established its own legitimacy as the 'correct' or 'standard' form of an overall German language (Billig 1995: 32–3). In reality, print rather than spoken languages united people and 'permitted the continued existence of very dissimilar spoken varieties of the language in the different regions of the state' (Wright 2000a: 41).

The German focus on the significance of language for nationhood should be set against the status of French as the language of a civilised Europe in the eighteenth century. In 1635, France had established the *Académie Française* for the purpose of nurturing the 'French' language. Within a century, French was established as the international language on the continent. The French Revolution introduced the notion of citizenship, but interestingly it also provided a strong impetus for cultural and linguistic unification. A language census in 1790 revealed that only one-fifth could speak French confidently while less than two-thirds actually knew some French (Alcock 2000: 11). Yet, the message of the Revolution was carried in French.

In this instance, the concept of official language was closely allied with the state. 'It is in the process of state formation that the conditions are created for the constitutions of a unified linguistic marker, dominated by an official language' (Bourdieu 1991: 45). A state language becomes the theoretical norm against which different linguistic variations are measured. The language becomes obligatory on official occasions, in state institutions and public administration. In the case of France, 'promotion of the official language to the status of national language gave them that *de facto* monopoly of politics, and more generally of communication with central government and its representatives, that has defined local notables under all the French republics' (Bourdieu 1991: 47).

State education was one of the state's primary mechanisms of homogenisation and the Rights of Man and the Citizen did not apply to the Occitans and Bretons who wished to use their own language as the medium of instruction in schools (Billig 1995). Compulsory and free education ensured that all children received their primary schooling solely through the medium of French. Moreover, the content of the curriculum was designed to inculcate French nationality. 'The education system set out quite consciously to turn the disparate elements of France into a nation' (Wright 2000a: 38). The histories of Lavisse and

Michelet had a tremendous influence on the sense of identity among French schoolchildren. The spirit of Republicanism ensured that civics replaced religion in the French curriculum. History texts in French schools from 1860 onwards focused on eras when Frenchmen shared a common destiny. There was a neglect of other actors in the national space which allowed French history 'to be presented as if it were the story of one group' (Wright 2000a: 38).

Participation in the revolutionary army was also a vital force as military commands were delivered in one language. Soldiers returning home had acquired fluency in French. In subsequent decades and centuries, the nation state pursued an official assimilationist policy (Ager 1999; Judge and Judge 2000). French was authorised as the sole medium of communication in public life. Languages and cultures such as Breton, Basque or Occitan were regarded as divisive and a danger to the territorial unity of the nation state.

The key to membership in France was the acceptance of its secular republican values on the part of would-be citizens. In theory, civic nations in Western Europe such as France are culturally neutral – as states which emphasise civic rather than cultural values. Traditionally, the concept of citizenship has emphasised a reciprocal political relationship between individual and state and 'is intimately related to the question of belonging to a nation' (Rex 1991: 5). Despite its obvious link with national identity, citizenship has largely been considered a culture-blind concept, particularly in the civic republican tradition – yet this is hardly the case. In the French example of 'civic' nationalism, there was (and is) an inextricable link between language, culture and imagined community.

Scandinavia provides further examples of the historic importance of language for nation-building. McWhorter (2002: 69) argues that in fact 'there was no such thing as "Swedish"' until Sweden acquired its independence from its Scandinavian neighbours in 1526. When Norway asserted its independence from Denmark in the early years of the nineteenth century it immediately set about generating a language that was recognisably different from Danish and 'what is today "Norwegian" was just "the way they speak Danish in Norway"' until Norway broke with Denmark in 1814' (McWhorter 2002: 69). In consequence, contemporary Norway has two languages. While Nyorsh, the artificial standard, is somewhat different from Danish, the language commonly spoken is remarkably similar. Yet all are commonly accepted as different and distinct languages and the question of whether they are dialects of a single continental language is rarely raised.

Such case studies are hardly confined to history and there are several examples of a more than significant link between language, nation and statehood from recent times such as that of Slovak (Daftary and Gál 2003) and Ukraine (Stepanenko 2003). In some instances, newly established states have endeavoured to transform a language that was shared by several nations into a symbol of one particular group – a process which frequently generates tension and sometimes casts aspersions on the actual linguistic status of such speech forms. (Disputed languages will be given further attention in Chapter 6.) Here the focus is on a case study from the Balkans which illustrates the use of a language as a political tool in the quest for independent statehood.

Language and statehood: A case study from the Balkans

The politics of language in the region of the former Yugoslavia is an essential component of South Slav relations (Pupavac 2003: 138). Language boundaries have reflected ethnic divisions in the Balkans and language status has been intimately connected with political boundaries. Serbo-Croatian language policy is particularly interesting as it illustrates the attempts of two, then three and ultimately four nations to 'borrow' a language from a linguistic group and develop it as a symbol of separate statehood (Škiljan 2000: 9).

The Croat desire to distinguish themselves from the Serbs hardly stems simply from the violent collapse of Yugoslavia in the 1990s. The bitterness of the Second World War earlier in the twentieth century was a contributory factor when Croatia was allied with the Germans and Italians whereas Serbs were resisters. Even before then, Croatian civilisation was regarded as 'Western' and Croatia once formed part of the Western Roman, that is Austrian Empire. The Croats were Catholic and used the Latin script whereas Serbs were 'Eastern', Orthodox, used the Cyrillic script and were supported by Russia. When separate nations were united in a common federation, emphasis was placed on a 'common language'. The attempts to unite the language were a real effort to merge two possibly quite different civilisations. In contrast the assertion of politically distinct tongues reflected times when the desire for separate states had come to the fore.

This section focuses on the emergence of a distinct Croatian language, which has been central to the national question in Croatia. The following statement issued by a journalist in the newspaper *Vjesnik* illustrates the significance of language as a tool of separate statehood in Croatia: 'First we defended the constitutional provisions on the

Croatian language, then we formed an independent Croatian state, then we made the Croatian literary language completely independent, we established a military force and then we created chaos in the once shared language' (cited in Pupavac 2003: 139). This journalist compared the destruction of Serbo-Croat as a literary language to the compression of an old tin can.

Recognition of a common Serbo-Croat language can be traced to March 1850 when several Serb and Croat intellectuals signed the 'Literary Agreement' in Vienna. Serbs and Croats stood to gain from an agreement which symbolised the unity of South Slavic power in the context of the then Austrian Empire. From the Serb perspective the Agreement had an added political dimension as language unity could be used as proof of dominance of Serb ethnicity. Vuk Karadžič viewed the Agreement as evidence that all speakers of the Štovakian dialect were essentially Serb. 'He considered the Croat Štovakian speakers to be "Catholic Serbs", the Muslim Štovakian speakers to be "Muslim Serbs", and the Orthodox Štovakian speakers to be "Orthodox Serbs"' (Greenberg 2001: 18–9).

The commonality of language was reinforced sociolinguistically in the late nineteenth century with the publication of a Serbo-Croat grammar book, dictionary and orthographic manual. Serbo-Croat was subjected to hard unifying pressure with the establishment of a kingdom of the Serbs, Croats and Slovenes in the aftermath of the First World War, but language policy in Yugoslavia slackened somewhat after the Second World War and recognised to a limited extent traditional, ethnic and linguistic differences. Although the impulse towards communicative and symbolic unity continued, post-war Yugoslavia endeavoured to defuse ethnicity through the limited recognition of identity in matters such as the codification of Macedonian as a literary language and under the rule of Tito (1944–80), Yugoslavia was widely held to be a model multi-national state.

Yet the importance of the Serbo-Croat language which was spoken by some three-quarters of the population was always considered central to the cohesion of the state and in Cold War Europe of the 1950s there were some attempts to reconcile the symbolic significance of the Croatian and Serbian linguistic traditions of the two predominant ethnic groups with the perceived need for a common state standard. In 1954 the Novi Sad Agreement declared that the language was one: 'the national language of Serbs, Croats and Montenegrins is one language, that is, the literary language which developed from its basis around two main centres, Belgrade and Zagreb, united, with two pronunciations, ijekavian and ekavian' (cited in Pupavac 2003: 144). The Agreement confirmed the equality of the Latin and Cyrillic scripts used by Croat and Serb populations respectively.

Following on this Agreement, the 1963 Constitutions of Bosnia and Herzegovina, Montenegro and Serbia pronounced Serbo-Croatian as the official language while Croatia reversed the order and declared their tongue to be Croato-Serbian. This was an early indication of the dissatisfaction that would later emerge publicly. Within a decade of the Novi Sad Agreement there was acrimony regarding the compilation of the first two volumes of the *Dictionary of the Serbo-Croatian Literary Language*. Croatian academics expressed serious dissatisfaction with what they regarded as the 'Serbianisation' of certain standard Croatian terms.

In the initial stages the debate focused purely on linguistics but quickly escalated to symbolise the discontent of Croatian academics generally with their position within the federation. This dissatisfaction served as the catalyst for a new Declaration on the Name and the Position of the Croatian Literary Language in 1967, which was endorsed by 18 Croatian institutions and 140 Croatian intellectuals, many of whom had previously signed the Novi Sad Agreement. In their rejection of the earlier Agreement, the intellectuals declared Croatian and Serbian as distinct and separate literary languages and challenged the Constitution to recognise four separate literary languages – namely Croatian, Macedonian, Serbian and Slovenian. In response, Serbian academics put forward a counter proposal designed to protect the Cyrillic script from infringement.

While the Croatian Declaration of 1967 focused on language, the document essentially demanded a revision of the status of Croatian within the federation and could be regarded as the declaration of the Croatian Spring nationalist movement. In 1971 the Croatian academic Radoslav Katičić wrote in the weekly *Hrvatski Tjednik* that the Novi Sad Agreement had relied on 'the unsupported assumption of an alleged Serbo-Croat linguistic unity, which has frequently been used to deny the independent existence of the Croat literary language and its historical and territorial continuity' (cited in Pupavac 2003: 145–6). The revised constitutional provisions in Yugoslavia of 1974 sought to affirm the existence of the Croatian literary language at an official level while maintaining a common spoken language throughout the federation.

The new Yugoslav Constitution did little to appease national sentiments and language disputes escalated over the following decade. A memorandum compiled by members of the Serbian Academy of Arts and Sciences criticised Croatian language aspirations as detrimental linguistically as well as politically to ethnic Serbs in Croatia. Tito reacted negatively to Croat attempts at linguistic independence and banned many Croatian language books including an orthographic manual published in 1971, a Croatian grammar issued in 1973, and several Croatian language school textbooks (Greenberg 1999: 145). However, this situation was reversed and the Croatian literary language became the official language of the Republic of Croatia soon after Tudjman was elected in 1990.

The cultural construction of the new Croatian State placed great emphasis on the distinctiveness of the Croatian language. In *The Fall of Yugoslavia: The Third Balkan War*, Glenny (1992: 145) describes the attempts to construct linguistic differences at a conference in a suburb of Sarajevo in the summer of 1991. On this occasion the leader of the Croatian Democratic Union (HDZ) delegation demanded simultaneous translation of conference proceedings from Serbian into Croatian:

> Jurica's request, which would be akin to somebody from Glasgow requesting that a Londoner's speech be translated into Scottish English, provoked uproar and laughter. An avalanche of fists thumped the table, one delegate walked out in disgust never to return, the assembled observers had tears of laughter in their eyes but there was more to come as one of the delegates from Sarajevo stood up and screamed above the commotion in all seriousness, 'I demand a translation into Bosnian!' (The equivalent of Irish English)

Since the proclamation of Croatian independence, Croatian has become the language of general public communication and Croat linguists have launched a quest to purify their language, a process which has involved the 'ethnic cleansing' of the language from Serbian influence. Much of the vocabulary relating to state institutions has been revised including the words for 'embassy' and 'passport'. In some instances the process has focused on perceived rather than real Serbian influence and international terms such as *aerodrom* 'airport' or *avion* 'aeroplane' have been replaced with native Croatian words. This new Croatian terminology has been accepted by Croatian government and the media which has actively campaigned against former 'Serbian' influences (Greenberg 2001).

Although theoretically a linguistic process, the matter of language purification is essentially political and features in many nationalist movements. 'Philological nationalism' is the term given by Hobsbawm (1990: 56) to such activity. Within the independent Croat state, language has become a boundary marker that distinguishes insiders and outsiders, Croats and Serbs. 'Applying these general rules to the domain of language policy, it tends to symbolically assemble all of Us, i.e. all the Croats, and – at the same time – to exclude from the symbolic space all the Others, i.e. above all, the Serbs' (Škiljan 2000: 12). The process of exclusion appears to have been entirely effective within the independent Croat state. While initially the Serb minority refused to accept the idea of living in an independent Croatian state, ultimately they have accepted (for now at least) a status which determines Serbian as a minority language with restricted areas of use within Croatia. Of course, it also implies that their language is separate and 'Serbs of Croatia, who have apparently spoken the same language as the Croats', request translations of school texts from Croatian into Serbian 'although they understand the Croatian texts'. Thus they are willing partners in 'their exclusion from the symbolic Croatian space, having as a perspective, integration into Serbian space' (Škiljan 2000: 12).

Serbs in Croatia and particularly in the Krajina region where they formed a minority of 12 per cent complained initially that the HDZ failed to give them cultural and linguistic autonomy. In particular, they sought separate instruction in Serbian in schools, and the right to display bilingual signs in both Latin (Croatian) and Cyrillic (Serbian) scripts (Greenberg 2001: 27). Script became an issue of tremendous political significance as Serbs experienced many problems with a lack of enthusiasm among state officials to recognise documents written or printed in Cyrillic. In the early years of the HDZ many ethnic Serbian children were denied Croatian citizenship for a number of years (Pupavac 2003: 151–2).

The issue of minority language rights has been taken up at several levels. At a national level Milorad Pupovac of the Serbian Democratic Forum demanded formal recognition of Serbian language rights. Human rights advocates from Amnesty International and other international organisations criticised Croatia for failing to provide special language provision for the Serb minority and to respect their language rights. Yet there have been some suggestions that it is neither fair nor sensible to expect the Croatian Republic to afford special provision in language matters for the Serbs. The first of these arguments relies on the similarity of Croatian and Serbian: 'Yet would one demand special language provision for ethnic Britains in the United States or vice versa?' (Pupavac 2003: 149). In my view this argument lacks merit as the ruling party rather than the ethnic Serbs have determined that Croat and Serbian are two independent languages. The logical consequence of this government decision is to render Serbian a minority language with associated rights.

The second argument requires more attention as it relates to public recognition of a minority identity and the consequences of such recognition in specific areas. In the case of ethnic Serbs outside Eastern Slavonia, for instance, individual teachers have been reluctant to offer courses in schools which identify them as Serb rather than Croat. Parents have also been reluctant to mark their children as different by sending them to separate classes in Serbian language. Public identification of Serb ethnicity might engender bullying at local level. Memories of former Serbian dominance are still vibrant and ethnic Serbs in certain regions would prefer to integrate and even assimilate rather than seek special status (Pupavac 2003: 151).

However, Serbs are not the sole minority group who are caught up in these linguistic tensions. Greenberg (2001: 25) has identified Yugoslavs as 'the most forgotten victims' of wars and tensions in former Yugoslavia. These individuals have often refused to become involved in ethnic politics and may have married 'across the ethnic divide' or may themselves be children of mixed marriages. Many such persons are stateless as a result of Yugoslavia's disintegration and despite official recognition and even insistence on separate Croatian and Serbian languages, these individuals are likely to remain speakers of 'Serbo-Croatian' or 'Croato-Serbian'.

The future of Croatian and Serbian as distinct languages seems to rely entirely on the continued existence of separate independent states. In the case of Croatia in particular, language politics and statehood are intimately connected and the question of language will remain a contested issue until national insecurities are resolved. Here as in many other historical and contemporary examples, language debates are essentially matters for politicians rather than linguists and demands for language rights are essentially requests for political accommodation.

While linguistically there appears to be little (albeit a growing) difference between Croatian and Serbian, the political affirmation of a separate Croatian language raises many questions regarding accommodation of real or actual difference which takes on special significance in newly established states that are still asserting their independence. The next case study focuses on a similar timeframe since the Baltic States and Balkans acquired their independence at the same time. In all these instances there has been a determination to ensure the pervasiveness of the official, indigenous language at all realms of society but the process of normalisation of the official language has had very different consequences for minority groups. In the case of the Baltic States, the question of citizenship has been a particular issue.

Citizenship and language: The Baltic states

The politics of language in Estonia, Latvia and Lithuania form an interesting case study of the contemporary link between language and citizenship. The Estonian people who inhabit the most northerly of the three Baltic States are Finno-Ugric and are most closely related to the Finns. Their Finno-Ugric language is completely distinct from Latvian and Lithuanian which belong to the Baltic group of Indo-European along with the now-extinct Old Prussian. All three languages are quite different from Slavic languages such as Russian, Belorussian, Ukrainian which are also spoken in the Baltic States.

Prior to independence (for the second time) from the Soviet Union, the three Baltic States had begun to claim some degree of autonomy. Initially they confined their demands to cultural self-determination and each of the three introduced language laws in the late 1980s. In the case of Estonia, for example, legislation in 1989 established Estonian as the state language and required that all official personnel be competent in the language within 4 years. Despite the denial of official status for Russian, it was given a lot of attention in the law. 'Citizens in their relations with authorities, subordinates in their relations with superiors at the workplace, as well as clients in the service sector, were given the right to choose either Estonian or Russian as the language of communication' (Järve 2003: 78–9).

This Estonian language law could be read in one context as simply part of the process of nation-building. However there was much more to it than that. 'It was also the first legislative move aimed at containing the Russian language and monolingual Russian-speakers in Estonia, while promoting Estonian instead' (Järve 2003: 79). From this point forward, Russian-speakers were confronted with the stark choice of acquiring Estonian or ultimately losing their jobs.

In March 1990, Lithuania declared its independence from the former Soviet Union. A year later, Latvia and Estonia followed suit. At that point in their history Estonia and Latvia in particular had experienced large-scale planned migration of Soviets and in common with many other analysts this chapter focuses on the impact of language and citizenship for Russian-speaking minorities in these countries. However, it is important to note at this point that the Russian-speaking minority includes members of many nationalities such as Ukrainians and Belarussians as well as immigrants from various other Soviet republics who had been assimilated into Soviet culture (Hogan-Brun and Ramonienè: 2005).

Planned migration had an inevitable impact on the indigenous population in the Baltic States. In the late 1980s, the share of ethnic Estonians in Estonia had fallen to 62 per cent and that of ethnic Latvians in Latvia to 52 per cent. Since then, proportions of Soviet Russians have decreased and censuses at the turn of the twenty-first century indicate that they form 25.6 per cent of the population in Estonia and 29.6 per cent in Latvia (Hogan-Brun 2003: 122). Lithuania had not experienced such a comparable degree of planned immigration and the proportion of indigenous Lithuanians remained at 80 per cent (Tsilevich 2001). 'The higher proportion of indigenous people in Lithuania relative to the other Baltic Republics means that unlike the Latvians and Estonians, the Lithuanians do not fact the danger of becoming a minority in their own land' (Fernández-Armesto 1994: 283).

After independence in the early 1990s, the newly established states sought to re-establish Baltic cultures and languages as the national norm which turned the formerly dominant group, the Russians, into a marginal position culturally. Lithuania, where the proportion of Russians was relatively low, opted for inclusive policies offering citizenship to everyone who was resident there at the time of the restitution of independence. In contrast, Estonia and Latvia adopted a position whereby only those residents who had been living in Estonia and Latvia before the annexation of 1940 were automatically entitled to citizenship (Hogan-Brun 2003: 129). This excluded Russians who arrived during and after the Second World War from automatic citizenship and effectively prevented them from having any major input into the formulation of the new linguistic legislation. However, this was not an entirely exclusive process and a linguistic qualification for citizenship was introduced. Individuals prepared to learn the new state languages and pass certain basic examinations in linguistic competence could earn citizenship. With this requirement the Baltic Republics were ensuring that the new states were political expressions of the indigenous culture and language (Tsilevich 2001).

The link between language and citizenship in Estonia and Latvia had significant consequences for Russians as they were effectively deprived of certain key rights. In the case of Estonia, for example, Russians were ineligible to vote in national elections or to hold any elective office.

They were not free to join political parities or to serve in the higher civil service or police force. Perhaps even more significantly, they were unable to own land (Laitin 1996). All citizens in certain public spheres were required to rely on their use of Estonian.

In Latvia, where some half a million or more Russians were potentially stateless the issue was even more complex and various revisions of the language bill were discussed at parliament. After the restoration of independence, the Latvian Government amended the language law and adjusted the hierarchy of languages to further increase the significance of Latvian and to reduce rights to speak Russian in the public sector. However, the Latvian Parliament was conscious of the relatively large proportion of non-Latvian-speaking population – approximately 700,000 of the total population of 2.5 million and embarked on the provision of Latvian language training to enable the non-Latvian-speaking population overcome its disadvantages.

Conscious of international interest in their regime, the Prime Minister of the Republic of Latvia requested the assistance of the United Nations Development Programme in the summer of 1994 to organise a programme of experts who would be involved in drafting a National Programme for Latvian Language Training. Representatives from eight countries – Canada, Denmark, Finland, Germany, Israel, Norway, Sweden and the United States – became involved as well-representatives of international organisations such as the CoE, the United Nations Educational, Scientific and Cultural Organisation (UNESCO) and the Organisation for Security and Co-Operation in Europe (OSCE).

Following various amendments, the Latvian Constitution confirmed Latvian as the sole official state language in 1998 which paved the way for a new language law. In May 2002, the Latvian Parliament (*Saeima*) amended the election laws and made Latvian the working language of Parliament – a position which is interesting when one notes that this amendment also dropped proficiency in the Latvian language as a prerequisite for standing in parliamentary or municipal elections! (Hansson 2002: 19).

Since the introduction of these laws, the process of naturalisation has hardly taken place on a large scale. From 1992–96 just over 80,000 individuals in Estonia acquired citizenship through naturalisation. Of these, approximately 30,000 became citizens following an examination of their knowledge of the Estonian language and the Constitution of the country (Permanent Representative of the Russian Federation to the United Nations 1996). In the case of Latvia, early figures for the period from 1995 to June 1997 revealed that of the 120,000 individuals eligible to apply for citizenship, only 7512 had actually applied. Of these some 5944 had succeeded in acquiring citizenship (Ozolins 1999).

Research conducted in 1997 and 1998 for a project entitled *On the Way to a Civil Society* in Latvia was quite illuminating in revealing people's interest in learning the history and culture of Latvia and in acquiring the indigenous language. Of those responding to the survey, some 40 per cent of non-citizens aged 15–30, and 55 per cent of non-citizens in the older age groups did not believe they could pass the naturalisation exams of Latvian language and history. (*Promotion of Integration of Society in Latvia* 2001).

One should not assume that the slow take up of citizenship is simply a language issue and other factors may also have an impact. For example, citizens are liable for military service which may explain the reluctance on the part of young males to apply. A more significant factor perhaps is the lack of provision for dual citizenship. The acquisition of a state passport in Estonia or Latvia will inevitably entail the loss of the old Soviet passport. This means that visits to Russia for Soviet Russians holding Baltic citizenship would involve applying for a visa.

One intriguing factor in this entire process is the terminology that has been used to deal with the Russian language. Categories such as 'minority language' are generally avoided in Latvia and Estonia and terms such as 'state language' or 'foreign languages' are preferred. The Language Act of Estonia deals explicitly with this issue and determines that any language other than the Estonian, the official state language, is effectively a foreign language. This has a severe impact on speakers in the state who commonly use Russian.

In Latvia, the new and revised law adopted in December 1999 guaranteed the rights of national minorities to speak their mother tongue (Art. 4). However, it was quite clear that languages apart from Latvian and Liv were to be categorised as 'foreign' although it did concede that the Latgalian written language did not fall into this category as it was effectively a historically established variety of Latvian (Hansson 2002). This complex system of categorisation was designed to place Russian in the category of foreign rather than minority languages – which would hinder speakers of Russian claiming official protection for their language on the basis of minority rights.

The linking of language competency with citizenship in the Baltic States was probably inevitable when one considers that the drive for independence had its roots in the language movement. Prior to the acquisition of self-determination there were serious concerns about the decline and possible extinction of Estonian and Latvian in particular in the context of the huge numbers of speakers of Slavic languages in and near these regions. Historical factors were also at work and there is no doubt that tensions between the Balts and the Russians are not entirely due to linguistic difference. Instead they are a consequence of historical power relationships between the dominant and the dominated.

While at first glance the language laws may seem an over-reaction to a historical situation, it is important to set these in the context of a process designed to reverse rather than simply protect that status quo. In some Baltic regions such as the city of Narva in the northeast of Estonia, Russian is spoken more widely than the official national language. This situation is hardly an incentive for Russian-speakers to acquire the new state language. Moreover, Soviet Russians are not necessarily inclined to take an interest in the new state language. For this reason the political changes were designed to overturn the privileges enjoyed by the formerly dominant group and to serve as the catalyst for the regeneration of the indigenous languages (Ozolins 1999).

Moreover, one must appreciate that the Russian language was spoken as mother tongue by almost 20 per cent of the population in the Baltic States at the time of independence and was perceived as a genuine threat to indigenous, official state languages. Balts were conscious of the vast linguistic resources available to speakers of Russian due to the sheer numbers of native speakers of Russian world-wide and the Soviet practice of imposing Russian as the second language on non-Russian peoples. Russian newspapers and television were widely available. There were also minority programmes on the radio. For this reason the language situation in the newly established Baltic States was treated as a zero-sum game which involved the non-recognition of Russian in state sectors. This was a reversal of the previous situation when Russian had full use in the official domain.

Inevitably such policies have generated numerous criticisms – many of which have come from Russia itself. One Russian objector claimed that the practice in Latvia and Estonia was becoming 'more and more overtly discriminatory in character', and that 'its objective of forcing out the Russian-speaking population' was becoming 'ever more thinly disguised'. Apparently over 100,000 non-citizens left Estonia between 1991 and 1996 and some 116,000 Russian-speaking former residents of Estonia became Russian citizens (Permanent Representative of the Russian Federation to the United Nations 1996). From the Russian perspective the situation in Latvia was equally dismal.

The Russians took the case of their minorities to several international organisations such as the UN, OSCE and the CoE (Hogan-Brun 2003). These responded with various criticisms, which were eventually acknowledged by the Baltic States. For example, the State Language draft law which appeared in Latvia in 1995 was delayed and amended following harsh criticism from the OSCE High Commissioner on National Minorities and other international organisations. Ultimately some provisions of the new State Language Law actually appeared to be even more liberal than those in force before its adoption (Tsilevich 2001).

The OSCE continued to monitor the Latvian citizenship law and severely criticised subsequent proposed language legislation in the private economic sector. Entry into the EU would be jeopardised, they warned, unless Latvia reconsidered language legislation in this area. In 1999, the Latvian Parliament passed a new language law which effectively repeated the earlier provisions for the law to apply to the private economic sphere, but ultimately this law was returned to parliament by the President for further consideration (Ozolins 1999). Overall it would appear that pressure from the OSCE has had the effect of liberalising the language laws to some extent (Hogan-Brun 2003).

In all three Baltic Republics, the indigenous language is a prerequisite for business in both private and public sectors. In the case of Latvia, for example, fluency in the Latvian language is a precondition for work in public and monolingual speakers of other languages frequently become unemployed (*Promotion of Integration of Society in Latvia* 2001). Language legislation here in 1999 sought to extend the use of Latvian to all business sectors, private and public, by advocating that where even one participant requested it, private business meetings and correspondence should be conducted in the official state language.

One point that should be made is that the required level of language competency in all three Baltic States differs with respect to the job involved. (Different levels of language competence also apply to public employment in South Tyrol.) In the case of Latvia, new regulations in 2000 determined six levels of language competency. Those in more highly skilled professions such as lawyers and notaries are required to have a greater degree of fluency in the Baltic languages compared with those in lower skilled occupations, such as public transport conductors and taxi-drivers. The state determines the necessary requirements for employees in state and municipal institutions whereas private institutions had greater flexibility in this regard (Hansson 2002).

There is no doubt that 'this hotly contested law enforcement can arguably have a segregationist effect on the labour market in the private sector' (Hogan-Brun 2003: 130) as it reserves the better paid jobs in government for the more fluent speakers of official languages of the Baltic States. On the other hand, the essential link between language and economy does serve to enhance the will to learn the language. In the case of both Estonia and Latvia, it is more economically expedient to learn the respective Baltic language and engage with indigenous Baltic success rather than follow Russian cultural or political groups (Ozolins 1999).

Overall one can identify several trends with regard to language politics in the Baltic States. The first of these is the dramatic efforts to protect and promote official state languages, which were seriously undermined during the Soviet period when they were excluded from important state sectors such as military affairs, industry and transport. 'Harsh language legislation is seen as a tool for preserving the titular languages and ensuring their competitiveness, or as combating "linguistic Darwinism", as one leading linguistic expert in Latvia described' (Tsilevich 2001).

There is a perceived reciprocal relationship between language and state in these regions. While languages in the Baltic are regarded as symbols of state sovereignty, the state is perceived as protector of the language. However, the rights of minority representatives to foster their languages and culture are guaranteed and the law on state language in Lithuania states that the Republic 'shall guarantee the right of persons, belonging to ethnic communities to foster their language, culture and customs' (Hogan-Brun and Ramonienè 2003: 43).

Promotion of Estonian and Latvian rather than Russian symbolises the new geopolitical orientation of these Republics and their rejection of former Russian domination. Accession to the EU could be perceived as evidence of the Balts 'turning their back' on Russia and the curtailment and suppression of the Russian languages is further evidence of Baltic attempts to eradicate any traces of former Russian domination. Modern Baltic citizens wish to be associated with progressiveness in Europe and are more tolerant of the use of other Western languages than they are of Russian. Moreover, the learning of foreign languages is highly encouraged, particularly in the context of membership of the EU (cf. Hogan-Brun and Ramonienè 2004: 77).

The size of the various ethnicities is of major significance in this context. While ethnic Balts are more numerous than Speakers of Russian in the respective Baltic States, the proportions acquire an altogether different significance in a wider international context. Soviet Russians are a minority in the Baltic States but they are related to a federation of gigantic proportions. In contrast, the extent of Baltic cultures and languages is geographically and politically small. Druviete (1999: 270) reinforces this point by arguing that Russian and English 'possess two crucial features: they are widely spoken and function as languages of international communication'. In contrast, Latvian 'has no such "carrots" to offer'. For this reason, 'the only compensatory mechanisms for Latvian can be of a legal nature'. However, some analysts have contended that this situation hardly justifies the restrictive language laws. The Latvian language which is spoken by 1.4 million citizens can hardly be regarded as under threat – even in an international context (Dobson 2001).

Sometimes it is argued that these restrictive laws are designed to hinder the prospects of Soviet Russians who are not really committed to the independence of these newly established Republics. Instead it is assumed that Soviet Russians in Estonia constitute a case of 'long-distance nationalism' (Schiller and Fouron 2002) or in this instance are an example of cross-border nationalism. The implication here is that immigrants are inevitably more loyal to the homeland of their ancestors rather than their country of residence. (A similar argument is used against the inclusion of speakers of non-European languages in Europe cf. Chapter 8.) However, there is little genuine evidence that ethnic Russians in the Baltic States either expect or desire re-unification with Russia and it is not certain that they actually identify with their ancestral homeland.

It has also been suggested that the new citizenship laws provide the basis for stability as they ensure that large numbers of Russians could not have a political input into state legislation. From this perspective the inclusion of a high proportion of Russians could split the state into two with a large minority seeking a two-nation, two-language state (Ozolins 1999: 253). This is an argument with which I personally am not in favour as the implementation of political hegemony in other contexts such as Northern Ireland ultimately engendered riots, violence and terrorism on an ongoing basis (cf. Nic Craith 2002a, 2003a). But more significantly, there was a fear in Latvia in particular that 'if citizenship was granted to non-Latvians any change in the composition of the population might lead to Latvia being voted back to Russia. The example of Belarus more or less returning to the Russian fold in 1999 was not encouraging (Alcock 2000: 189).

Moreover, a counter argument would suggest that no-one (Russian or otherwise) is actually barred from acquiring citizenship once the requirements are fulfilled. Furthermore, the strong support given to state languages in the economic and employment sectors effectively persuades ambitious non-speakers of the Baltic languages to acquire the state tongue. Interestingly, gender differences also appear to impact on the desire to learn the language. Young Russian males from prosperous families appear least likely to opt to learn the local Baltic language whereas Russian women are much more favourably disposed to acquiring the language in Lithuania (Hogan-Brun and Ramonienè 2005; Ozolins 1999). Sociolinguistically it appears that Russians in the Baltic States are gradually learning the official state language. The total proportion speaking the state language has risen from 67 to 80 per cent in Estonia, from 62 to 80 per cent in Latvia and from 85 to 94 per cent in Lithuania (Hogan-Brun 2003: 125).

English is also gaining ground in these countries. As early as 1991, David Laitin observed with shock the efforts of all participants at an inter-Baltic conference to speak English rather than Russian as a medium of communication. He also recorded the serious attempts in Narva schools to procure teaching materials in English rather than Estonian and commented on the efforts of the local schoolboy with which he lived to learn English (Laitin 1996). (But as already noted, there is not much impetus to learn Estonian in Narva where the environment is essentially Russian.)

Conclusion

For now it appears that official status at national level seems to satisfy nationalists in the Baltic States for whom language has proved an intricate part of the process of state-building. In an increasingly globalised world, states are operating in a transnational rather than a national context. Yet the implications of national status have enormous consequences for languages within the EU. Ultimately membership of the EU is perceived as an opportunity for speakers of Estonian, Latvian and Lithuanian as these languages have now acquired status as official, working languages at international level. While the promotion of multilingualism within the Union is regarded as a positive challenge, there is also the issue of the impact of more widely spoken languages within the Union such as English, French or German (Hogan-Brun 2004). This more transnational context provides the focus for the next chapter.

3
European Elites: Official Languages in the EU

Although the concept of 'nation state' is increasingly challenged at the beginning of the twenty-first century, there is no doubt that it will legitimate and demarcate significant cultural and social differences for the present (Hannerz 1996). Indeed the link between official language and nation state is effectively endorsed by EU institutions. When a nation state joins the Union, its official language is (with few exceptions) given the status of official, working language of the EU. Theoretically at least, national languages of member states have equal and significant status within the EU although reality does not always match the rhetoric and a small number of official languages have gained primary working status.

Official, working languages

The concepts of 'official' and 'working' language originally derive from their use within the League of Nations, the forerunner of the United Nations (UN). Initially the UN gave official language status to major world languages such as Chinese, English, French, Russian and Spanish. After the 1973 oil crisis, Arabic was added to the list. However, English and French were given the additional status of working languages (Phillipson 2003). With few exceptions the EU does not distinguish between official and working languages and, in principle, national and official languages of new nation states acquire official and working status upon entry to the EU.

This policy has been in place since its inception, and the principle of parity for the languages of participating states was established at the beginning. The rules of procedure of the European Court of Justice of 7 March 1953 state that its official languages are French, German, Italian and Dutch, which constitute the primary languages of the initial six member states. Even at this early stage, however, there were some intimations that the four languages were hardly equal. 'Listing the languages not alphabetically, but naming French first, suggests that French was assumed to have a greater role to play' (Phillipson 2003: 54).

Initially the situation appeared uncomplicated, but difficulties arose with enlargement and the situation became ambiguous with the accession of Ireland and the UK in 1973. When Ireland became a member of the EEC in 1973, its government advised against granting the status of a working language to Irish (Ó Murchú 1992; Nic Craith 1994, 2000a). As English is the second official language of the nation state, Irish parliamentarians did not wish administrative services to be overburdened with translation duties. For this reason, a special status of treaty language had to be created to accommodate Irish.

Treaty status implies that all EU treaties are published in Irish and are regarded as authentic. Irish can also be used by Irish citizens for making certain contacts with the EU institutions. But the ambiguous position of Irish has been raised by the Irish Government in July 2004 following a vigorous campaign by Irish-speakers in Ireland spearheaded by a group called *Stádus* (Status). Later that year Ireland's permanent secretary to the EU, Ms Anne Anderson, told a meeting of ambassadors from various member states that the Irish Government wished to revisit this question. This request received a 'cautiously positive' response from those present at the meeting. Since then the Irish Government has been notified that Irish will become the 21st official language of the EU. On 13 June 2005 Irish was given the status of an official and working language of the EU. This status will apply from January 2007 and has been widely welcomed by Irish-speakers.

The accession of the UK to the EU raised issues in relation to Celtic languages other than Irish. Although Welsh has national and official status within Wales, it is not a national language of the UK as a whole and consequently never obtained EU official, working status. Until recently no Celtic language achieved working status within the Union. The acceptance of Irish as an official, working language will have 'a major psychological impact' on speakers of all Celtic languages (Ó Riagáin 2004).

Irish and UK accession triggered some anxieties in relation to the potential impact of English on languages spoken in the EU. When President Pompidou agreed in 1972 to Britain's entry to the EEC, he insisted on the pre-eminence of French as the dominant language of EEC institutions (Phillipson 2003). Moreover, it appears that a former British Minister Edward Heath agreed that all British civil servants connected to the Community would have fluency in French.

The accession of Spain in 1986 raised further difficult questions. Although Basque, Catalan and Galician are recognised as official languages on a regional basis, their lack of recognition on a national basis within Spain disqualified them from official, working status within the EU. This angered Catalans in particular who argued strongly for the inclusion of Catalan as an official, working language of the Community on the pragmatic basis of the extent to which it is spoken throughout the continent. Catalans have consistently pointed to the fact that numbers speaking the Catalan language greatly exceed that of Danish which was given official, working status with Denmark's entry to the EU in 1973.

Catalans have received some sympathy for their position from the European Parliament. In December 1990, the European Parliament passed resolution A3–169/90 on languages in the (European) Community and the situation of Catalan (OJ-C19, 28 January 1991), which called on the Council to support the case for the translation of the Community's treaties and other basic documents into Catalan. It also called for the use of Catalan in disseminating public information about the European institutions in the media. Moreover the resolution supported the case for the inclusion of Catalan in the list of languages supported by Lingua and Erasmus programmes. It backed the case for the use of Catalan in all Community dealings with the Autonomous Regions of Catalonia and the Balearic Islands. Such concessions have hardly calmed the Spanish Government's quest for recognition of Basque, Catalan, Galician and Basque and they have again raised this issue.

With the accession of Finland and Sweden to the EU on 1 January 1995, the number of official, working EU languages increased from 9 to 11 (Table 3.1) and ensured automatic rights for speakers of these languages. For example, the official journal of the European Community

Table 3.1   Official, working languages of the EU 1995

Danish
Dutch
English
Finnish
French
German
Greek
Italian
Portuguese
Spanish
Swedish

was drafted in all official languages. Moreover, individuals in respective member states who sent documents to the Community in any of the 11 official languages were entitled to written replies in the same language.

As noted in Chapter 1, the most significant enlargement to the Union occurred in 2004 with the accession of 10 new member states. At this time, a further nine languages were added to the list of official, working languages within the EU. The new official, working languages are represented in Table 3.2. During the process of accession, applicant states ensured that they were guaranteed the same rights as member states, and could not be pressurised into having their language rights restricted upon entry to full membership. Despite such guarantees, however, a narrow language policy was implemented during the actual process of negotiation for membership, and English featured as the key language.

In the case of Poland, for example, the Multi-annual Financing Agreement (Special Accession Programme for Agriculture and Rural Development) between the Commission and Poland stipulated that the Agreement be drawn up in English and Polish. A similar situation occurred in the case of the Czech Republic when it was stipulated that the Czech Republic should ensure that all relevant national legislation, written procedures, manuals, guidelines and so on, relating to this Agreement be made available in English upon request from the Commission (Phillipson 2003: 123). Such provisions effectively ensured that representatives of both the Commission and the applicant states functioned in English, although they may have been more comfortable operating in German or French or in their mother tongue. More seriously it ensured that the monitoring of key issues such as agricultural subsidies, or the movement of labour, was filtered through the English language, making it more difficult for civil servants in the respective new states to participate.

Table 3.2 New official, working languages of the EU (May 2004)

Czech
Estonian
Hungarian
Latvian
Lithuanian
Maltese
Polish
Slovak
Slovenian

The process of increasing the number of official, working languages from 11 to 20 was controversial for speakers of minority languages. Although the EU as an institution supports multilingualism, this primarily applies to its official rather than its minority languages. Enlargement ensured that languages such as Estonian and Latvian which are spoken by little more than one million qualified for official status, whereas Catalan, with speakers of many millions, is still excluded from this elite club.

Of particular annoyance to speakers of Irish in Ireland has been the case of Maltese which is spoken by an even smaller number than that of Estonian or Latvian. The Maltese example is considered an appropriate benchmark for Irish for several reasons. In the first instance, English is an official language in both Ireland and Malta but Irish and Maltese are recognised as national languages. The number speaking Maltese on a daily basis is similar to that of Irish, although there are four times as many individuals who can speak Irish as there are people in Malta. However, Maltese is spoken by the majority of the population in Malta on a daily basis. This is not the case in Ireland where English predominates. Yet Irish (unlike Maltese) is recognised as the first official language, both constitutionally and legally.

For speakers of Irish the acquisition of official, working status by a language such as Maltese is 'proof' that the case of Irish needed to be reconsidered. Ultimately, however, the lack of official, working status for Irish to date was a consequence of the behaviour of the Irish Government rather than a consequence of any action at EU level. In the case of Maltese, the Government of Malta requested official, working status for the language, and even this has not been without problems. Although Maltese acquired official status within the EU on 1 May 2004, the Maltese Government asked for a 3-year derogation on translating EU legislation. Effectively this means some acts (including judgments of the European Court of Justice) will not necessarily be translated into Maltese in the initial 3 years. This decision will be reviewed in December 2006 when the Council of Ministers will determine whether to extend the transitional period further.

Towards a Lingua Franca

Some governments have become alarmed at the increase in the number of official, working languages within the Union, and cases for the restriction of the number of official languages have been made at every stage throughout its short history. This issue arose as early as 1973 when Denmark was prepared to forego official, working status for Danish, and agreed to the restriction of the number of languages to English and French on one condition – that no member was permitted to use his or her mother tongue in EU institutions. While this proposal had great merit in ensuring that all members were equally disadvantaged, it was inevitably rejected by both the British and the French. In consequence the Danes claimed official EU status for their national language (Wright 2000a).

Subsequent accessions of Greece, Spain and Portugal ensured that the number of official, working languages was again on the agenda. Between 1979 and 1982 a number of individual members of the European Parliament and parliamentary committees studied the language question and expressed concern at the implications of the increase in the number of pairs of languages for translation and interpretation from 30 to 72. (The accession of Greece alone caused a 12.5 per cent increase in language staff at the Commission.) In 1994, before the accession of Finland, Austria and Sweden to the EU, Alain Lamassoure, the Minister for European Affairs in France, indicated that France would avail of its presidency (from January to June 1995) to propose limiting the number of official, working languages to five.

Neither initiative succeeded in changing the rhetoric of equality for national languages and the 1979–82 initiative served as the catalyst for a debate on linguistic democracy which concluded that members of the EU were best served by the principle of multilingualism. The French initiative of late 1994–95 was received negatively both within the European Parliament and outside. Greeks were especially incensed at the potential loss of status for their language and embarked on a vigorous campaign of protection. The writer, Pavlos Matessis, supported the campaign for the protection of Greek and called for a movement prepared to take the French government to the European Court of Justice if it failed to drop the proposal.

In each instance, proponents on both sides of the argument were making the case from a position of sincerity with a concern to promote democratic principles. However, their perception of the process of democracy differed. Those in favour of restricting the number of languages suggested that the EU would shortly resemble the Tower of Babel and could hardly remain articulate as the number of official languages increased. Those against restricting the number of official languages pointed to the need for ordinary individuals to understand the operations of the EU. This could hardly be achieved if the institutions operated in a language which they did not comprehend and would seriously impact on speakers of languages which were 'small' within the EU although not necessarily small in a more global context (Phillipson 2003).

As the EU expands to the East and the South, the mechanics of the plurilinguistic regime will become more urgent and complicated. In such circumstances the EU will probably maintain the fiction of equality of status for official, working languages while at the same time informally encouraging greater use of a limited number of languages. While the commitment to linguistic and cultural diversity will be maintained in principle, pragmatics will determine that less, rather than more, languages are spoken at meetings of EU institutions. As it stands, plurilingual arrangements are already under threat, and the determination in principle not to yield to a smaller number of languages will ensure that those lingua franca which come to the fore are determined by national interests rather than political discussion. This is not a satisfactory situation.

Theoretically official, working languages have equal status, but this largely applies to print material rather than the spoken word. Anderson (1991) identified print capitalism as an important factor in the establishment of linguistic hierarchies. In the context of the EU the power of print designates official languages as being more important than others, but it does not guarantee equality in other sectors. The Union's commitment to a plurilingual regime has dissipated and at a practical level, a new hierarchy of language has emerged within the realm of 'official languages'. While the Council of Ministers uses all official languages in its formal proceedings and the EU has a range of translators and interpreters to deal with key documents, the languages of French and English have come to dominate in less formal situations and the predominance of these languages has varied over time.

Before the accession of Ireland and Britain to the EU, most informal documents were drafted primarily in German and French. Although the Dutch and Italians could have demanded the translation of all materials into their respective languages, they seldom exercised the right to do so and French predominated in informal proceedings in these early stages. As many of the institutions of the EU are located in French-speaking territory, French prevailed in the European courts, although defendants, plaintiffs and witnesses still retained the right to speak their national language at court proceedings.

This singular use of French within the EU in its infancy was merely a reinforcement of its primacy within Europe, that is at least 400-years old. By 1600, French was already developing a leading role in Europe under Henry IV and had become 'the inner-circle language of cultivated German courts'. In contrast, English at this time was regarded as a local rather than a European language. John Florio, the compiler of an English–Italian dictionary in 1598 remarked of it that it was 'a language that will do you good in England, but past Dover it is worth nothing' (Hale 1993: 50).

French was maintained as the sole language of international diplomacy until the end of the First World War, when American (rather than UK) influence ensured a strong profile for English. Prior to the establishment of the EEC, the French endeavoured vigorously to establish their national language as the sole official language of embryo European organisations, but were forced under pressure from other member states to concede the principle of the equality for all four national languages, including German (Phillipson 2003).

However, the linguistic hierarchy has changed over time. In 1970 some 60 per cent of documents were translated into French whereas 40 per cent were translated into German. Since then German has begun to lose its predominant position and by 1989 a mere 9 per cent of unofficial documents were translated in German whereas the proportion translated into English had risen to 30 per cent. The German Government has occasionally complained about the lack of use of their language. In the summer of 1999, for example, they boycotted informal meetings of ministers when German interpretation was not available (Wright 2000a).

Generally speaking, however, they seldom voice such complaints with any energy as to do so could be perceived as a return to Nazi tactics. 'Since 1945, the German government has been concerned to establish its democratic credentials and refrain from any promotion of the German language that could recall Nazi ideology, which attributed almost mythical properties to the language' (Phillipson 2003: 90). The lack of dominance of German is also reflected in the business community. Texts on microbiology, for example, are no longer published in German effectively restricting the development of a German technical vocabulary in this field. Commands on computers in German are also expressed in English (Schröder 1993: 31).

Since the 1970s the circumstances of English have changed dramatically and its increasingly global use has ensured that it now also dominates transactions within EU institutions. The ascendancy of French in the internal operations of the EU was unchallenged until recently but English is now spoken more widely at informal transactions. In 1997 the proportion of languages translated into English was 45 per cent which compares favourably with the figure of 40 per cent for French. Three years later the gap between the two had extended considerably and some 55 per cent of documents were translated into English whereas a mere one-third was rendered into French. The expectation is that the 2004 enlargement will enhance rather than diminish the status of English within EU institutions although it may also favour German to a lesser extent.

The increasing predominance of English within the EU is merely a reflection of the status of English globally. English is the mother tongue of some 300 million people worldwide. A further 300 million speak English as a second language. Another 100 million speak English fluently as a foreign language. Although there are more first and second language speakers of Mandarin Chinese in a global context, English has a higher social and political significance in several key areas. English is used at official and semi-official levels in over 60 countries and has significant status in another 20. It has established a presence in all six continents and is the primary language of newspapers, books, airports and air-traffic control, science, technology and medicine. More than two-thirds of the world's scientists write in English. Some three-quarters of the world's mail is composed in English. Of the information stored in the world's electronic retrieval system 80 per cent is in English and it is the primary language used on the Internet. Over 50 million children learn English as an additional language and a further 80 million study English at secondary levels of education (Crystal 1997b: 360).

Although English may appear naturally suitable for post-modern society, it is important to note that it did not derive its national and inter-national status without intense planning. Instead a publication on the British Council website explains that ' "national" languages in Europe had to be politically planned. The English language was self-consciously expanded and reconstructed to serve the purposes of a national language' (Graddol 1997: 6).

By implication, lesser-used languages are not inherently inferior because they failed to achieve national status. They merely have not had the benefit of official support over a number of centuries (cf. Chapter 4). 'A language does not become a global language because of its intrinsic structural properties, or because of the size of its vocabulary, or because it has been a vehicle of great literature in the past, or because it was once associated with a great culture or religion'. Instead 'a language becomes an international language for one chief reason: the political power of its people – especially their military power' (Crystal 1997a: 7).

Several factors aided the development of English as a language of state in the post-1660 period. Modern institutions of science such as the Royal Society in Britain were established and language became part of their scientific agenda. New terms and ways of writing in English were developed. 'National' systems of education throughout Britain and Ireland promoted the use of English and demoted the status of Celtic languages (Durkacz 1983; Withers 1984). English was adopted as the language of government, of commerce, of law and of social status. Speakers of English were regarded as prestigious, contrasting with speakers of Celtic languages who were perceived as backward and traditional (Nic Craith 1993). Emigration and colonisation were significant factors in the development of English as a global language.

Contemporary society associates English with modernity and progress but this association is not accidental and 'the development model with capitalism and English as both the means and the goal has been exported worldwide' (Skutnabb-Kangas 1999: 194). The colonisation process was a significant factor in the spread of English in the past. Substantial contemporary aid from British and American donors consolidates the dominant role of English in much of Africa and Asia.

The home page of the British Council explicitly links the acquisition of English with respected values in contemporary society. Visitors to the website are invited to ascertain the benefits associated with the acquisition of English. Terms such as 'democracy', 'equality', 'freedom', 'friendship', 'inspiration' and 'independence' flash across a world map. By implication, the visitor associates English language skills with opportunities for progress, liberty and success. A Keltic on-line bookshop invites the learner to purchase English language aids. (In choosing the acronym 'Keltic', the Kensington English Language Teaching Information Centre may have deliberately wished to tap into the positive vibes towards Celticity at the end of the twentieth century!)

Of notable interest in publications on this website is the lack of complacency regarding the future of English. Although, English is widely regarded as the global language, visitors are encouraged to query whether it will retain its pre-eminence in the twenty-first century. They are advised that the next 20 years will be critical for English. It would be 'foolhardy to imagine that its pre-eminent position as a world language will not be challenged in some world regions and domains of use as the economic, demographic and political shape of the world is transformed' (Graddol 1997: 2). This note of caution may surprise speakers of lesser-used languages as it implies that advocates of the use of English work hard at maintaining its world status even when that is unlikely to be threatened.

The status of English within the EU is unlikely to decrease and although the significance of French for the purposes of translation has diminished somewhat, it still remains considerable. French and English are frequently used in informal contexts and when used for such purposes, they are sometimes referred to as 'procedural languages' (Phillipson 2003: 120). Speakers of other official languages do not object to such restrictions as their 'equality' of status is theoretically guaranteed, although 'there is a certain dishonesty in maintaining the fiction that the EU gives equal weight and respect to all official languages of the member states if, in reality, the languages which permit access to the European centres of power are one, perhaps two, dominant lingua francas: English and French' (Smith and Wright 1999: 9).

Effectively, a new hierarchy of state languages has emerged and some official, working languages are deemed more useful than others. At the level of the print community all official languages are considered equal but the increasing use of French and English in informal contexts has led to the de-territorialisation of these languages. According to Lull (2000: 239) de-territorialisation constitutes the initial step in the formation of new cultural territories. He defines this process as the 'partial tearing apart of cultural structures, relationships, settings and representations'. There is a severing of the obvious or natural connection between a cultural concept and a specific territory or social space. Cultural signs are separated from particular locations in time and space and are uprooted from the places we expect them to be (Giddens 1991; Rowe and Schelling 1991).

This is particularly the case with English as ownership of that language is increasingly challenged. Many countries adopting English as their second language are asserting that it is '*their* language, through which they can express their own values and identities, create their own intellectual property and export goods and services to other countries' (italics original in Graddol 1997: 2). When speaking of her 'multicultural English', for example, Rajendran (1999) asserts that her English is basically a Malaysian English. Whichever accent she chooses to use or whatever lexical items she chooses to incorporate, it is her English and it is Malaysian, because she is Malaysian.

A similar view has been expressed by several prominent Indian writers such as Salman Rushdie who has argued that the debate about the appropriateness of English in post-British India has 'meaning only for the older generation. The children of independent India seem not to think of English as being irredeemably tainted by its colonial provenance. They use it as an Indian language, as one of the tools they have to hand' (Crystal 1997a: 136).

In the context of the European Parliament, English is increasingly perceived as European or global rather than a national speech form. Although the globalisation of culture is regarded in the late twentieth century as a paramount trend, commentators usually refer to it in the context of the increasing dominance of Western, and particularly American cultural practices throughout the rest of the world, but this process is also occurring within the EU. With the increasing prominence of English and French, the status of these two languages is enhanced and in the case of English in particular, the links with Britain and England have weakened.

In some sense English no longer reflects the status of its speakers in England and the English no longer have a language of their own. One could not assert that the English spoken by the Irish, the Australians of Japanese descent or Afro-Americans, for example, really belongs to the Anglo-Saxons. The title of the language is frequently qualified as American-English, British-English or Hiberno-English and computers regularly offer spell-checks in at least nine varieties of English (Nic Craith 2002a).

While the globalisation of cultural resources is regarded by many as a natural consequence of high modernity (Giddens 1991), the increasing informal use of French and English within the EU has had implications for the status of other working languages of participating nation states. Inevitably this has created an internal hierarchical structure. Bauman (1998) suggests that progress never moves forward in an egalitarian manner. For that reason globalisation frequently reinforces social divisiveness rather than generating social harmony and unity. 'Globalization divides as much as it unites; its divides as it unites' (1998: 2). It appears that to integrate means making a compromise.

Despite the rhetoric of equality there has been a tacit acceptance of a hierarchy of 'in-house languages' within EU institutions. In the early decades the dominant language was largely French. Now it is primarily English, although to some extent the language preference can vary from region to region. While there is a preference for English as a lingua franca in the mainly Germanic north, the tendency is largely towards French in the south of the continent.

Although a linguistic hierarchy is generally rationalised as the inevitable outcome of pragmatic constraints, it may also be 'underpinned by a belief in the greater appropriacy of these languages (the purported superiority of French, or the role of the French in building up the EU, English now being thought of as a universal open sesame)' (Phillipson 2003: 136). The fact that documents are usually available in French and English at a much earlier stage than other language versions reinforces the impression of this apparent superiority and gives individuals with access to those languages more time to prepare responses compared with others who must wait for translations which they can access (Wright 2000a). Thus we have de jure linguistic equality within EU institutions but de facto two lingua francas, English and French.

Citizens and their languages

At an official level the EU remains committed to the principle of multi-lingualism and this official commitment serves to promote mutual recognition and respect for the equal integrity of all national cultures (Habermas 2001). Overall, support for multilingualism within the EU refers to the institution and its employees but not necessarily to citizens in different member states. While the EU actively encourages citizens to acquire new languages, they can choose to remain monolingual and demand service in their respective national languages. 'Support for multilingualism within the EU must be understood as referring to institutional multilingualism. These serve to "foster language diversity" by enabling member states to continue to function monolingually' (Phillipson 2003: 129).

Sometimes it is argued that restrictions on the number of official and working languages would simplify matters and that a limited number of languages would serve EU citizens equally well. The range of languages could perhaps be reduced to include English, French and possibly German or Spanish. The Spanish situation is particularly interesting as globally it is outstripping French rapidly. In the future it is hard to imagine Spain accepting a continued privileged position for French and to a lesser extent German which is still in decline.

Proponents for a restriction in the number of working languages are usually fluent in one of the more global languages and do not necessarily appreciate the inevitable difficulties for citizens that would have to operate entirely in a foreign language. For these arguments to have any tenacity, the EU should opt for 'smaller' rather than 'larger' languages in such a situation, thereby spreading the burden of disadvantage more equally and generating a genuine appreciation of the problems for those not permitted to operate in their mother tongue.

The arguments against restricting the number of official languages are powerful. In the first instance, it would increase the sense of alienation felt by many citizens in different member states if they could only deal with EU institutions in a foreign language. Members of the public are primarily interested in hearing about EU institutions and regulations in their own language. While the use of an official language does not necessarily guarantee that citizens in member states can deal with the

EU in their mother tongue, the ability to engage with the process in one's national language helps ensure that Brussels is not completely detached from EU citizens (Mackiewicz 2003). 'To put it bluntly, the average citizen in any Member State is not interested in knowing that the Union functions in many languages. People want to know that it speaks their language – and listens to them in their language' (Cunningham 2001: 12).

If the EU aspires to be a meaningful body for all its citizens, then its legislation must have real currency for individuals in different member states. The translation of legislation into national languages goes some way towards ensuring the relevance of these laws for individuals in different countries. EU citizens could hardly be expected to adhere to laws which they cannot understand. Moreover, the translation of these laws into the respective national languages serves as some guarantee of equality before the law (Cunningham 2001; McCloskey 2001).

There is also the issue of work within the EU. Currently every citizen is entitled to become an MEP. As long as s/he can communicate in one of the official languages of the EU, s/he is in a position to operate effectively within Parliament. Restrictions on the number of languages spoken within this institution would necessarily discriminate against those citizens who do not speak one of these limited numbers of languages and could in effect prevent them from aspiring to membership of Parliament. Ultimately this could be perceived as education or class restriction.

Sometime the issue of the cost of language services is raised in relation to the number of official, working languages. This applies particularly to the operation of the translation service. However, there are several arguments to counteract this. The first relates to the actual process of translation as practised in the European Commission. On a day-to-day basis, the Commission uses three working languages – English, French and German. Draft legislations and policy papers are usually produced in one or more of these three languages. It is only at the final stages that documents are translated into all official languages.

Moreover, the European Parliament has devised a time-and cost-effective system for dealing with the translation issue in that it has developed a system of six 'pivot' languages, which are English, French, German, Italian, Polish and Spanish. 'A document presented in say, Slovak or Swedish will not be translated directly into all other 19 languages. Instead it will be translated into the pivot languages and then retranslated from one of them into the others.' This effectively removes the need for translators to work directly from each of the current 20 EU official languages to all of the others which would give a total of 380 bilateral combinations

(European Commission 2004: 19). It also results in a considerable reduction in expenditure. In 1999 the total cost of the interpretation and translation services for all the institutions was 685.9 million euro. When one divides this by the population of the EU, it amounts to less than two euro per citizen, which is hardly a significant liability.

An increase in the number of official languages will not necessarily incur a greater financial burden on EU citizens as the introduction of new, official languages to date has also implied the entry of new taxpayers and an increase in resources within the EU (Cunningham 2001). Moreover, the cost of the translation service is minute in relation to the potential cost of wars and disharmony across EU nations. The EU operates on the basis of 'unity in diversity'. If the recognition and maintenance of linguistic and cultural diversity contributes in a significant manner to peaceful relations, then the number of official, working languages is actually cost-effective and ultimately represents a saving (Mackiewicz 2003).

The process of translation and interpretation brings further benefits to 'smaller' languages in particular. In some countries there has been very little tradition of translating the type of material generated by the EU into and out of various national languages (McCloskey 2001). As language services of the Union interpret and translate new ideas from major official languages into other working languages they make a significant contribution to the ethno-linguistic vitality of these languages (Mackiewicz 2003). Ultimately, there is considerable expectation that the development of appropriate technology will ease the process of translation within the Union. Both EUROTRA and SYSTRAN are used for the translation of basic technical documents, where absolute accuracy is not essential. Although machine translation has a limited capacity, it saves time for individual translators who can refine the first draft produced by the machine (Wright 2000a: 175).

The EU has also highlighted the importance of languages through other initiatives. On 17 July 2000 the European Parliament declared 2001 as the 'European Year of Languages', suggesting that the acquisition of new languages would generate increased awareness of cultural diversity, thereby contributing to the eradication of anti-Semitism, intolerance, racism and xenophobia. One of the primary objectives of the initiative was to emphasise the importance of knowledge of languages as a skill necessary for participation in the European knowledge society and for integration into society.

This principle was further reinforced with the publication of the *Action Plan 2004–2006* which called attention to the principle of 'mother tongue plus two other languages' as the guiding principle for EU citizens. The Commission concluded that the range of foreign languages currently spoken by Europeans was narrow, and confined primarily to English, French, German and Spanish. In consequence, 'member states agree that pupils should master at least two foreign languages, with the emphasis on effective communicative ability: active skills rather than passive know-ledge' (Commission of the European Communities 2003: 6). This is a very optimistic objective.

Moreover the Action Plan specifies that efforts to learn new languages should not be confined to the acquisition of official, working languages. Instead 'the range on offer should include the smaller European languages as well as all the larger ones, regional, minority and migrant languages as well as those with "national" status, and the languages of our major trading partners throughout the world' (Commission of the European Communities 2003: 9). While new initiatives are laudable, a cynic could view them as a necessary stage before the formal reduction of the number of official, working languages of the EU. As long as citizens are primarily monolingual, the EU will be required to offer services in all national languages. If, however, most citizens are competent in two or three languages, then it might be feasible to reduce the number of official, working languages.

The Action Plan was quite explicit in its concern about the impact of the spread of English on national languages in particular. 'In non-Anglophone countries recent trends to provide teaching in English may have unforeseen consequences on the vitality of the national language.' In these circumstances it argued that university language policies should include 'explicit actions to promote the national or regional language' (Commission of the European Communities 2003: 8). While there was general agreement on the benefits of multilingualism for all European citizens, the Commission proposed that 'English alone is not enough' (Commission of the European Communities 2003: 4). Instead lessons should be available in a wide variety of languages.

There are several other points of interest in this Action Plan. Of particular note is the issue of equality of all European languages. The Draft Resolution declared that 'all European languages are equal in value and dignity from the cultural point of view and form an integral part of European culture and civilisation' (Phillipson 2003: 196). While this statement admits the equality of official and non-official languages from a cultural perspective, the lack of reference to the economic perspective merely serves to highlight the lack of economic opportunities in minority language sectors (cf. Chapter 4).

Conclusion

At the time of writing, the draft European Constitution is available in the 20 institution languages plus Irish, as well as the languages of three candidate countries: Bulgarian, Romanian and Turkish. The European Council has also agreed that the Treaty may be translated by individual member states into other languages which enjoy official constitutional status in all or part of their territory. This simply requires that a certified copy of such translations should be provided by the member states concerned and should be deposited in the archives of the Council. Spain has already taken advantage of this article and undertakes to provide certified translations of the constitution in Basque, Catalan and Galician.

Official, working languages are members of an elite club which excludes lesser-used language groups. Minority linguistic groups are not only angry at being left out of the 'elite club' of languages within the EU, but also surprised and irritated when political elites in member states who in the cause of national homogeneity had long suppressed or discouraged cultural and linguistic diversity within their own borders' champion diversity at European level. There appears to be a certain lack of logic in finding plurilingualism divisive and disadvantageous at national level but a source of cultural capital within a broader context. Numerous regional groups and linguistic minorities have pointed out the anomaly and used it in their own struggle for linguistic maintenance and cultural recognition.

4
'A Hierarchy of Legitimacies': Minority Languages

Academics and policy makers usually organise languages into several distinct categories. English, Chinese, Arabic, German, French or Spanish are easily identified as majority or dominant languages, but a variety of groupings are used to order 'middle-sized' languages, which may be characterised as 'minorised', 'lesser-used', 'less-widely spoken' or even the convoluted 'less-widely taught, less-widely used' languages. These categories are entirely contextual and the ascription of minority or majority status to a language depends on specific political contexts. French is spoken as a first language by over 50 million speakers and is clearly a world language, yet in the context of Italy, it is considered a 'minority' language. German is the majority language in Germany and Austria and is spoken in many countries worldwide but is a minority language in Denmark.

Logic hardly applies in the use of these designations. Although there are some 6,565,000 speakers of Catalan and 5,326,000 speakers of Danish (Grimes 2000), Catalan is classed as a lesser-used language while Danish enjoys the advantages of officialdom in the context of the EU. Other more intriguing examples include the case of German in Switzerland. Although German is the most widely used official language of Switzerland, there are individual cantons where it is a minority language. At the same time, Italian is a minority language in the confederation as a whole, but within the canton of Ticino, it is the sole official language. Then there is the case of Russian in the Baltic States. Although Russian has no official status here, it is actually more widely used than the state language in some regions (Blair 2003).

Many of these categories exclude any reference to non-indigenous and non-European languages. 'There are more speakers of Turkish living in the EU than of Danish, but no government insists that the [EU] documentation be available to them in their first language' (Barbour 1996: 38). This exclusion of non-European languages from the general terms of reference will be explored in Chapter 8.

While the distinction between majority and minority languages in the Western world usually refers to relative numerical size, it is more appropriate to think of it in terms of access to power in a specific political context (see Nelde *et al.* 1996, Skutnabb-Kangas 2000). The primary difference between dominant and minority languages pertains to rights, privileges and planning, and perhaps the primary common factors uniting speakers of minority languages is that in established nation states they do not have majority status and have not had the benefit of decades and centuries of state language planning. Arguably, where there is a strong element of devolution, this situation may be redressed somewhat as is the case with German in South Tyrol (cf. Chapter 5).

'Linguicism' is the term used to describe this categorisation of languages and it has been defined as 'ideologies, structures and practices which are used to legitimate, effectuate and reproduce an unequal division of power and resources (material and immaterial) between groups which are defined on the basis of language' (Phillipson 1992: 47). The process of linguicism is of significant influence in determining political and economic advantages for dominant languages. It is also used to construct some languages negatively as non-resources, even as handicaps, which may prevent children from enjoying the 'full benefits' of majority languages.

Minority languages and national ideologies

Dominant languages invariably have government support and have emerged in the world scene in consequence of their political strength. Such languages are constructions of the nation state in the first instance and have enjoyed state sponsorship over decades and centuries. They appear eminently suitable for contemporary society as the linguistic and educational processes employed in the construction of nation states have linked them 'inexorably to modernity and progress while consigning their minority counterparts to the realms of primitivism and stasis' (May 2001: 310).

Essentially dominant languages are given state recognition and affirmation in the public space. Society imagines that these languages are naturally advantaged rather than socially constructed. In contrast, minority languages are deemed to be inherently handicapped and unworthy of state respect or planning. Official recognition is frequently withheld from such languages, which are perceived as simply incapable of dealing with modern contexts. This is not simply a matter of non-recognition. Instead it is a process of 'mis-recognition' (Bourdieu 1991) as it denies the inherent potential of such languages.

If the establishment of chosen 'national' languages was a deliberate, political act, so too was the process by which other language varieties were subsequently 'minoritised' within these same nation states. These minoritised language varieties were, in effect, deemed to be of lesser political worth by the newly formed polities. 'Measured *de facto* against the single standard of the "common" language, they are found wanting and cast into the outer darkness or *regionalisms*, the "corrupt expressions and mispronunciations" which schoolmasters decry' (italics original in Bourdieu 1991: 54).

National languages came to be associated with modernity and progress, while their less fortunate counterparts were associated with tradition, purity and ultimately disappearance. The association of national languages with logic and rationality ensured that they 'were to be deployed in pursuing "modern" activities demanding the essence of reason'. In contrast, regional or minority languages 'could be deployed for the emotive context of the "traditional"' (Nelde *et al.* 1996: 3).

More often than not, regional or minority languages were also constructed as problematic – as '*obstacles* to the political project of nation-building – as threats to the "unity" of the state – thus providing the *raison d'être* for the consistent derogation, diminution and ascription of minority languages that have characterised the last three centuries of nationalism' (italics in original, May 2003: 213). This has applied to Breton and Occitan, for example.

Minority languages became a political issue in many contexts. For example, in the late 1980s, the German government estimated that there were at least one million German-speakers in Poland, whereas the Polish government suggested this minority to be less than 3000 speakers (Nelde 2000: 442). While the situation of the German-speaking minority in Poland has not generated conflict and terrorism, there are many instances in contemporary Europe where a minority language is still associated with physical violence. In the case of Northern Ireland the violence has reputedly ended whereas in the Basque example, continuing violence impacts negatively on the use of the language.

The Basque language is one of three main regional languages in Spain and has traditionally been spoken in an area called *Euskal Herria* the Basque Country (Stuijt *et al.* 1998; Gardner 2000). In contemporary times, this name is applied to an area comprising seven historical provinces;

four of these (Araba/Álava, Bizkaia/Vizcaya, Gipuzkoa/Guipúzcoa and Nafarroa/Navarra) are located in Spain and the remaining three (Lapurdi/ Labourd, Nafarroa Beherea/Basse Navarre and Zuberoa/Soule) are across the border in France (Map 4.1).

The history of Basque-speaking provinces has to be set in the context of the policies of regionalism versus centralism. By the Middle Ages Castille had taken control of the three Basque Provinces in Spain but Navarre maintained its independent status until 1512 when it was captured by Ferdinand of Aragon and Regent of Castille. Less than 20 years later the territory on the French side of the border was relinquished. Although Basques retained their autonomous rights at this time, the Basque language was abandoned by the middle classes (Alcock 2000: 17).

Map 4.1   Basque-speaking historical provinces. *Source*: Adapted from Kockel (1999).

In 1807 Napoleon was given the right to set up garrisons in Spain. However, the following year, the French Emperor intervened in a dispute which effectively placed his own brother on the Spanish throne. Emphasis on the role of ordinary individuals in saving the nation in the subsequent war reopened the debate on centralism versus regionalism. The role of the individual effort was later re-emphasised after the French Revolution in 1789. After the first Carlist War (1841), Navarre lost the status of kingdom to become a province of Spain. Following the second Carlist War in 1876, the linguistic rights of Spanish Basques were abolished. Those living in Navarre were not affected as severely at this time and while their fuero was not abolished, it did suffer a gradual process of erosion.

In this political context Basque nationalism flourished and placed great emphasis on the distinctiveness and uniqueness of the Basque people as crucial to the nationalist cause. Nationalist leaders sought public affirmation of and recognition for Basque identity. At different times, nationalist leaders emphasised the significance of Euskera, the Basque language which is the only non-Indo-European language spoken in Western Europe. As with Ireland, the earliest organisers of Basque nationalism were members of the middle classes. These *petit bourgeoisie* viewed the rapid industrialisation of the Basque country as a threat both to their local status and to the traditional way of life.

Sabino Arana, the founder and leader of the Basque Nationalist Party (PNV) was somewhat ambivalent towards the language but recognised its usefulness as a significant cultural marker of the Basque people. From his perspective, the originality of Euskera and its resistance to influence or corruption from other languages was conclusive proof of the purity of the Basque people. Arana was determined to cleanse Basque of its Spanish borrowing and one of his legacies was to 'distort and complicate Euskara while attempting to purify it' (Conversi 1997: 64). Arana pursued this goal with such vigour that it led him 'to "invent" a purified idiom virtually alien from the language spoken by the common people', although many of these were subsequently adopted by other nationalists and Basque-speakers.

For Arana, the Basque language was subordinate to the concept of race and there may have been practical reasons for this stance. Euskara was a minority language and 'was barely spoken in the urban centres, especially in his home city of Bilbao where he was most politically active and created the first nuclei of Basque nationalism' (Conversi 1997: 65). Although Arana did not conceive of Euskara as the primary vehicle of Basque worldviews, he was aware of its traditional importance as a signifier of Basqueness, although preferring to subordinate it to the concept of race.

As with many other regional and minority languages in Europe, the use of Basque was primarily confined to fishing communities and the rural peasantry by the middle of the nineteenth century. Its social status declined further with the establishment of primary schools in the 1880s which used Castilian or Spanish as the medium of instruction. The lack of recognition of Basque within a national system of education generated the stigmatisation of Basque as a tongue for the uneducated.

The negativity implied in the classification of some languages as non-national had severe impacts on many speech communities throughout Europe at this time. Speakers of lesser-used languages frequently become active themselves in the process of jettisoning or abandoning their traditional languages and cultures. 'The negative attitudes may be so entrenched that even when the authorities get around to doing something about it – introducing community projects, protective measures, or official language policies – the indigenous community may greet their effort with unenthusiasm, scepticism, or outright hostility' (Crystal 2000: 84).

In the past, minority communities frequently consented to the 'symbolic violence' that was visited upon them and presupposed their traditional languages to be inherently inferior and incapable of dealing with the modern technological world. Grillo (1989) has called this the 'ideology of contempt'. In nineteenth-century Ireland, for example, the Irish language (majority at the time) was associated with backwardness and a peasant lifestyle whereas English was perceived as the language of modernisation (Nic Craith 1993) 'English was, practically, the sole language of administration, law, literacy and commerce. It was almost universally the language needed by the urban immigrant and the emigrant overseas. Conversely Gaelic has become associated with igno-rance, struggle and distress' (MacDonagh 1983: 105). In many instances the decline of language usage was a direct consequence of the association of the language with traditionality. It derived 'from a rejection of the language associated with a negative identity that links the relegation of the language and the language group into a world which is conceived of as "traditional"' (Nelde *et al.* 1996: 22).

In the case of Basque, speakers of the language refused to accept the stigmatisation of their language. There was also an attempt to standardise the seven dialects of writing in the Basque language, but these efforts ceased with the outbreak of civil war and the process was not completed until the 1960s. By this time Spain was under the control of the dictator General Franco who took control from 1939 to 1975. During this period, the Basque Government which had been formed 3 years earlier went into exile and the PNV effectively went into hiding. Franco introduced many severe measures to curb the speaking of Basque and to suppress any distinctive emblems of Basque identity.

In the late 1950s Basque youths reacted against what they perceived as the passivity of their parents by setting up *Euskadi ta Askatasuna* (The Basque Country and Freedom), more commonly known as ETA. In its initial period, ETA was a broad cultural and humanist movement but it gradually evolved into an armed organisation with separatist and revolutionary aims. In the course of its evolution it went through a series of schisms but in each case, the original name of ETA was retained by those who kept their arms and believed in the process of violence to achieve independence. During the final years of the Franco's dictatorship, the PNV not only re-emerged as the major political force in the area but also fractured into various schisms.

Members of ETA and their sympathisers tend to think in terms of culture, territory or class ('Basque labour'). To them the Basque language is the central cultural symbol, a form of distinctiveness and singularity, which was suppressed but rescued from the Francoist regime. ETA's perspective on the language reinforced the Whorfian (1956) determinist view that a language effectively filters a culture and reflects it. In its strong form this theory is no longer generally supported, but language is still regarded as the authentic marker of culture by many. In their promotion of Euskera, Basque nationalists affirmed an inextricable link between language and worldview. The loss of their ancestral tongue would result in the disappearance of a distinctively Basque mode of thought.

In the 1960s the Franco regime took a more tolerant view of regional languages and after its fall, the new democratic Spanish State adopted a more positive position on its minority languages in the 1978 constitution. While the constitution established Spanish as the official language of the state, it permitted co-official local languages in the autonomous communities or regions of Spain. Basque autonomy was established with the Statute of Guernica in 1979 and Basque was given co-official status throughout the Basque Autonomous Community and in part of Navarre (Gardner 2000: 3). Basque acquired a strong presence in the educational sector and pupils could choose Basque and/or Spanish as their medium of instruction in schools.

Although the Basque Autonomous Community was given sole jurisdiction in 39 areas, the laws of the Basque Parliament were dependent on the State Constitutional Tribunal for their legitimacy and constitutionality. This ability of the State Constitutional Tribunal angered members of

ETA and served as one justification for a continuation of political violence (Alcock 2000: 148). From their perspective there were also the issue of the denial of the right of self-determination as well as the imposition of limited autonomy.

The political wing of ETA has consciously striven to raise public consciousness of the significance of the Basque nation and regard Basque patriotism as a status defined by performance rather than birth. Radical leaders think and speak in terms of the grand Basque nation. They seek to increase the numbers speaking Basque and to afford greater public recognition of its vitality, which has resulted in many new ventures.

In recent years the language has gained a new significance in defining Basque identity and this is not confined to those of Basque descent. A spirit of inclusivity embraces learners of the Basque language and has generated the term *Euskaldunberri*, that is new Basque-speaker. In the mid-1960s the term referred to all those (native and immigrant) who were voluntarily acquiring the language, and 'contemporary nationalists have chosen to stress the participation of "all new Basque-speakers" in the making of the Basque *Herria*' (Conversi 1997: 67).

The majority of Basques enjoy their culture and its reinvention and fusion with other elements of modern society. Fiestas are one of the main cultural expressions of Basque culture. The nationalist left and particularly its youth are more active in the community than the average Basque and tend to politicise some cultural events. But it is important to emphasise here that the speaking of the Basque language and the celebration of Basque culture is not inherently or necessarily political although in some instances it has been politicised by those seeking political independence.

While this can benefit the language by increasing the numbers speaking the language, it can also have the opposite effect. Some Basques who oppose Basque nationalism have reacted against the language movement which they link to nationalist politics, 'and non-nationalists have become increasingly belligerent with regard to what they consider expansionist language policies' (Gardner 2000: 19).

This debate concerning the politicisation of language is hardly confined to the Basque example and the situation in Spain can be compared with that of Irish in Northern Ireland. Irish cultural nationalism came to the fore in the late nineteenth century and largely dissipated with independence for the Southern 26 counties in the early 1920s. In the case of the remaining six in Northern Ireland, nationalist ideology re-emerged in the second half of the twentieth century. In the mid-80s when violence abounded in Northern Ireland, the Irish language proved extremely significant for individuals who were unhappy with their British status and strove for re-unification with the Republic of Ireland.

Gerry Adams (1986: 143), the political leader of the Republican, Nationalist party, Sinn Féin, argued that 'the restoration of our culture must be a crucial part of our political struggle and that the restoration of the Irish language must be a central part of the cultural struggle'. Before the onset of power-sharing in the national assembly, the use of Irish was often perceived as a powerful political act. 'The Irish language is the reconquest of Ireland and the reconquest of Ireland is the Irish language. The language of the people shall revive the people' (Adams 1986: 147).

For many Irish republicans in the 1980s speaking Irish generated sentiments of protest and that community was familiar with examples of alleged discrimination against speakers of Irish. For example, Éamonn McCann (1974) recounted the case of the Irish language teacher, Frankie Meehan, who was stopped by the police in 1957 and answered in Irish. Meehan was subsequently imprisoned for 7 months without trial. Other stories of alleged harassment abound. One commentator wrote that if 'people were not harassed [by officials of the British State] over using Irish names, speaking Irish or whatever, Irish probably would not have been as important according to some'. When youths shouted 'tiocfaidh ár lá' (our day will come) at individual members of the British security forces, 'the fact that it was in Irish was as much an act of defiance as the actual words' (Ó hAdhmaill 1990: 328).

Republicans pursuing the nationalist cause regarded Irish as 'the rightful language of the nation' (Sands 1982: 150). Its use by prisoners in the 1980s in the H-Block prison considerably enhanced the appeal of the language to the republican community at large. The subsequent deaths of some of these Irish-speaking republican prisoners elevated them and the language itself to a heroic level. Learning and speaking Irish was perceived as an affirmation of the republican cause.

In the case of Northern Ireland many nationalists regard Irish as their mother tongue. This applies even when they do not speak the language fluently. Irish may not be the language of their childhood, yet it is perceived as their own language, as describing and interpreting the Irish worldview. Tolkien regarded Welsh in a similar fashion. He distinguished it as his native rather than his cradle tongue. Interestingly, many loyalists who are utterly committed to unity with Britain believe that Irish represents their own native tongue. (In this they refer to the Gaelic language spoken by their ancestors in Scotland.) A former loyalist prisoner,

William Smith (1994: 17) describes the effect of Irish in the prison camps as follows: 'I was listening to a language that I couldn't understand, that I had never heard before, but it was not a foreign language. It was my own native tongue.'

In the early 1980s the Irish language strengthened a sense of community in a variety of sectors in Northern Ireland. For the republican tradition it easily identified members of their own community within the Maze prison and one of its principal advantages was that of separating 'insiders' from 'outsiders', of placing a linguistic barrier between Irish republican prisoners and British wardens but the efficacy of the language as a boundary marker was always in danger as prison wardens frequently 'threatened' that they were learning it, that they would soon know what republican prisoners were saying.

McKeown (1996: 46), a former republican prisoner, recounts the anxiety of prisoners when it appeared that on one occasion a new officer was familiar with Irish. He refers to a specific incident when a new prison officer opened the door of one of the cells and recited the prayer 'Hail Mary' in Irish. As the prayer finished, the prison officers slammed the cell door shut and went up the wing 'hooting and cheering'. For a time the republican prisoners were very concerned but quickly established that the officer's knowledge of Irish was superficial. Following a few brief meetings with the new warden, they 'addressed him in Irish in what appeared to be a serious manner but which was in reality heaping abuse upon him, it became obvious that his grasp of the language did not extend beyond the solitary prayer'.

A revival of interest in Irish in the community at large linked the Irish-speaking republicans in the Maze prisons with their supporters in the community at large. In the wider Northern Irish community the use of Irish in street signs and in murals served to identify nationalist areas. At this stage in its evolution, republicans were accused of using the language as a tool of exclusion and many of those who spoke the language were politically motivated. Their cultural and political commitments were inseparable.

However, in an era of peace and reconciliation, such images have altered and the British Government recognises Irish for the purpose of funding and so on. The director of the ULTACH Trust, an organisation for the promotion of the language across all communities, conceives of Irish as a tool of integration rather than segregation and explains that the inclusion/exclusion dichotomy will not be alleviated by the de-politicisation of Irish. Instead it is more appropriate to multi-politicise the language and render it acceptable to all political traditions (ULTACH Trust 1994: 15).

Although speakers of Irish are not completely free from the suspicion that they espouse republican ideologies as a matter of course, the Irish language has gained some credibility within the official realm, not merely as a symbol of nationalist or republican ideology but as a linguistic human right that can be enjoyed by those who wish to speak it in a non-confrontational manner.

In both these examples of Basque and Irish, proponents of minority languages clashed with the ideology of the nation state which in the past at least presupposed the notion of one national language for the nation. Moreover, the existence of minority languages appeared to threaten the security of the state. The recognition of minority languages was deemed to be dangerous as 'it may encourage linguistic minorities to think that they "own" a part of the country and therefore have a right to choose to break away from the state' (Kymlicka and Grin 2003: 15). With the emergence of the EU, the context for minority languages has changed considerably, and speakers of such languages operate in a transnational rather than a national context. For many this has proved an advantage rather than a difficulty.

A hierarchy of minority languages

Ultimately the term 'minority' refers to a group or community of people who share a language. It refers to speakers of a language rather than the language itself. As the context (or the location!) changes, so does language status. 'In some cases the term "minority" language is in fact an official language of the European Union, for political borders do not always follow the main cultural divides' (Directorate-General for Research 2002: 22). Moreover, with the exception of some major languages such as English, and possibly French, all languages in the EU are minority languages because in a transnational context they are spoken by a numerical minority.

There are different ways of categorising minority languages in the EU (Nic Craith 2004). One could, for example, categorise the autochthonous communities into four main groups that have emerged in the course of recent history. The first of these refers to a minority in a member state who speak a language that is one of the official and working languages of the EU. This would apply to German-speakers in Eastern Belgium or South Tyrol and to Greek-speakers in Puglia and Calabria or to Finnish-speakers in Sweden.

The second category refers to those who speak one of the two 'semi-official' languages of the EU. In the previous chapter we noted the position of Irish which, despite its treaty status, has not been an official, working language of the Union. Luxemburgish is also in an anomalous position. Although it is a national language of Luxembourg, French is the sole language for legislative purposes. While Luxemburgish can be used for administrative or judicial purposes, it is generally marginalised in its written form (Warasin 2003). Yet Luxemburgish is one of the languages covered by the Lingua Action of the Socrates Programme – an advantage which also applies to Icelandic and Norwegian because Socrates extends to the non-EU members of the European Economic Area (EEA).

The third transnational category refers to speakers of minority languages which enjoy some degree of official recognition in the states in which they are spoken. Here one would include the cases of Basque, Catalan and Galician in Spain as well as some of the Celtic languages in Britain and in Ireland such as Welsh, Scottish-Gaelic and Irish and the indigenous Sámi languages in the Nordic Countries.

The final category of minority language encompasses those which do not enjoy official recognition within the EU or in the member state in which they are spoken. Examples here would include Aroumainian, Arvanite, Pomak and Slavo-Macedonian in Greece (Grin and Moring 2002).

The previous chapter noted discrepancies with regard to the respective status of official languages in the EU. The same proposition holds for minority languages in a transnational context. Although they may appear to face similar issues, speakers of minority languages are rarely in similar positions and the recognition or non-recognition of their language in home and other territories may have significant implications for progress in different contexts.

One can illustrate selected examples of the differential status in table format: Table 4.1 offers examples of languages which are dominant and official in one state but have regional, minority in positions several others

Table 4.1 Languages with official status in one state but minority positions in others

Official language	Minority language
Albanian	Italy, Greece
Croatian	Italy, Austria
German	France, Italy, Belgium, Denmark
Greek	Albania, Italy
Slovenian	Austria, Italy

while Table 4.2 provides examples of languages that are official in one country state and have a minority position in merely one other. Table 4.3 refers to regional languages spoken in more than one member state of the EU. Table 4.4 offers selected examples of minority languages that are spoken in one member state only.

Table 4.2   Languages with official status in one state but a minority position in one other

Official language	Minority context
Czech	Austria
Danish	Germany
Dutch	France
Finnish	Sweden
French	Italy
Greece	Italy
Macedonian	Greece
Portuguese	Spain
Slovak	Austria
Swedish	Finland
Turkish	Greece

Table 4.3   Regional languages spoken in more than one member state of the EU

Language	Spoken in
Basque	Spain, France
Catalan	Andorra, Spain, France, Italy
Limburgian	Netherlands, Belgium
Low-Saxon/Low-German	Netherlands, Germany
Occitan	Spain, France, Italy
Sámi	Norway, Sweden, Finland, Kola Peninsula

Table 4.4   Minority languages spoken in only one member state of the EU

State	Minority Languages
France	Breton, Corsican
Germany	North Frisian, Saterfrisian, Sorbian
Great Britain	Welsh, Scots-Gaelic, Scots, Ulster-Scots
Italy	Friulan, Ladin, Sardinian
Portugal	Mirandes
Spain	Galician, Aragonese, Asturian
The Netherlands	Frisian

In the past two decades, there have been many attempts to ascertain the precise strengths and weaknesses of many of these minority languages, primarily with a view to deciphering how such languages could be revitalised. One of the better-known case studies is that of Joshua Fishman who introduced the graded intergenerational disruption scale (GIDS) in 1991 with the publication of his *Reversing Language Shift*. Fishman suggested that there are essentially eight stages of 'threatened-ness' that make up GIDS. Reversing language shift can then be seen as a process whereby a minority language group moves from stage eight, which is extreme disruption, to the first stage. The eight stages of the GIDS can be briefly characterised as follows.

Stage eight represents the weakest possible situation and refers to a language that has merely ancient speakers and no written standard. Stage seven is hardly a significant improvement in that it refers to a language context where speakers are past child-bearing age and can no longer contribute numerically to the future of the language. In stage six, intergenerational family functioning is potentially possible. Fishman regards this stage as very important strategically as 'the lion's share of the world's intergenerationally continuous languages are at this very stage and they continue to survive and, in most cases, even to thrive, without going on to subsequent ("higher") stages' (1991: 92). Stage five includes minority language literacy at home, in the school and local community, but as it has no official recognition or support, such literacy remains confined to the locality.

The remaining stages focus on the reclamation of the language in different sectors. Stage four represents a major break, because at this point the minority language gains some official recognition and becomes part of mainstream formal education. In stage three the minority language is reclaimed in the 'lower work sphere'. This situation improves yet again in stage two, where the language is used in 'lower governmental services' and the mass media. Although the minority language is not used in the higher spheres of either governmental services or the media at this stage, it represents an important point in the process towards full recognition in formal spheres.

At the uppermost and first stage, the minority language is used in higher education and in the higher realms of government, media and professional life. This does not necessarily imply that the process of language reversal is complete or that language planning is no longer necessary, but at least it ensures that the mechanism for the reproduction of the language community is in place and the language has a real chance of survival. In 2002, Grin and Moring endeavoured to assign a

GIDS score to minority languages within the EU. Selected results are illustrated in Table 4.5:

The EU has also made some attempt to categorise the minority languages within its boundaries and the Euromosaic Report (1996) aimed to set minority language groups within the conceptual framework of a multicultural Europe. The primary focus of the authors was on speakers and communities of minority languages rather than on the languages themselves. Their purpose was to acknowledge the strong and persistent economic and social pressures on speakers of minority languages to assimilate into a majority group. To focus on the language itself would result in the reification of language, as if it had a life of its own, and the avoidance of the real issues – that is, problems for speakers of these languages.

Table 4.5 Selected minority languages in the EU according to GIDS

Stage	Language
One (strongest)	Catalan in Catalonia
	Welsh in Wales
	Basque in the BAC
Two	Catalan in Mallorca
	German in Belgium
	Danish in Germany
Three	Sámi in Sweden
	Basque in Navarre
	Turkish in Greece
Four	Basque in France
	Ladin
	Slovenian in Austria
Five	Irish in Northern Ireland
	Franco-Provençal in Italy
	Slovak in Austria
Six	Berber in Spain
	(Slavo) Macedonian in Greece
	Hungarian in Austria
Seven	Portuguese in Spain
	Albanian in Greece
	Greek in Italy
Eight (weakest)	Aroumanian
	Cornish

Source: Adapted from Grin and Moring (2002).

The Euromosaic Report was similar in format to the GIDS research in that it produced a scaled rating of different language communities on the basis of seven variables which the authors regarded as essential for the healthy survival of a specific language group. As was the case with GIDS, the higher rating implies a healthier position. Many language planners place great emphasis on the educational sphere and the most significant variable from the perspective of the authors of Euromosaic was education and the extent to which the language was either taught as a subject or used as a medium of instruction.

The second variable focused on the family and the degree to which the language was transmitted from one generation to the next. Reproduction also featured prominently in the third stage although in this instance the focus was on cultural rather than physical activities. In particular, the authors explored the extent to which there was a range of programmes, radio stations, TV channels in the language, as well as published press.

The authors considered official status for the language (i.e. legitimation) as a vital fourth variable and included bodies established for the development and promotion of the language community within this contextual framework. The institutionalisation of the language constituted the fifth variable. Here the authors considered the extent to which the use of the language in various public spheres was considered habitual or normal, rather than exceptional.

The final two variables focused on prestige and community. The sixth variable explored the significance attached to fluency in the language for the purposes of socio-economic advancement. The link between language and economy is a vital and frequently under-researched issue (Nic Craith 2002b). They also considered the extent to which the language is used in informal social community relations, and by associations and clubs in the immediate environment (Grin and Moring 2002).

Overall the Euromosaic Report concluded that one cannot essentialise the process of language shift, but it was clear from their report that many of the smaller linguistic minorities were in serious decline and their future prospects were extremely doubtful. On the other hand their report concluded that languages in cross-border situations (the focus of the next chapter) gained from the majority status in another country. For example, German-speaking groups in minority contexts frequently had access to majority German media which in turn served to empower the minority language community.

Grin and Moring (2002) combined the GIDS and Euromosaic scales for each of the 55 RML (Regional or Minority Languages) communities

Table 4.6   Selected minority languages in the EU according to Euromosaic and GIDS

Cluster 1 (strongest)	Cluster 2	Cluster 3
Swedish in Finland	Turkish in Greece	Frisian
Catalan in Catalonia	Basque in Navarre	Croatian in Austria
Luxemburgish	Danish in Germany	Sorbian
Welsh	German in Denmark	Basque in France
Basque in the BAC	Irish	Sámi in Finland

Cluster 4	Cluster 5 (weakest)
Irish in Northern Ireland	North Frisian
Albanian in Italy	(Slavo)Macedonian
Sámi in Sweden	East Frisian
Czech, Slovak in Austria	Albanian in Greece
Breton	Cornish

Source: Adapted from Grin and Moring (2002).

identified in the Euromosaic report and found them to be concentrated primarily in five clusters. While Table 4.6 offers a unique overview of the relative strengths and weaknesses of selected languages in each cluster, one must be aware of the fact that they are based on a survey conducted some 10 years ago. The situation of some of these language communities has altered in the intervening period.

The authors of this table acknowledge that many developments have occurred since the collection of the data which may impact on the scoring of the languages. However, they are also quite emphatic that few would actually change cluster as a result. Irish in Northern Ireland is one possible exception here.

There are many languages in contemporary Europe that are not included in this table. These include the minority languages of those countries which joined the EU in 2004 as well as non-European languages which were not included within the terms of reference of the Euromosaic Report. Non-territorial languages such as those of the Roma and Sinti are excluded and the table also omits languages which did not have recognition at the time of the survey such as Scots (Lallans) and Ulster-Scots in the UK and Lower German in Germany (cf. Chapter 6). For this reason the table serves as an indicator rather than an absolute criterion for language strength but it does provide a useful overview.

The transnational context

For many minority language groups, the EU offers a transnational context that is an opportunity rather than a threat. In a transnational context, the relevance of a nation state for a minority language community is diminished. This is a happy scenario for speakers of many minority languages as the formation of nation states have generally hampered rather than consolidated minority cultures and languages. Minority groups were frequently involuntary members of specific nation states and their membership was determined by conquest rather than integration. Accession to the EU changes the context considerably and minority groups no longer have to operate solely within national structures. 'A unified Europe offers all the potential for economic and monetary cohesion, redistribution of money, transport infrastructure and educational standards that in the past had to be filtered through a larger nation' (Mundy 1997: 50).

Since its inception the EU has primarily focused on official, working languages rather than on minority groups but there have been some specific initiatives in relation to minority language policy (Nic Shuibhne 2002, 2003). In 1979, Gaetano Arfè MEP presented a motion for a resolution on a 'Charter of Ethnic Minorities'. Some months later, a second motion was tabled by John Hume MEP, calling for a Community Charter of Regional Languages and Cultures. For our purposes the second of these was extremely important as it drew attention to languages as an integral part of Europe's diversity.

Over the years a number of resolutions have drawn the attention of MEPs to the role of minority languages within the Union. The Arfè 1981 resolution on a Community Charter of Regional Languages and Cultures and on a Charter of Rights of Ethnic Minorities called on authorities at national, regional and local levels to take measures in education, in the media, in public life and social affairs, in courts and in other official bodies. The resolution recommended that regional funds be allocated for the support of folk and regional cultures and for regional economic projects. Moreover, the Commission was asked to review all Community legislation or practices which operated against minority languages (European Commission 1981).

Two years later, another Arfè resolution in favour of minority languages and cultures highlighted the significance of the previous resolution and called upon the Commission to intensify its efforts in this sphere. The Commission was asked to inform the Parliament about practical measures that could help speakers of minority languages. One proposal was for the establishment of an organisation which would represent the 30–40 million speakers of minority languages at European level (European Commission 1983).

The following year the European Bureau for Lesser Used Languages (EBLUL) was established, setting the stage for great improvement. Yet many initiatives failed to have any real impact at this time and the Kuijpers resolution of 1987 on the Languages and Cultures of Regional and Ethnic Minorities in the European Community formally regretted the lack of progress (European Commission 1987). The resolution urged member states to provide a legal basis for the use of regional and minority languages and proposed a review of national practices that prejudiced minority languages. It also urged government services to use national, regional and minority languages in specific areas such as the official recognition of place names and surnames in a minority language in postal services, in consumer information and in product labelling. It highlighted the significance of economic support for minority languages and granted the Intergroup on Lesser Used Languages full official status in the European Parliament.

In 1991 the Viviane Reding resolution on the position of languages within the community was passed. This resolution had a special focus on speakers of Catalan who have consistently sought official status on the basis of the sheer numbers speaking the language (European Commission 1991). A report accompanying this resolution included a general consideration of the multilingual institutional context of Europe, before looking into specifically at the case of Catalan.

The following year the CoE concluded its draft of a charter specifically for the purpose of encouraging preservation and promotion of Europe's indigenous, minority languages. This European Charter for Regional and Minority Languages (ECRML) has had a significant, long-term impact and is quite precise in its definition of regional or minority languages (Blair 2003). It pertains to languages that are 'traditionally used within a given territory of a State by nationals of that State who form a group numerically smaller than the rest of the State's population', and to those that are 'different from the official language(s) of the State'. It is quite clear from the text that the Charter does not pertain to dialects of the official state languages. Moreover it confines itself solely to autochthonous languages and does not include languages of migrants within its terms of reference.

In 1994 the Killilea resolution urged member states of the EU to ratify this Charter and to enact legislation for the use of minority languages in fields identified in the document such as education, justice, public administration and the media (European Commission 1994). This resolution also favoured increased financial support for the national committees of EBLUL and adequate budgetary provision for programmes in favour of minority languages, including languages of non-territorial, indigenous minorities.

The Charter formally came into force in March 1998. This was a significant period for regional and minority languages generally as the USA passed two Native American Languages Acts at this time. These Acts were designed to promote the freedom of Native Americans to speak and develop their mother tongue (Crystal 2000: 135). The ECRML is divided into five parts. Part I, General Provisions, is primarily concerned with definitions and practical arrangements. Part II obliges acceding states to accept the general objectives and principles of the Charter. Part III outlines appropriate measures to promote and enhance the use of regional or minority languages in public life. This section offers details on the practical measures that are required of states ratifying the Charter. These arrangements pertain to various public spheres where languages are spoken, including education, the judicial and administrative authorities and the public services. The document is also concerned with the media, cultural activities and facilities and with the status of languages in the economic and social life within and between nation states.

There are two levels of adherence to the Charter. A signature commits member states to the principles of the Charter as set out in the initial sections. States signing the Charter are not obliged to immediately extend its terms of reference to all languages within their boundaries. Instead they identify the languages to which it will first apply and are free to extend the number of nominated languages at a later stage. At the time of writing, 30 member states of the CoE have signed the document, and 17 of these have actually ratified it. (Of notable interest here are the examples of Caucasian countries such as Azerbaijan who have joined this European club!)

Ratification of the Charter is a more intensive commitment and obliges member states to the application of a minimum of 35 paragraphs or sub-paragraphs from the 65 options given in Part III. At least one of the 35 must be chosen from Article 9 which relates to judicial authorities. Table 4.7 outlines the details of countries that have signed or ratified this document to date.

The implications of this international covenant are gradually being acknowledged by member states of the CoE and vary considerably from country to country. In the case of the UK, for example, the Government signed the Charter initially in relation to five languages: Scots, Ulster-Scots,

Table 4.7 Nation states that have signed or ratified the ECRML (July 2005)

Member state	Signature	Ratification	Entry into force
Armenia	11/05/2001	25/01/2002	01/05/2002
Austria	05/11/1992	28/06/2001	01/10/2001
Azerbaijan	21/12/2001		
Croatia	05/11/1997	05/11/1997	01/03/1998
Cyprus	12/11/1992	26/08/2002	1/12/2002
Czech Republic	09/11/2000		
Denmark	05/11/1992	08/09/2000	01/01/2001
Finland	05/11/1992	09/11/1994	01/03/1998
France	07/05/1999		
Germany	05/11/1992	16/09/1998	01/01/1999
Hungary	05/11/1992	26/04/1995	01/03/1998
Iceland	07/05/1999		
Italy	27/06/2000		
Liechtenstein	05/11/1992	18/11/1997	01/03/1998
Luxembourg	05/11/1992	22/06/2005	01/10/2005
Malta	05/11/1992		
Moldova	11/07/2002		
Netherlands	05/11/1992	02/05/1996	01/03/1998
Norway	05/11/1992	10/11/1993	01/03/1998
Poland	12/05/2003		
Romania	17/07/1995		
Russia	10/05/2001		
Siberia and Montenegro	22/03/2005		
Slovakia	20/02/2001	05/09/2001	01/01/2002
Slovenia	03/07/1997	04/10/2000	01/01/2001
Spain	05/11/1992	09/04/2001	01/08/2001
Sweden	09/02/2000	09/02/2000	01/06/2000
Switzerland	08/10/1993	23/12/1997	01/04/1998
FYR of Macedonia	25/07/1996		
Ukraine	02/05/1996		
United Kingdom	02/03/2000	27/03/2001	01/07/2001

Welsh, Scots-Gaelic and Irish. Cornish has recently been included. More controversially the issue of Sign Language has also been raised (cf. Chapter 6). When the British Government ratified this Charter in 2001, it applied Part III to the three nominated Celtic languages within its boundaries and Part II to Scots and Ulster-Scots.

While the implications of these practical measures outlined in Part III of the Charter are generally appreciated by the linguistic groups that benefit from such arrangements, I think it is important to also highlight the consequences of the mere signature of this document. All contracting states are obliged to accept Part II of the Charter even if the provisions of Part III are difficult to apply to a particular language. The more significant elements of the initial section are recognition of regional or minority languages as an expression of cultural wealth along with respect for the geographical areas of each such language. Paragraph 3 of this initial section obliges states to promote mutual understanding and especially tolerance and respect between all linguistic groups of the state.

In some instances this act of signing has generated a new respect for specific languages and has encouraged their greater use. This applies, for example, to Sater Frisian, which is spoken in the villages of Ramsloh, Scharrel and Strücklingen in the Community of the Saterland in Cloppenburg, Germany. According to their website, three factors have generated a great increase in the numbers of Frisian-speakers in these regions. These include the emergence of the Frisian movement in the 1960s, the establishment of the Frisians as a recognised minority and the inclusion of Frisian by Germany in the European Charter of Regional Languages. Speakers of this language in Germany exceed 2000 and are on the increase.

The mere signature of the Charter has also generated difficulties for certain nation states with centralised structures. In the case of France, for example, it stated in its Declaration that when ratifying the Charter it would explicitly pronounce that the document was not designed to protect minorities. Instead it aimed to promote the European language heritage. It was also explicit that the ratification of the Charter in the case of France would not imply collective rights for speakers of regional or minority languages. Instead France would interpret the Charter in the context of equality of French citizens without distinction (Directorate-General for Research 2002: 169). To date France has failed to ratify the Charter (Wright 2000b) but the debate was regarded as highly significant for speakers of minority languages, especially for those who speak a non-European language such as Berber (cf. Chapter 8).

The Charter also suggested that parties should undertake to apply, mutates mutandis, the principles of tolerance and respect for non-territorial languages.

> However, as far as these languages are concerned, the nature and scope of the measures to be taken to give effect to this Charter shall be determined in a flexible manner, bearing in mind the needs and wishes, and respecting the traditions and characteristics, of their groups which use the languages concerned.

Many states have specifically addressed non-territorial languages within the terms of reference of the Charter. In the case of Germany, for example, the Romany language of the German Sinti and Roma were explicitly identified in January 1998 as minority languages to be included within its terms of reference. In the year 2000, Sweden made a declaration identifying Sámi, Finnish and Meänkieli (Tornedal Finnish) as regional or minority languages; and Romani Chib and Yiddish as non-territorial minority languages within state boundaries (Directorate-General for Research 2002: 169). (The significance of place for language shall be explored in Chapter 7.)

Ultimately citizens speaking a minority language have benefited enormously from the international framework and a resolution by Eluned Morgan to the European Parliament in 2001 considered the promotion of linguistic diversity and language learning in the context of the European Year of Languages. Since that time, there have been a series of meetings to discuss the development of a new European Constitution. The language issue has been constantly championed by EBLUL who argued that for 'EU-based speakers of regional and minority languages, the notion of European citizenship has an important additional dimension' in those circumstances 'when the European Union respects its lesser-used languages as an important part of – and an added value to – the European heritage and culture'. In this they were making an explicit link between language and citizenship (European Bureau for Lesser Used Languages 2001).

In a resolution adopted at a council meeting in Ljouwert/Leeuwardern on 15 June 2002, EBLUL argued that European identity and European citizenship as defined by the Treaty on EU should incorporate the notion of cultural and linguistic diversity. For speakers of regional or minority languages in particular, 'the notion of European citizenship has an important dimension only if the European Union effectively respects its lesser-used languages as an important part of – and an added value to – the European heritage and culture' (European Bureau for Lesser Used Languages 2002).

At a meeting in April 2004, EBLUL took the opportunity to re-affirm the significance of linguistic diversity among EU citizens and included in its recommendations that the anti-discrimination articles of the existing treaty be adapted to include the concept of discrimination based on language. Unlike the Charter of Fundamental Rights and the European Convention of Human Rights, European Treaties had ignored discrimination based on language (EBLUL 2004). This situation has since been addressed.

Conclusion

Although the future for minority languages is generally precarious, there have been some success stories within the context of the EU, and the greatest of these has surely been the signature and ratification of ECRML by an ever-increasing number of countries within Europe, thereby reminding national states of their obligations towards cultural and linguistic minorities.

Since its establishment the EBLUL has acquired the status of Non-Governmental Organisation (NGO) at the levels of the European Council and the United Nations. Over the years it received about 85 per cent of its whole budget from the European Commission (Brezigar 2004b). It has also got support from the Irish and the Luxembourg governments as well as from the government of the Province of Fryslan in the Netherlands, the Community of Wallonia-Brussels, the German-speaking Community in Belgium, the Autonomous Province of South-Tyrol in Italy, the Swedish Assembly in Finland and many others.

However, the funding prospects are always precarious and in 2004 EBLUL encountered serious financial difficulties when they failed to deliver a programme which sought to integrate the newer EU members. In October, Bojan Brezigar, the chairman, issued a statement (2004b) indicating that EBLUL was in a financial crisis, which could threaten its existence. The lack of finance resulted in the dismissal of several employees from the office in Brussels and the General Secretary Markus Warasin decided to quit his job.

However, the tone of the press release was not entirely dismal and a general assembly meeting in Stockholm formulated a new direction for EBLUL. Members decided to decrease the organisation's activities in Brussels and strengthen the network instead. A policy of decentralisation would ensure the future of EBLUL and would involve member state committees more strongly. This would also increase the potential for sponsorship at national levels. Ultimately EBLUL faces difficulties from two quarters. The first of these is the EU directly which cannot guarantee any funding in the longterm. The second is that they face competition from the European Language Board networks.

Many minority language groups receive limited funding from the EU, but it is the recognition of their language at an international level that is really significant for most of them as it encourages greater standing at local and national levels. In some instances, recognition from kin or neighbouring states can also prove useful. Cross-border co-operation between different language communities provides the focus for the next chapter.

5
Languages across Borders

Regional and minority languages generally acquired their disadvantaged status during the process of nation state formation in the nineteenth century. 'They found themselves excluded from the state level, in particular from general education' (Extra and Yagmur 2002: 19). New political boundaries divided medieval empires and long-established language communities. Physical movement of population did not necessarily occur, but the change in nation-state borders generated new national minorities (Kockel 1999: 265). For example, the Danish minority in Schleswig-Holstein was created by changes in the border between Denmark and Germany rather than by any movement of the people.

Although two groups on either side of a state border may speak the same language one cannot automatically infer that they are kin groups. This situation may apply for example to speakers of Hungarian in Slovakia or Romania who identify more with Hungary than with their country of residence. But it clearly does not operate in other circumstances. Swedish-speaking Finns do not consider themselves to be Swedish. Instead they are Finnish. Similarly, French-speaking Swiss maintain their allegiance with Switzerland rather than with France (Grin and Moring 2002).

In a chapter that focuses on cross-border co-operation it is important to clarify that while the 'kin state' concept has some validity in certain circumstances, it does not have a general application across all borders. One should also note that cross-border co-operation is not necessarily confined to groups speaking the same language but can also operate in communities which have no linguistic relationship with one another.

Ethnic conflicts and state boundaries

Many of the better-known examples of cross-border co-operation in contemporary Europe are a consequence of peace initiatives designed to resolve conflict and serve as the catalyst for better understanding and communication between groups with different historical perspectives (Nic Craith 2004). They may also reflect difficulties that have arisen in consequence of revised state boundaries. The latter applies to all three examples citied in this section – the examples of Trentino-South Tryol in Austria, the Schleswig-Holstein region on the border between Denmark and Germany and the case of Irish in Ireland, north and south of the border.

Following the First World War, the Trentino-South Tyrol region of Austria was designated as part of Italy in accordance with the Treaty of St German in 1919. The region is divided into the provinces of Trento and Bolzano/Bozen or South Tyrol and comprises a territory of 3600 km^2 with some 950,000 inhabitants. Three ethnic-linguistic groups (Germans, Italians and Ladins) live here. Speakers of Italian constitute the majority in Trentino and form 97 per cent of the population. A mere 2 per cent are Ladins while a very small proportion speaks German. Demographical statistics are quite different in South Tyrol. There, German-speakers form 69 per cent of the population, 26.5 per cent are Italian-speakers and less than 5 per cent speak Ladin.

Cross-border co-operation in this region serves as a model for the peaceful resolution of ethnic integration although progress was not automatic and many difficulties had to be resolved. Following the Second World War, the German minority in South Tyrol fully expected their land to return to Austria but by 1946 it became clear that this would not happen. The failure to regain South Tyrol served as the catalyst for Italian–Austrian negotiations and resulted in a series of legislative instruments for the protection of the German minority in South Tyrol.

The first of these, the De Gasperi-Gruber Agreement was signed on 5 September 1946 and contained many key clauses guaranteeing important rights for speakers of German in South Tyrol (Alcock 2000: 98). In this Agreement, the Italian state undertook to guarantee the cultural and economic protection of its German-speaking minority in several sectors. The first Article of the Agreement stipulated that 'the objective was to safeguard the German ethnic character of the South Tyrolese people but not to safeguard as German the ethnic character of South Tyrol' (Alcock 2000: 99). This issue had already been discussed in

1920 but the most significant element of the De Gasperi-Gruber Agreement was the emphasis on economic as well as cultural development of the South Tyrolese.

Essentially the Agreement proposed equality of rights for the German-speaking inhabitants in the province of Bolzano and the townships of the Trento province with their Italian-speaking counterparts within the framework of special provisions designed to protect the ethnical character of the German-speaking population, such as legislation that guaranteed the right to elementary and secondary education in the respective mother tongues. It provided for parity of German and Italian languages in public offices as well as in place names. Significantly it assured the right to re-establish equal status and equality of rights for speakers of German and Italian in public offices.

Although it was designed to ease tensions, the Agreement generated widespread shock and dissatisfaction among the South Tyrolese who had failed to obtain self-determination. The Austrian Government argued that the Agreement offered the best possible solution under the circumstances and was not meant to imply any rejection of the South Tyrolese by Austria. However, the South Tyrolese were particularly angry that regional autonomy was designed to include not only the Province of Bolzano in South Tyrol where the majority were clearly German-speaking but also extended to the Province of Trento. This ensured that Italians had an overall two-thirds majority in the region Trentino-Alto Adige although Bolzano itself was two-thirds German-speaking. Since the primary legislative power for the most important economic and social sectors was assigned to the region rather than the individual provinces, it appeared that speakers of Italian had gained autonomy at the expense of speakers of German. 'The South Tyrolese complained bitterly and with justification, that the autonomy should be for them. They were the minority. The Italians in the region did not need autonomy since they had the state behind them' (Alcock 2000: 108).

Anxieties lessened somewhat with the amendment of the 1948 Statute which came into force in 1972. This second statute transferred legislative and administrative power for several important sectors including agriculture and tourism directly to the Provinces of Trento and Bolzano/Bozen although industrial development generally remained with the region. A decision was taken to ensure proportional representation of all the ethnic groups in all state bodies with the exception of the Ministry of Defence and various police forces in South Tyrol. Ethnic proportions were based on a census of population. Overall jobs in various administrations are divided into percentages of speakers of German, Italian and Ladin, and competence in both German and Italian is required for entry, promotion or transfer at every grade. This is a situation not unlike that which now pertains in the Baltic States (cf. Chapter 2).

In South Tyrol the issue of ethnic identity was extremely important. It not only determined the school which children would attend, but also governed access to employment at all levels in the public administration and the allocation of housing. Ethnic proportions were determined according to national census results in which every citizen was required to officially declare his or her ethnic group.

It was not until 1992 that the South Tyrolese declared their satisfaction with the implementation of these measures. On 11th June the Austrian government confirmed receipt of a resolution from the South Tyrolese declaring that any disputes over the implementation of the De Gasperi-Gruber Agreement were over. However, this state of contentment among the South Tyrolese should be set in the context of distinct unease among their Italian-speaking counterparts. The economic boom which had benefited the South-Tyrolese countryside through all-the-year-round tourism and funds from the Common Agricultural Policy had done little to help the Italian industrial sector which had suffered great difficulties. Many Italian-speakers were so disheartened with their economic prospects that they had begun to declare themselves as South-Tyrolese in the census. While this could be viewed on the one hand as South-Tyrolese assimilation of the Italians, German-speakers were very concerned with its practical consequences such as large numbers of Italian-speakers in German-speaking schools.

It was not long before South Tyrolese ambitions to be reunited with their North Tyrolese kin became obvious. On 19 March 1970 members of the parliaments of North Tyrol and Südtirol/Alto Adige assembled in Bozen/Bolzano for their first joint session after more than 50 years. A year later, a meeting in Innsbruck united members from North, South and East Tyrol. In 1991 members from Trentino were included in these meetings. The provincial parliaments of North Tyrol, Südtirol/Alto Adige and Trentino sat together in 1991 and 1993 with the provincial parliament of Vorarlberg in Meran/Merano and Innsbruck respectively although the province of Vorarlberg subsequently opted to have observer status.

In October 1994 the North and South Tyrolese parliaments set out to create an autonomous European Region Tyrol (AERT) but their far-reaching proposals to organise the transfer of power from the three provinces to AERT were vetoed by both Vienna and Rome. On 19 May

1998, the three provincial parliaments met in Meran/Merano, the former capital of Tyrol. The central theme of this meeting was the convention on cross-border co-operation within a Euroregion between the Autonomous Province of Südtirol/Alto Adige, the Autonomous Province of Trento and the Province of North Tyrol. This convention represented a pilot agreement of the 'Three Provinces' Parliament and can be regarded as the catalyst for the establishment of organisational structures for the Euroregion Tyrol-Südtirol/Alto Adige-Trentino. The provincial parliaments have had several meetings since then.

Cross-border co-operation between the three provinces has become well established. South Tyrolese have the right to go for treatment to North Tyrolese hospitals, and direct the bills to Bolzano. Co-operation has been established in many sectors including communication services, culture, education, the economy, the environment, traffic and tourism. Current issues of interest include common initiatives of the three universities in the field of information technology and the organisation of big thematic exhibitions.

Many of these projects have been located at the European Academy of Bolzano/Bozen which has spearheaded much of the research for speakers of minority languages. In 1998, for example, the local government at South Tyrol commissioned a research project which would examine new mechanisms for the protection of speakers of minority languages within the EU. This resulted in a package of primarily soft-law measures which recommended the establishment of a European Monitoring Centre and an EU Action programme. The project was sponsored by the Autonomous Province of Bolzano/Bozen and has since been employed by local authorities as a basis for dialogue with members of both the European Commission and the European Parliament.

In 1999 the European Academy of Bolzano/Bozen hosted a 2-week summer academy on the theme of 'Trans-national Regionalism and Minority Protection in Europe'. This residential course on cross-border co-operation was attended by civil servants of different levels of government as well as by representatives of minorities. There was also strong interest from academic circles, and students from EU member states as well as from countries of Central and Eastern Europe participated in the venture. The European Commission sponsored the initiative along with the Autonomous Province of Bolzano/Bozen. Partners to the project included the Universities of Bratislava, Graz, Ljubljana, Olomouc and Szeged.

Several international partners have come together to establish a European network of minority dailies. This initiative is designed to enhance the co-operation and exchange of information between European minority daily newspapers which often have limited resources and an inadequate infrastructure for gathering information. Representatives from different European minority dailies met in Bolzano in 2000 at a meeting sponsored by the European Academy. This led to the drafting of a Statute for the Association of Minority Dailies which was adopted in July 2001. Initial costs associated with the project were partly covered by a grant from the European Commission but are now fully financed by members.

One of the most important initiatives from a linguistic perspective context has been the development of an Italian–German dictionary (Grin and Moring 2002: 150*ff*). The *Dizionario Terminologico del diritto societario italiano/tedesco* is a unique reference dictionary which is of great significance for champions of minority language rights in the region. Published jointly in Bern, Bolzano-Bozen, Munich and Vienna, the idea for the dictionary came from the project 'Terminologia e lingua speciali' which was located in the European Academy in Bozen/ Bolzano. The publication of a bilingual dictionary of administrative, economic and legal terminology was designed to overcome linguistic difficulties in the Alpine region. The project focuses on legal and social affairs, and is useful for analysts and civil servants, lawyers and politicians. Effectively, the Dictionary facilitates the functioning of a regional assembly (the 70 members of the South Tyrol Council). The project secured EU funding from the European INTERREG II programme and was co-funded by the Autonomous Province of Bolzano-Bozen.

The success of cross-border co-operation in Trentino-South Tyrol is matched in the Schleswig-Holstein region on the border between Germany and Denmark (Nic Craith 2004) (Map 5.1). Here a 1920 border referendum under British supervision generated much controversy. Following partition, German-speakers in the Northern part (now part of Denmark) campaigned for a complete review of the border, and for distinct cultural autonomy. The *Bodenkampf* (fight for the soil) over the proportion of land owned by German farmers generated huge controversy (Kockel 1999: 202). In the Southern part of the region that remained with Germany, ethnic discrimination became considerably worse. Anti-Danish activities were often violent. Hostilities also happened, albeit at a smaller scale, on the Danish side of the border.

The determination of ethnic group membership by self-definition was introduced in the decades between the two World Wars and ultimately highlighted a rather unusual position in Südschleswig. Prior to the Second World War, German-speakers in Sønderjylland

Map 5.1 Schleswig-Holstein. *Source*: Adapted from Kockel (1999).

outnumbered the Danish group south of the border by a ratio of about 4:1. In the late 1940s, this position was virtually reversed. Following the Second World War, there was much hostility towards the 20,000 Germans in Schleswig because of their co-operation with the German occupying forces during the hostilities. 2000 had opted to join the German army. When the conflict was over, 3500 were imprisoned for their collaboration with the occupying forces. German schools were closed and their property was confiscated.

The situation in Germany was hardly better. There the emigration of Danes after the war along with one million refugees from the East was perceived as a threat to the national balance. A *Land* election law ensured that any parliamentary party that received less than 5 per cent of the vote would be eliminated from the *Land* Parliament. This effectively ensured that the Danish in Germany lost their representation at an official level which angered Denmark to such an extent that it threatened to veto West Germany's accession to NATO (Alcock 2000: 115).

The decline in relations spurred both parties to arrive at a solution and to solve issues relating to the border between these two countries. In the 1950s the border was finally agreed and accepted by the national minorities in both countries. The conditions for future peaceful coexistence were set out in the Copenhagen–Bonn Declarations of 1955. These Declarations set out the individual rights to be enjoyed by members of both national minorities on an equal basis. They also contained provisions for the cultivation of Danish and German traditions, languages and cultures.

In the case of Schleswig, the Declarations acknowledged the right of the German minority to set up institutions for general education in German and the entitlement to sustain cultural, professional and religious relations with Germany as well as the right to use German in court and in public offices. These rights were reciprocated for the Danish-speaking population in Germany. Significantly the 5 per cent rule was abolished for political representatives of the Danish minority.

The Danish minority in contemporary Schleswig-Holstein numbers about 50,000. While they are all are fluent speakers of Danish they also speak German. In some localities, these Danes speak *Plattdeutsch* or Low German. In areas close to the border, some of the Danish minority speak Sønderjysk, a regional Danish dialect. The German minority across the border in Denmark is smaller and numbers some 15,000 members. They mainly reside in the border region in the Southern and Eastern parts of Sønderjylland/North Schleswig. Altogether they make up between 5 and 20 per cent of the general population. While the

German community is fluent in German, most of them can also speak Danish. Many individuals in the rural community speak Sønderjysk while the rest traditionally speak High German.

Cross-border co-operation is very extensive in Schleswig-Holstein, and most of the ethnic and cultural minority organisations can locate their origins to the time of partition. Both Danish and German minorities have maintained close links with their respective ancestral home and receive comprehensive support from their 'motherland'. In consequence a range of parallel institutions has been developed, and this range from education and health services through to sporting and trade associations. In fact 'it is practically possible for members of either minority to lead their lives through each group's own social infrastructure, with a minimum of contact between minority and host society' (Kockel 1999: 205).

Some 14,000 Danes in Germany belong to the *Sydslesvigsk Forening* SSF (South Schleswig Association) which is committed to the promotion of the Danish language. This organisation is committed to the protection of the interest of the minority as well as to the promotion of a sense of community among its members. It clearly aims to promote the Danish language and way of life and places great emphasis on Nordic culture generally. It endeavours to maintain a strong link between the Danish minority in Germany with Denmark and Scandinavia.

Danes in Germany are supported by the *Generalsekretariat* (Danish General Secretariat) which is located in Flensburg. *Dansk Skoleforening for Sydslesvig* (The Danish School Association for South Schleswig) holds responsibility for matters concerning the Danish schools and kindergarten schools in South Schleswig. The Danish minority has published *Flensborg Avis*, a daily newspaper in Danish since 1869. This newspaper also has a German column. In addition to this, *Flensborg Avis* co-owns Radio Schleswig-Holstein which broadcasts news in Danish on a daily basis. As one might expect, Danish newspapers, TV and radio channels are available in the region.

The Germans in Denmark also enjoy cultural benefits on a similar level. The German *Bund Deutscher Nordschleswiger* emphasises the significance of cultural links with Germany while also being aware of the importance of social commitment to Denmark. Members aim to co-operate with the Danish state in minority affairs; and are keen to reduce the emphasis on the border with a view to European unity (Kockel 1999: 208).

The *Deutscher Schul- and Sprachverein für Nordschleswig* (German School and Language Association for North Schleswig) operates a number of kindergartens, private schools and schools of further education which teach through the medium of German. Pupils in these *Deutscher*

Schul- and *Sprachverein für Nordschleswig* schools are also required to study Danish. The German minority issues *Der Nordschleswiger*, a bilingual daily newspaper which provides information on local, regional and national levels. The German minority can receive German television and radio channels in South-Jutland.

Cross-Border co-operation in the region was enhanced with the formal establishment of the Sønderjylland/Schleswig Region in the town of Aabenraa in September 1997. This area of more than 8000 sq. km has approximately equal Danish and German territories although the population distribution is decidedly uneven. This new foundation for co-operation was established with the signing of an agreement involving the Counties of Nordfriesland, Schleswig-Flensburg, Sønderjylland and the town of Flensburg. The agreement was intended to foster active, positive coexistence between the respective minorities in the areas of culture, environment, trade and politics, and it is also designed to establish a joint, regional profile with enhanced potential in a competitive European context.

Principles of equality and mutual respect for the special cultural features of the German and Danish peoples are set out in the Agreement and several bodies have been established to ensure the success of this co-operation. Working parties have also been set up to develop initiatives and projects of mutual interest. Languages, culture and tourism have been highlighted as areas of priority for mutual co-operation. Sixteen Danish and German members from cultural and educational backgrounds serve on the committee dealing with languages and inter-cultural understanding. They offer advice on experience exchange and discuss initiatives designed to enhance Danish/German co-operation for culture and language on both sides of the border. Its members are active in schools and within the cultural life of the region generally. The group has initiated many projects including common courses for Danish and German teachers and established common arrangements for Danish and German schools. They have also engaged in the production and publication of educational material in Danish and German about the region.

While cross-border co-operation in the Schleswig-Holstein region is often cited as a model for post-conflict ventures, one could argue that ethnic integration has ultimately 'taken the form of either complete assimilation, or an almost complete isolation, while cultural interaction remains rather limited on either side of the border' (Kockel 1999: 209). To a certain extent this 'parallel but distinct' model also operates in Northern Ireland.

Arrangements for cross-border co-operation in Northern Ireland are more recent than those in either Trentino-Süd-Tyrol or Schleswig-Holstein. From the foundation of the Northern Irish State in the early 1920s there was little official British State recognition of the existence of the Irish language. This changed in August 1988 when the British Government published a preliminary report on a survey of the Irish language in Northern Ireland (Sweeney 1988). Three years later a question on Irish was included for the first time in the Northern Irish census form and the returns offered fresh insights into the extent of the Irish linguistic community in Northern Ireland (Mac Póilin 1996; Nic Craith and Shuttleworth 1996; Nic Craith 1999).

The 1991 Census explored the ability of individuals to speak, read and/or write Irish. Those with no knowledge of the language were also asked to respond. According to the published reports a sizeable minority had some understanding of Irish (Department of Health and Social Services 1993). 9.35 per cent of the male and 9.64 per cent of the female population were familiar with it and both genders could speak, read and write it in virtually equal proportions.

One of the more interesting findings of the census was the level of education of the 'typical' speaker of Irish. Historically, Irish has become associated with poverty and a lack of formal educations, but the 1991 Census rejected such stereotypes (Table 5.1). Over 20 per cent of the most highly proficient sector has some knowledge of Irish. A similar proportion of the student population and almost 17 per cent of professionals were familiar with the language. (High levels of education also pertain to Irish-speakers in the Republic of Ireland and may indicate

Table 5.1 Knowledge of Irish in Northern Ireland in 1991 Census

All ages 3 +	Number
Total population	1,502,385
Can speak Irish	45,338
Can read Irish	5,887
Can write Irish	1,340
Can read and speak Irish	6,593
Can read and write Irish	2,802
Can speak and write Irish	1,031
Can speak, read and write Irish	79,012
Do not know Irish	1,320,657
Not stated	39,725

that many have acquired their understanding of the language in the classroom rather than in the home.)

The Northern Irish Census also contained a table linking religious affiliation with linguistic skills. Although the question on Irish was obligatory, it was not necessary to provide a response to the religious question. According to the results almost 22 per cent of the Catholic population were speakers of Irish. This was hardly surprising as the language has traditionally been associated with the Roman Catholic denomination. However, a further 5500 Irish speakers identified themselves as belonging to a different denomination and almost 10,000 Irish-speakers did not declare any religious affiliation.

These results may have satisfied those keen to emphasise the extent of the Irish-speaking minority in Northern Ireland. However, they would not necessarily convince the sceptic. As with any census question concerning language, there was no objective assessment of the accuracy of claims regarding linguistic skills and nothing prevented individual persons with limited skills in Irish from classifying themselves as being competent in the language.

The accuracy of self-assessment in census forms is a question that is frequently raised and many sociologists ask whether any individual is sufficiently aware of his or her own language usage to report it. Unfortunately, this dilemma is not resolved by a simplification of the inquiry on a census form. Even if questions were restricted to asking merely which languages were spoken, it would still be open to a degree of ambiguity (Beardsmore 1982).

Although 9.4 per cent of the population classified themselves as Irish-speakers in the Northern Ireland census of 1991, one cannot assume that all of them were necessarily competent in the language. It merely indicated that these respondents wished to portray themselves as Irish-speakers. On the other hand, it is also possible that some with a little knowledge of the language may have regarded that as insufficient to justify claiming a competency of Irish and may have returned themselves as being unable to speak it.

A vigorous campaign had served as the catalyst for the reintroduction of the language question in 1991 and it is doubtful whether any opportunity to emphasise the size of the Irish language community was missed. If the figures could not be regarded as an absolute indicator of linguistic ability in Irish it can be assumed that they illustrated a very positive attitude towards the language. Regardless of their actual language skills a substantial proportion wished to be identified as Irish-speakers (Nic Craith 1999).

Seven years after the Census, the majority of political parties in Northern Ireland arrived at a form of political compromise. The talks conducted over 2 years under the chairmanship of Senator George Mitchell included representatives of both unionist and nationalist communities. The document published as a result of the talks has become known as the Good Friday or the Belfast Agreement. This document proposed changes in a range of sectors including the cultural arena. With regard to linguistic diversity in Northern Ireland it affirmed that participants recognised 'the importance of respect, understanding and tolerance in relation to linguistic diversity, including in Northern Ireland, the Irish language, Ulster-Scots and the languages of the various ethnic communities, all of which are part of the cultural wealth of the island of Ireland' (Government of the United Kingdom of Great Britain and Northern Ireland and Government of Ireland 1998: 22).

The Agreement's endorsement of linguistic diversity represented progress from the perspective of those seeking to enhance the status of Irish in the community. The fact that Irish was placed on a par with Ulster-Scots surprised some unfamiliar with linguistic diversity in Northern Ireland or those who react with incredulity to the suggestion that Ulster-Scots constitutes a unique and distinct language (cf. Chapter 6). Moreover, there was absolutely no reference to Welsh, Scots-Gaelic or Cornish in the Good Friday Agreement. Although Irish has been placed on an equal level with Ulster-Scots, no comparison was made between Irish and other Celtic languages of the United Kingdom. Many nationalist politicians had sought parity of esteem between Irish and these related languages and had particularly requested that Irish be accorded a similar status to Welsh.

The lack of reference to other Celtic languages could infer that the British Government wished to develop an Ulster solution to an Ulster problem. Perhaps it was also felt that such a comparison would offend some Irish-speakers, who might perceive it as an attempted 'redefinition' of the language as an element of British Celtic culture. Possibly the omission indicates some unwillingness among unionist politicians to accept Irish as a recognised Celtic language of the United Kingdom.

However, the Agreement represented considerable progress for speakers of the language. Apart from its proposed ratification of the ECRML, the British Government has made other specific offers in relation to Irish. It indicated that it would 'take resolute action to promote the language' and 'facilitate and encourage the use of the language in speech and writing in public and private life where there is appropriate demand'. The British Government also specified that it would 'seek to remove, where possible, restrictions which would discourage or work against the maintenance or development of the language' and 'make provision for liaising with the Irish language community, representing their views to public authorities and investigating complaints'.

There were also concessions in the area of education. The demand for Irish-medium education since the late 1970s in Northern Ireland has been unprecedented (cf. Chapter 9). In acknowledgement of this interest the British Government stated that it would 'place a statutory duty on the Department of Education to encourage and facilitate Irish medium education in line with the current provision for integrated education'. It also undertook to 'explore urgently with the relevant British authorities, and in co-operation with the Irish broadcasting authorities, the scope for achieving more widespread availability of *Teilifís na Gaeilge* [Irish language television in the Republic] in Northern Ireland' and to 'seek more effective ways to encourage and provide financial support for Irish language film and television production in Northern Ireland'.

The most significant consequence of the Agreement was the establishment of several cross-border implementation bodies between Northern Ireland and the Republic (Nic Craith 2004). These included a Language Board, known in English as the North/South Language Body which had two separate parts designed to deal with Irish and Ulster-Scots respectively. Sixteen members were appointed to attend to *An Foras Teanga* (the Irish language agency). A further eight were appointed to cater to Ulster-Scots (cf. Chapter 6).

Schedule 1, Article 3 of the North/South Co-operation/Implementation Bodies (Northern Ireland) Order issued in 1999 stipulated that board members should promote the Irish language north and south of the border, although the political context in each jurisdiction was different. In the case of the Republic of Ireland, where Irish is the first national language, board members were encouraged to facilitate the use of Irish in public and private life. In the North, they were asked to promote the language in the context of the Part III of the ECRML which the British Government has signed and in those instances where there was public demand.

The Irish Government responded favourably to the new language agency and transferred all responsibilities for the language from the Irish Minister for Arts, Heritage, Gaeltacht and the Islands to the new cross-border body. The new Agency acquired responsibility for funding eight voluntary Irish language groups. However, its cross-border activities have hardly been confined to the direction of financial support.

Foras na Gaeilge has conducted research on the visibility of Irish in several sectors including the independent broadcasting sector. It set up a working party to examine policy in the media. *Foras na Gaeilge* has provided funding for programmes such as *Ros na Rún*, the Irish language soap drama. It has allocated financial resources to Irish language festivals such as *Féile an Phobail* which is held annually in West Belfast. The Agency has also supported weekly and daily Irish language newspapers such as *Lá* and *Foinse*. Overall, *Foras na Gaeilge* is determined to increase the visibility of Irish in the public sphere.

Education is a significant resource for any minority language and *Foras na Gaeilge* has funded the development of educational resource materials in Irish with the aim of ensuring that Irish can be used as easily as English in any school context. The Body has also allocated funding to information technology ventures such as *Digiscoil* and with the help of *Coláiste Mhuire* in Belfast is preparing education resource materials for school. *Foras na Gaeilge* has subsidised training courses for teachers in Irish and prepared booklets for parents of children going to Irish-medium schools. It has sponsored Irish language prizes at third level. *Foras na Gaeilge* has funded several educational organisations such as *Forbairt Naonraí Teo and Gaelscoileanna*, and has given funding to *Gaelscolaíocht* and *Gaeloiliúnt* for Irish-medium education in Northern Ireland.

Foras na Gaeilge has become involved in the funding of various cultural initiatives such as the CDRom *Éist Arís* (Listen Again) which promotes singers from Scotland as well as throughout the island of Ireland. A particularly successful venture has been the Columba Initiative which supports speakers of Scots-Gaelic with speakers of Irish Gaelic, north and south of the border. Gaelic festivals in Scotland have also received funding from *Foras na Gaeilge* which has organised a series of seminars north and south of the Irish border on terminology in Irish. Theatre groups north and south of the border such as *Aisling Ghéar, An Taibhdhearc* and The Armagh Rhymers have also benefited financially from this organisation.

The cross-border body has provided a translation service for certain state sectors and become involved in the re-issuing of certain classic texts which have gone out of print. *Foras* has appointed Development Officers for Irish in Health Boards and Local Government Offices. (To date these have primarily operated south of the border.) It has also promoted Irish among the *Garda Síochána* (Irish police force) and has allocated funding for research which aims to promote Irish in the state sector.

The cross-border body has acknowledged the challenge of reviving the language on a cross-border basis and focused much of its human and financial resources on strategic planning. Members of the body regard the status of Irish as extremely significant and are very keen to enhance opportunities for speaking Irish in the public sector north and south of the border. It will be a significant challenge to develop an integrated policy for Irish under the auspices of both British and Irish Governments to develop the language throughout the Island of Ireland.

In each of the instances mentioned above cross-border co-operation has had significant benefits – not just for the languages themselves but for those who speak the language especially in a minority setting. Transfrontier co-operation can have a positive impact on any negative legacies of a border, such as the development of a poor, physical or cultural infrastructure, lack of communication and so on. However, not all instances of cross-border co-operation are this successful and some examples have encountered greater difficulties than others. Such impediments would apply to the case of Basque.

Impediments to cross-border co-operation

Transfrontier co-operation in the Basque Country does not take place between equals in terms either of numbers or official status (Nic Craith 2004). There are 2,623,318 inhabitants in the Basque regions in Spain. Of these, 594,568 are familiar with the language. Figures for the French Basque area are considerably lower. Of the 249,275 inhabitants there, a mere 56,200 are Basque-speakers (Gardner 2000: 11). As noted in the previous chapter, Basque has co-official status with Castilian in the Basque Autonomous Country in Spain. Basque is also co-official with Spanish in certain areas of Navarre since 1982. In contrast, Basque is not officially recognised as a language with any rights in the French Basque regions. Basques on the French side of the border have a 'limited capacity to develop initiatives to promote and safeguard their culture.... They need to rely heavily on support from the other side of the border, at least in linguistic, cultural, educational and media initiatives' (Grin and Moring 2002: 160).

The lack of a common status and language policy for the different regions impacts negatively on cross-border co-operation between the two Basque-speaking communities. There is also the issue of the ECRML which was signed by Spain in 1992 and ratified in 2001, but has never been ratified by France. As noted in the previous chapter, the French Constitution regards recognition of any language other than French as unconstitutional. In consequence, Basque is not recognised as a language with any rights in France.

The attitude towards language normalisation in general and transfrontier co-operation in particular is highly dependent on the political agenda of those in charge of the respective districts. Since its constitution in 1979, the Basque Autonomous Community has been governed by moderate Basque nationalists either as a sole party or in coalition with others and they have been more proactively involved in cross-border initiatives than the Navarre Charter Community which is governed by Spanish nationalists.

There are also political implications for those with a nationalist ideology. Basque nationalists poll around 55 per cent of the vote in the Basque Autonomous Community, over 20 per cent in Navarre and over 10 per cent in the French Basque Country. From the perspective of many Basque nationalists, the national border through Basque-speaking regions is not legitimate and they would hardly view their work in a cross-border context. Instead, organisations with membership from both North and South are working in a national rather than an international context. This issue of recognition of an international border is hardly confined to the Basque community. Individuals in the Republic of Ireland and in Northern Ireland, for example, may not necessarily view Irish as a cross-border language. Instead they may see it simply as an all-Island language which is facilitated by the cross-border body.

Linguistic factors also impact negatively on the cross-border partnership in the Basque Country. In common with many minority languages 'Basque has a number of flourishing dialects. This is hardly surprising in a minority language which is still undergoing a process of standardisation and does not enjoy political unity of its territory.' Although 'literate users have relatively little difficulty in understanding each other's written texts, particularly as the use of the 30-year old written standard has spread rapidly, comprehension difficulties do occur at the oral level, particularly between speakers of geographically distant dialects who have little contact with each other' (Gardner 2000: 10–11).

Despite these impediments there have been many international agreements, resolutions and programmes that form the framework of transfrontier co-operation in the Basque Provinces in Spain – with the exception of Navarre. Although cross-border co-operation agreements have been signed by authorities there, there is little evidence of any action or outcomes apart from a sound archive of the Basque Language which resulted from co-operation between the Navarre Government and the Institute *Culturel Basque-Euskal Kultur Erakundea* based in the

North. This archive aims to conserve the recordings of Basque dialects in Navarre and to make these recordings available to any person who may be interested in this audio material. Parts of the French Basque Country use Navarre dialects of Basque.

Some cross-border initiatives have suffered from the political context. The principal Southern Basque nationalist parties (*Eusko Alderdi Jeltzailea* and *Eusko Alkartasuna*) have branches and premises on both sides of the international border but the nationalist left party *Batasuna* was banned by the Spanish authorities in 2002 and can operate legally only from across the border with headquarters in Bayonne. Various organisations of the nationalist left such as the youth organisations *Haika* (a result of the fusion of the Southern *Jarrai* and the Northern *Gazteriak*) and *Segi*, the anti-repressive *Gestoras Pro-Amnistía*, had similar experiences. The Basque language has been central to all of these cross-border activities.

Another organisation that has suffered the consequences of political tensions is Demoak, a Northern social movement for democratic rights in the Basque Country. Members use active non-violence to denounce the lack of Basque linguistic rights, among other issues. For example, one of their last direct actions was directed against the French railway company SNCF for its refusal to feature Basque in their services (announcements, signs, tickets etc.) in the French Basque Country.

In November 2003, Demoak and its sympathisers including several Southerners disrupted the railway system across the French Basque Country. They sat down to play a game of cards on the rails. Sixty-three people were subsequently arrested and tried and judged in Bayonne. Twelve of these came from the Basque Country in Spain. In court, the judge allowed those from the Spanish Basque Country to deal with proceedings in Basque using an interpreter, whereas those from the French Basque region were not permitted to use the interpreting service. The latter were denied the right to speak Basque on the basis of their French citizenship. French is the only official language for French people. When the accused from the French Basque region insisted on their right to use the interpreter's services, the judge ordered the police to clear the courtroom. In consequence five people required medical assistance.

Publications have also been affected by political tensions. The Basque language newspaper *Berria* which is produced in the Basque regions in Spain features journalists from north and the south of the international border. Its central informative scope is the Basque Country in both

France and Spain and it is distributed on both sides of the border. Its predecessor, *Euskaldunon Egunkaria*, was shut down in February 2002 by the Spanish authorities, causing great concern and provoking a massive reaction of anger and support. The paper's board denounced the use of torture during interrogation of its members by the Spanish security forces.

Such protests are not exceptional. In 1998 the Spanish–Basque bilingual daily *Egin* – published in Spain but distributed on both sides of the border – was shut down for its alleged relation with ETA. At the time of writing, the case has not been taken to court. The bilingual daily *Gara* replaced *Egin*. However, other publications have not been affected. Since 1977, other Basque language books and music have been produced by the publishing company Elkar which is based in the South in San Sebastian. The publications are distributed on both sides of the French/Spanish border.

Although the case of Basque has been used to serve as an example of potential impediments to cross-border co-operation, this is not to imply that it is the sole cross-border community to encounter such difficulties, nor are the problems confined to the illustrations above. In some instances, communities speaking the same language in different territories may be imbued with different ideologies. This would apply in Ireland, for example, where speaking Irish can have different interpretations north and south of the border. As noted in the previous chapter, minority languages in some locations have become politicised and speakers of the same language in a different state may unwittingly be drawn into a political situation.

Sometimes communities across borders may not wish to engage in co-operative ventures for historical reasons. This particularly applies in contexts where one of the partners represents a former imperial power. In can also be the case that communities across borders lack common histories or narratives of identity. In these circumstances the border may represent a meeting of differences rather than commonalities which makes co-operation more difficult.

Finally, enthusiasm to become involved in cross-border initiatives is frequently dampened by the sheer complexity of many European programme participation requirements. In particular, regulations regarding the minimum size of the project and the number of partners from different member states have made applications to the EU for funding quite difficult for smaller language communities. Despite these difficulties, the EU has generally been supportive of cross-border co-operation.

European support for transfrontier co-operation

The process of cross-border co-operation has been endorsed in several
agreements and charters at European level in recent decades. The
European Charter of Border and Cross-Border Regions, which was
adopted by the Assembly of European Border Regions (AERB) in 1981
and revised in 1995, gives some attention to the promotion of cross-border
co-operation in cultural affairs. It suggests that 'cross-border co-operation
in cultural matters is an important prerequisite for any measures
designed to establish a relationship of trust'. For that reason a 'wide
knowledge of cross-border regions, their geographical, structural,
economic, socio-cultural and historical conditions is a prerequisite for
active participation of the citizens and all other partners' (AERB 1995: 15).
In drawing attention to the significance of information on cross-border
regions, the AERB was also highlighting its own relevance as a body of
expertise.

The Charter adopted by the AERB sought a range of developments at
regional level, many of which refer explicitly to cross-border co-operation
among language groups on either side of an international border.
Interestingly this document does not necessarily focus on 'kin' state
languages or even on groups speaking the same language across the
border. In fact it almost assumes that there are different languages in
question and advocates 'the widest possible knowledge about the
language of the neighbouring country or the dialects as part of the
regional cross-border development and a precondition for communication'. It proposes strategies for the acquisition of the language of the
neighbouring state including 'the incorporation of the language of the
neighbouring country in the teaching plans for all school forms' (AERB
1995: 16).

This interpretation of cross-border co-operation was far broader than
that assumed in the ECRML. Here, cross-border co-operation was interpreted as co-operation across borders between groups speaking more or
less that same language on either side of an international border rather
than co-operation between neighbouring states in relation to different
or related language groups.

Article 7 of the Charter suggested that in respect of regional or
minority languages, parties should base their policies on several principles and objectives including the 'maintenance and development of
links' between 'groups using a regional or minority language and other
groups in the State employing a language used in identical or similar
form, as well as the establishment of cultural relations with other

groups in the State using different languages'. It also suggested that parties should consider 'the promotion of appropriate types of trans-national exchanges' for speakers of 'regional or minority languages used in identical or similar form in two or more States'.

In the field of media, the Charter suggested that parties agree 'to guarantee freedom of direct reception of radio and television broadcasts from neighbouring countries in a language used in identical or similar form to a regional or minority language'. Moreover they are requested 'not to oppose the retransmission of radio and television broadcasts from neighbouring countries in such a language'. (This issue has particular relevance in Northern Ireland where there have been problems with the transmission of Irish language television programmes to Northern Ireland from TG4, the Irish language television service based in the Republic.)

Article 14 declared that parties to the Charter would undertake 'to apply existing bilateral and multilateral agreements which bind them with the States in which the same language is used in identical or similar form'. It suggested that parties should conclude agreements 'in such a way as to foster contacts between the users of the same language in the States concerned in the fields of culture, education, information, vocational training and permanent education' for the benefit of 'regional or minority languages'. These actions would be designed 'to facilitate and/or promote co-operation across borders, in particular between regional or local authorities in whose territory the same language is used in identical or similar form' (CoE 1992).

The Framework Convention for the Protection of National Minorities (adopted in November 1994) had a similarly narrow interpretation of cross-border co-operation but emphasised the significance of transfrontier co-operation at all levels. It suggested that 'the realisation of a tolerant and prosperous Europe does not depend solely on co-operation between States but also requires transfrontier co-operation between local and regional authorities without prejudice to the constitution and territorial integrity of each State'. This is a highly significant point as effective cross-border co-operation often functions at local level or at the level of non-governmental organisation.

The interpretation of transfrontier co-operation in the Framework document seems to focus on the concept of 'kin' groups. Article 17 of this convention requires that

> parties undertake not to interfere with the right of persons belonging
> to national minorities to establish and maintain free and peaceful

contacts across frontiers with persons lawfully staying in other States, in particular those with whom they share an ethnic, cultural, linguistic or religious identity, or a common cultural heritage.

It also suggests that parties 'undertake not to interfere with the right of persons belonging to national minorities to participate in the activities of non-governmental organisations, both at the national and inter-national levels'.

The subsequent article requires that parties 'shall endeavour to conclude, where necessary, bilateral and multilateral agreements with other States, in particular neighbouring States, in order to ensure the protection of persons belonging to the national minorities concerned'. It suggested that 'where relevant', parties would 'take measures to encourage transfrontier co-operation' (CoE 1995).

The momentum for cross-border co-operation in the sphere of language has been maintained. In its first contribution to the Debate on the Future of the European Union, EBLUL placed great emphasis on the challenges posed by European diversity. EBLUL proposed that the EU should 'foster cross-border and inter-regional co-operation in cases where these languages are spoken in border areas or where they are official languages in a neighbouring State'.

The EBLUL also raised an important point in relation to the signifi-cance of language and culture for citizenship. It suggested that the notion of European citizenship has an important additional dimension under the following circumstances 'when real meaning is given to cross-border co-operation in the great multitude of cases where regional languages cover more than one EU Member State'. It suggested that speakers of lesser-used language from all over Europe should 'have the opportunity to get together, enabling them to learn from each other, to appreciate each other and to seek co-operation in a wide range of domains where they have similar interests and aims' (EBLUL 2001).

In its final document on the Declaration on Linguistic Diversity and the Future of the EU adopted in Ljouwert/Leeuwardern on 15 June 2002, EBLUL reiterated the significance of lesser-used languages for the concept of European citizenship in general. It proposed that 'the notion of European citizenship has an important dimension only if the European Union effectively respects its lesser-used languages as an important part of – and an added value to – European heritage and culture' (cf. Chapter 4).

The EBLUL sought the introduction of a specific article 'on linguistic diversity building' within the European Charter of Fundamental Rights which would require the Union to 'respect and promote linguistic diversity in Europe, including regional or minority languages as an expression of that diversity' and 'by encouraging cooperation among Member States' in order to achieve this objective. Community action would focus on the promotion of 'exchange of experiences and good practices' and would facilitate 'cooperation and joint projects between state, regional and local authorities'. EBLUL requested that the Community and member states would 'foster cooperation with competent international organisations in the promotion of linguistic diversity, in particular the Council of Europe' and would promote trans-border co-operation where appropriate (EBLUL 2002).

Since then a report issued by the Directorate-General for Research of the CoE endorsed the notion of cross-border co-operation among different language groups. In this instance the focus was on communities whose language is an official language of neighbouring kin state. In these circumstances it requests that 'the EU should support transfrontier co-operation in fields such as education, training, cultural production, literature, broadcasting, information and communication technology, thus facilitating exchanges and removing the remaining effects of the international boundaries, be they internal or external' (Directorate-General for Research 2002: 68).

This rhetoric in various treaties and agreements over the years has been supported with the implementation of several financial programmes, many of which need not be mentioned here. In some instances, financial support for EU cross-border co-operation was limited to specific regions. This applies to the Peace Programme which was adopted by the European Commission in 1995 in order to contribute to peaceful relations and to promote reconciliation in the whole of Northern Ireland and with the border counties in the Republic of Ireland. This was the biggest grant-making project within Northern Ireland and the border region. It encompasses the six counties of Northern Ireland and the six border counties of Donegal, Cavan, Monaghan, Leitrim, Sligo and Louth. The aim of the scheme was to address the social and economic issues identified by the Community Support Framework in the more specific context of Northern Ireland's current transition to a more peaceful and stable society. RML-related actions can be found in the sub-programme devoted to the social inclusion of children and young people, which among other measures seeks to promote common cultural aspects and awareness of cultural diversity by providing support for Irish language education.

Other EU funding programmes had a wider much remit. As early as 1989 the European Commission launched a new programme designed specifically to stimulate cross-border co-operation generally and to contribute to the development of border regions. Cross-border co-operation in this programme was interpreted in terms of contacts to direct neighbours in the border regions, which could be implemented through a whole series of measures, projects and institutions. The programme was also designed to promote inter-regional co-operation between regions that are not necessarily adjacent.

The primary objective of this INTERREG I initiative was to enhance cross-border co-operation in different regions and to unite the citizens of Europe more closely. It aimed to secure joint solutions to joint problems on border regions and to support cross-border initiatives between partners across borders. INTERREG's remit included the development of mutually supportive networks between border regions, lending them a concrete framework and considering new forms of co-operation and the initial phase lasted from 1990 to 1993.

INTERREG I's success served as the catalyst for the launch of a further phase of the program, entitled INTERREG II, for the period 1994 – 1999. This in turn led to a third phase for the period 2000–2006. All three phases have aimed to ensure that national political boundaries do not impede the sustained development of European regions. INTERREG III concentrates on co-operation between states, regions and cross-border areas. For example, it provides financial support for a joint initiative between coastal states of the Baltic. This project includes a cultural dimension which benefits speakers of different languages.

Linguistic diversity within the EU benefited from the Culture 2000 framework programme, which was instituted for 5 years (2000–2004). The aim of this programme was to encourage co-operation in order to contribute to the establishment of a common cultural area for Europeans, to develop artistic and literary creation, to promote knowledge of European history and culture, and to develop heritage sites and collections of European importance as well as intercultural dialogue and social integration. Several calls for proposals within this framework have specifically supported regional or minority language initiatives for literary translations of works published in the less widely used European languages or translated into these languages. A number of book translations to and from regional and minority languages have received the Union's support.

Conclusion

One could cite numerous other examples of cross-border co-operation in Europe (Nic Craith 2004) and many illuminating case studies could be drawn upon. Cross-border co-operation between Finland and Sweden is one of the more obvious examples (Sundback 1998; Tandefelt 1998; Wolf-Knits 2001; Eliasson 2003). The Nordic countries have agreed co-operation in the fields of culture (1971), between local authorities, on education aspects for language boards, and on the right to use their own language in other Nordic countries (1982).

In all instances cited above, contacts have been established between speakers of languages that have some legitimacy as either official or minority tongues. The next chapter will focus on languages which are seeking legitimacy at either local, national or international levels. In some cases, it has proved easier for such languages to acquire legitimacy at international rather than at local level.

6
The Quest for Recognition: Contested Languages

Inclusion/exclusion is one of the central themes of this book and the quest for recognition is essentially an expression of a desire for inclusion within the 'language club'. Chapter 2 explored the 'invention' of national languages during the construction of nation state and the demotion of others to the status of dialect. This chapter focuses on forms of communication whose linguistic status is or has been disputed in the recent past. In many of the examples explored here, speakers have little aspiration to establish a separate nation state – a fact which may actually hinder rather than help their case for language status.

Language, boundary, identity

'Invention' has become a buzzword in the past decade and Hobsbawm and Ranger's *Invention of Traditions* (1983) generated a plethora of debates regarding the authenticity of various cultural customs and emblems. In that book the authors focused on the construction of concepts that appear to have a primordial existence. It is commonly assumed that certain traditions and languages have existed since time immemorial. This applies particularly to national symbols that have been internalised and normalised for some centuries. Bourdieu (1977) coined the term 'habitus' to outline the usual process of remembering and forgetting in civic societies. It is also a useful expression to describe the manner whereby a person or community normalises symbols and concepts. Language is a concept that is increasingly recognised by political scientists and theorists as having been constructed in the era of nation states – as an idea that is closely linked to the erection of national boundaries.

Contested languages are frequently an unfortunate consequence of the establishment of national boundaries (Nic Craith 2000a). In the case of France, for example, once the decision was taken to elevate the Parisian dialect to the level of national language, all other forms of communication were considered detrimental to the territorial integrity of the state. 'This nationalist tide turned against the nations-within-nations that could foster alternate standard dialects, and Provençal and its *langue d'oc* kindred dialects were effectively banished from writing and official contexts' (McWhorter 2002: 70–1). With time the linguistic status of many of these forms of communication was questioned, despite the fact that cases such as Occitan had a long tradition of written literature.

Speakers of contested languages are generally unhappy with the lack of status for their speech form. Theoretically they could simply look for alternative classifications to the terms 'language' and 'dialect', but the use of other options can emphasise rather than reduce the hierarchical implications. Cohen (1971) classified languages in prestige terms and decided upon the categories of majestic, respected or depreciated languages. He selected Dutch as an example of a respected language, while he considered Frisian a depreciated tongue. In other words Dutch had legitimacy as a language in the international domain whereas speakers of Frisian had failed at that time to acquire international standing.

> The Dutch public in general, including the state government, would on average place Frisian in the latter category of discouraged, depreciated languages. They question perhaps if Frisian is really a language and rather see it as a dialect. This is a view that is even shared by Dutch linguistic scholars of some standing. (Gorter 1989: 41)

While Frisian-speakers generally reject the suggestion that their tongue is a dialect rather than a language, occasional speakers have internalised this depreciation of their tongue, demonstrating what Memmi (1965) designated as the classic colonial syndrome of feelings of mortification and inequality regarding one's native culture.

Another term that has come to the fore is that of *halbsprache* meaning a 'half-language' or a 'semi-language' referring to a speech form that is regarded as more than a dialect but less than a language (Nic Craith 2000a). This is sometimes used in the case of Scots (Lallans) in Scotland, which McClure (1997: 24) advises was once a language and 'has the potential to become one again'. He advocates that the enhancement of

Scots to the status of language will not require any inherent changes in the language itself. Instead the attitudes of speakers of Scots themselves will have to be changed. 'The task of those concerned for the future of Scots is to persuade the Scottish people that we have, as a unique national possession, a highly distinctive and expressive tongue which is also the vehicle for a literature of great antiquity, merit and durability.' More significantly he adds that 'if we wait until we have "proved" Scots to be a "language" before embarking on this task, we assuredly never will'.

Like Scots, many forms of communication in contemporary Europe can be classified as 'disputed languages'. Table 6.1 (below) provides some examples that have caused controversy at some stage in recent years. There are many other examples that could have been included in this table such as Picard and Champenois and the most striking feature about this list is that all the examples point to peoples without a distinct nation state. But one could also point to other examples such as Luxemburgish, Macedonian and Scottish which are now associated with distinct national boundaries – although the position of Macedonian remains controversial. Chapter 2 focused on examples of language status that were enhanced with the construction of nation states. Here the intention is to concentrate on forms of communication between different groups of people who do not form a separate nation state but have clearly a distinct ethnicity.

The Kashubs, for example, live in Northern Poland (cf. Map 6.1). The area inhabited by these people has diminished significantly over time. Their ancestors were the Slavic-speaking Pomeranians who inhabited the Baltic coast from the Vistula to the Elbe Rivers in the early Middle

Table 6.1   Disputed language varieties

Alsatian
Aragonese
Asturian
Franco-Provençal
Karelian
Kashubian
Low German
North-Italian (Friulian)
Sign Language
Ulster-Scots
Venetian
Walloon

Map 6.1 Kashubian-speaking area in Northern Poland. *Source*: Adapted from Wicherkiewicz (2000).

Ages. Later under pressure from German colonisers, the Pomeranians moved eastward (Wicherkiewicz 2000: 215).

It was not until the mid-nineteenth century that a sense of Kashubian identity re-emerged. The Spring of Nations and the pan-Slavic movement served as the catalyst for the modern history of Kashubian. Since that time, a sense of Kashubian ethnicity and linguistic identity has been re-enforced by the efforts of Kashubian writers (Wicherkiewicz 2004: 3). Although the Kashubs nurtured their sense of a distinctive identity, this has been despite, rather than because of, political administration.

One of the more decisive events for the Kashubs was the rebirth of the Polish State after the First World War when most Kashubian areas were incorporated into the Polish nation and Communist control impacted on all areas including language. Prior to 1989, Communist censorship prohibited the use of the term 'language' in connection with

Kashubian which was officially regarded as a distinct dialect of Polish. Many Kashubian scholars and writers of that period who did not support such a stance referred to Kashubian speech rather than dialect (Wicherkiewicz 2004: 7).

During the Communist era, there was no opportunity for any broader ethnic activity. All folk activities were strongly limited by the strict control and censorship of the Communist state which formalised many folk rituals. Folk arts and customs became the province of trained professionals such as dance instructors and musicians, rather than the product of the ethnic group from which they emerged. 'These kinds of processes tended to divorce ethnic traditions from ethnic identity' (Synak 1995: 158).

Estimates of numbers of contemporary Kashubians vary from half a million (Synak 1995) to 300 thousand (Wicherkiewicz 2000). The latter figure is derived from the first sociological and sociolinguistic research programme which was undertaken in the mid-1980s. According to those results, some 300 thousand identified themselves as Kashubian on the basis of four factors: (1) they were of Kashubian descent (i.e. kinship); (2) they had some territorial affiliation to the region where Kashubian is spoken; (3) they spoke the Kashubian language and (4) they felt themselves to be Kashubian. Although knowledge of Kashubian was apparently crucial as a marker of Kashubian identity, members of all generations are completely bilingual. Children whose mother tongue was Kashubian generally spoke Polish as their second language. Elderly people usually had a good knowledge of Low German and/or High German (Wicherkiewicz 2000).

Although the concept of a Kashubian language was disputed, the notion of Kashubian ethnicity had been gathering momentum for many decades. In 1956, *Zrzesenie Kaszubsko-Pomorskie* (the Kashubian Association) was founded to become the main advocate of reviving 'Kashubianess', at regional level. With the fall of Communism, there were many new opportunities and prospects for all minority groups in Poland and for the Kashubs in particular.

In 1992 a general Resolution at the Assembly of the Kashubs emphasised the necessity of stronger economic and social activities in favour of the Kashubian areas as well as the whole country. In particular it noted the importance of preservation and enrichment of cultural identity especially in relation to language (Synak 1995: 160). Generally speaking, however, 'the Kashubian leaders are careful to emphasise that the Kashubs are an ethnic group of the Polish nation' rather than a distinct nation state (Kamusella 2001: 240). They have no wish to secure national independence but are very keen that their distinctiveness should be recognised at national level, and to a certain extent they have already succeeded in this position.

With time the status of the Kashubian language in Poland has improved dramatically. The new Polish Language Law passed in 1999 allowed for minority languages (including Kashubian) to be used officially on a regional level. The adoption of the Law on National and Ethnic Minorities and on the Regional Language by the Polish Parliament provided for the use of the Kashubian (and other auxiliary) languages in respect of Christian and family names in private and public life as well as the use of these languages in geographical names and the names of public institutions. It also noted the rights of minorities to be taught in their minority language as well as the right to be taught the culture and history of their minority group (Wicherkiewicz 2004: 9).

In their quest for recognition of a distinct identity, the Kashubs can be compared with promoters of Ulster-Sots in Northern Ireland. Ulster-Scots ethnicity is less clear than that of the Kashubians but it is receiving significant endorsements with time. Those who consider themselves to be Ulster-Scot are descendants of Scots who migrated from the west coast of Scotland to Northern Ireland from the sixteenth century onwards. Speakers of Ulster-Scots are generally located along the east coast line of Northern Ireland, in areas congruent with what the Ulster Defence Association call the 'retainable homeland', the territory that they define as theirs. In this instance the language is linked to a particular territory but has no essential connection with a political border. This speech form has strong symbolic relevance both for those who speak it on a daily basis and for those who react with disbelief to its quest for legitimacy as a language.

An enhanced public awareness of the Ulster-Scots tongue can be attributed to the efforts of several non-governmental organisations in Northern Ireland, which have emerged from the culturalist wing of unionism and loyalism. These include the Ulster-Scots Academy and the Ulster-Scots Heritage Council (*Ulster-Scotch Heirskip Cooncil*). According to the Ulster-Scots Language Society, some 100,000 speak Ulster-Scots regularly. This represents less than 7 per cent of the total population of Northern Ireland and is smaller than the proportion of Irish-speakers, who now account for more than 10 per cent of the population. According to the 2001 Census in Northern Ireland, 10.1 per cent of males and 10.5 per cent of females have some knowledge of Irish. But in contrast to the Irish-speaking community, the Ulster-Scots Language Society claims that their language is dominated by native speakers of what may be 'a purer form of Lallans than that spoken in Scotland itself' (Adamson 1991: 76).

One of the more interesting aspects of Ulster-Scots is the relationship it affirms between language and boundary. In this case the quest for legitimate linguistic status is generating a boundary that is not separatist. Speakers of Ulster-Scots define themselves as different, yet distinctly British. In many circumstances the use of a language has been strongly associated with separatist intentions. This applies, for example, to the examples of Basque and Irish which were examined in the previous chapter. In those instances the use of a particular language has been perceived as the precursor of the quest for independence, but this is not the case with speakers of Ulster-Scots who wish to remain within the current political framework of the UK.

While it is generally true that many speakers of disputed languages are considered to have a distinct ethnicity, there is a particular problem for the Deaf community. In the late twentieth century, many deaf have endeavoured to counter the negativity associated with their disability and to emphasise instead their status as a separate cultural or ethnic group. Yet 'it appears to be impossible, in present circumstances, for Deaf people to be seen as *both* a linguistic minority *and* as disabled people' and the struggle will continue for many decades (italics original in Turner 2003: 181).

Although the Deaf community does not constitute a distinct nationality, the concept of national Sign languages has emerged in recent years and the EU has made a commitment to recognise Sign language as used by Deaf people within different member states. Perhaps the notion of a national Sign language reflects the common understanding of national languages – that is, particular languages associated with national boundaries – and one can reasonably talk about the Sign language of the Netherlands and Hungarian Sign language because these countries are committed to single Sign languages. But it is not always the case that there is a single Sign language within different national boundaries. In Northern Ireland, for example, there are two Sign languages in use reflecting affiliations with different political frameworks. There are also two Sign languages in Canada reflecting the different political allegiances here (Woll *et al.* 2001: 14).

Language and legitimacy

For many speakers of disputed languages, the quest for legitimacy is of real significance. In a social context there is greater prestige attached to languages rather than dialects and many contested language communities are profoundly aware of the significance of language status. No language is inherently handicapped or of less value than another. Yet the status of language confers greater legitimacy on some speech forms but denies it to others, which are relegated as dialects. The term 'dialect' implies a subordinate position 'that there are other dialects and a language to which they can be said to "belong". Hence every dialect is a language, but not every language is a dialect' (Haugen 1966: 923), but how does a speech form acquire legitimacy as a language?

Legitimacy itself is an elusive concept and can operate on two axes – the horizontal and/or vertical. At the horizontal level, legitimacy is self-affirmed and can be validated at a local, non-governmental level. It is a 'subject centred conception' (Theiler 1999: 13). Legitimacy can also be conferred vertically by an official or outside observer, such as a government organisation. In either instance, legitimacy becomes a 'prereflexive' concept (Bourdieu 1994: 127). It is internalised and treated as though it were natural or self-evident. But Lipset (1963: 77) has argued that a community only regards 'a political system as legitimate or illegitimate according to the way its values fit with theirs'. Since legitimacy is not an essential concept, its application to any tradition or custom can vary from one individual to another. Usually the degree of legitimacy acquired by a cultural concept depends on the extent to which a group or community has internalised it (Nic Craith 2000a).

The acquisition of legitimacy is a gradual process and is influenced by several factors. In the case of the concept of language – although it may be overstating the obvious – much depends on the degree to which speakers are aware of the status of their speech form and consider it in any sense significant. But in the context of contested languages, which are frequently classed as dialects, speakers are often patently aware of the disputed status of their tongues. While they may be uninterested in the role of grammar and syntax in differentiating a language from a dialect, speakers of these tongues are very concerned with the hierarchical implications, and the dimension of functional superiority and inferiority is very significant.

As in the case with other cultural concepts, groups can endeavour to confer legitimacy on their own speech form on a horizontal axis. Speakers of disputed languages and associated cultural organisations can simply define their own speech form as a language. This ideology is exemplified in the work of Boelens who writes that 'Frisian is a language because this is what the Frisians want.' He further argues that 'if the Frisians neglect their language it will become a dialect. It is absolutely necessary that the Frisian language keeps up with the times and continues to develop, because otherwise it will be pushed aside by other stronger languages' (Boelens 1990: 8*f.*).

Affirmations regarding the status of language or dialect do not necessarily refer to the grammatical structure and vocabulary of a speech form. Instead they are concerned with the symbolic status of the concept. As in all instances the language as symbol acts as a 'mnemotechnic aid' (Berger and Luckmann 1991: 88) or as marker of social roles or situations. The speech form signifies the social context of its speakers. When defining their tongue as a language rather than a dialect, speakers are conferring legitimacy not only on their medium of communication, but on their own social role. But what is that value of this self-affirmed legitimacy? Quite a lot as is illustrated in the example of Luxemburgish. In this instance, speakers of Luxemburgish began to think of themselves as a separate nation with a distinct language which has now acquired considerable status within the EU.

Many similar examples of self-affirmed legitimacy abound, although these are not necessarily as successful as the example of Luxemburgish. At the opening address of the sixth international conference on minority languages in the University of Gdansk, Prof. Józef Borzyszkowski (1996) noted with regret that 'still there are individuals and circles that question the status of the Kashubian language'. From his perspective there was no doubt but Kashubian is a distinct language in its own right. According to Kockel (1999: 55) 'whether the Kashubians speak a Polish dialect or a language of their own depends primarily on whom you ask, and although the Transylvanian question is unlikely to incite genocide, it remains a source of high tension in this post-homogenised part of the world'.

Sometimes the issue is fought on simple grounds. From a practical perspective one can ask what are the criteria that determine which form of communication is a real language. The most obvious answer is that it is spoken – but even this criterion has complications. Sign language is not 'spoken'. Does this disqualify it as a real language? Some people 'do not consider sign languages to be languages at all but merely non-linguistic system of gesture and pantomime' (Woll *et al.* 2001: 12). This is a debate that will be revisited later in the chapter but it should be noted at this point that the Ethnologue database lists more than hundred known Sign languages.

The sphere in which a language is spoken can also carry great import. Many Kashubs, for example, regard their own language as the primary medium of communication within their community, but in the recent past, at least, it has been confined to that intimate network and used only for 'informal' or 'unofficial' purposes. Many minority and contested languages have suffered from being identified as languages strictly for the home and ideally for use among the older generation. Younger members are often 'protected' against the native language by the older family members. 'The main reason for such parental and grandparental attitudes is the desire to ensure a better future for the younger generation. There is common conviction among the parents that the Kashubian vernacular as "everyday speak" is an important obstacle to learning Polish and achieving good results at school' (Synak 1995: 164).

Many contested languages lack a common standard version, and minor dialectical differences can be used to justify a switch to an altern-ative language. In the case of Kashubian, for example, 'dialect differ-ences, imperceptible to the outside observer, function in their consciousness as major barriers to communication, and these frequently justify conducting conversations in standard Polish (and in part also in German)' (Iskierski and Latoszek 1995: 145). In this instance, an apparent lack of mutual intelligibility justifies a switch in language.

Sometimes the lack of mutual intelligibility serves as the layman's criterion for linguistic status (i.e. if your language is very similar to mine then we do not speak separate languages). This is a measure that is frequently applied to Northern Ireland when Ulster-Scots is spoken. Individuals hostile to its linguistic status complain that they under-stand Ulster-Scots perfectly well; therefore it cannot be a separate language from English. But there are many examples of languages such as Danish and Swedish that are mutually intelligible, yet their linguistic status is hardly questioned.

In itself, mutual intelligibility is hardly a sufficient criterion on which to accept or reject the linguistic status of a specific form of communica-tion, and much depends on the everyday practical experience of language distance. In the case of Ireland, for example, the language distance between Irish and English is enormous since these two languages belong to separate Celtic and Germanic branches of Indo-European. For this reason, there can be an expectation at an everyday level that all languages are equally distant from one another. However, this element of language distance is not present for others who speak languages such as Spanish and Catalan or Italian and Friulan or Dutch and German.

There are many instances where 'dialects' which although not mutu-ally intelligible are still considered to be the same language. This would apply to Sámi languages in the Nordic countries and also to some Sign languages. 'It is possible that some national sign languages are made up of dialects that are to some extent mutually unintelligible. They are considered to be single languages by Deaf communities or hearing people working with Deaf communities because there are social, political or economic reasons for doing so' (Woll *et al.* 2001: 14).

However, there is some logic to the argument that a language that has evolved independently will be quite distinctive and linguists often avail of a technique called 'glottochronology' to examine the relationship between different languages. This technique operates on the principle that two languages which have evolved from the same 'parent' language should have approximately 86 per cent of their vocabulary in common after 1000 years of separation.

The same method can be applied to defining languages as either separate languages or as dialects of the same language. In 1972 the American linguist Morris Swadesh created a word list of 100 core terms common to all societies. These fundamental concepts related to people, animals, food items, numbers, weather conditions and so on. By finding the words for each of these 100 core items linguists could compare the coincidence between languages which can then be used as a test for separateness or independence.

Some linguists have already availed of this technique to make a point. In the case of Scots, for example, McClure argues that while many of Swadesh's basic concepts could be expressed by identical words in English and Scots (i.e. 'bird', 'egg', 'tree') one could also point to examples of Scots words that are unrelated to any English term (i.e. 'big/muckle', 'small/wee', 'ear/lug', 'mountain/ben'). Having applied Swadesh's test to the vocabularies of Scots and English, he concluded that the level of co-incidence between them was 89 per cent. While this may seem a rather high proportion it is less than that of Czech and Slovak, German and Dutch, Norwegian and Danish. He concludes that while 'not much weight can be put on this result; yet it does show that a form of Scots at least can be conceived of which is less closely related to English than Norwegian is to Danish' (McClure 1997: 17).

The Swadesh test is useful in that it is independent of personal bias or attitudes but some Sign linguists have found it completely inappropriate for contemporary Sign languages as the original list contains words such as 'louse' or 'dung' which are not core terms in Sign languages found in urban European or North American locations. Sign linguists have therefore adapted their lists. Overall, however, the Swadesh test is hardly conclusive evidence of linguistic independence.

Writing in a language can sometimes prove a significant element in the quest for linguistic independence, and a contested language that is not written down will have great difficulty in acquiring full linguistic status. This applies to contested languages such as Alsatian where the lack of a written code supports the view that it could hardly be considered an independent language. While there has been some attempt to adopt a written form of Alsatian based on phonetic representation, this is not considered sufficient and people respond with comments such as 'it is not written. There is no orthography. It's more phonetic' (Broadbridge 1998: 59–60). Similarly it has been argued that British Sign language (BSL) 'cannot be recognised as an official language because it has no written form' (McCullogh 2000: 93).

The art of writing has frequently been used by nation states to maintain tongues at the status of dialect. For example, several hundred dialects of spoken Chinese are usually classified into eight main subgroups. Despite extensive linguistic differences between the spoken dialects, many of them are regarded as varieties of a small number of languages. This situation is primarily a consequence of the similarity in the written forms of Chinese languages, although the spoken forms are mutually incomprehensible. But it may also reflect the political system in China, which encourages the concept of one nation and one people.

This also applies in a European context to several South German dialects which had functioned virtually as state languages in the multistate era of the Holy Roman Empire, but had eventually yielded up their status as written idioms. Gradually, these self-sustaining forms of communication were downgraded to vernacular variants of German and because there is only one written standard, they were considered to be one language. 'Yet at the time of their demotion, the main Southern German dialects could each claim several million speakers' (Schröder 1993: 32).

Martin Luther is usually credited with the standardisation of the German language in print with his translation of the New Testament. Although there had been many other German translations of the Bible before Luther's time, such efforts were 'mostly uncouth and not very easily understood by the common people'. Luther's translations 'may almost be said to have created the German language as a vehicle of literary expression'. His familiarity with both High and Low German was a consequence of his upbringing in Thuringia on the boundary between the two languages. In his translation he 'used neither High German nor Low German, but a third, which united the two' and his Bible 'gave Germany a common language' (Lindsay 1996: 116).

Although more than 75 per cent of the world's languages are not written down this does not necessarily imply that they are not languages. Yet the significance of writing down a language cannot be undervalued in a political context. In his much-quoted treatise on imagined communities, Anderson (1991) writes of the importance of the establishment of a print community (cf. Chapter 3). Hastings (1997: 12) suggests that many ethnicities become nations at the point when literature is produced in their own vernaculars. The literary form of almost every European language was developed from a small number of regional dialects. Hobsbawm (1990: 54) points to examples such as literary Bulgarian which is based on the West Bulgarian dialect and literary Ukrainian which was developed from dialects of its South-eastern region.

Many imperial powers have recognised the importance of a print community. When the Russians wished to Russify the Ukrainians, in the late nineteenth century for example, Aleksandr II signed a decree which prohibited all import and publication of Ukrainian books and newspapers and banned all teaching in Ukrainian even to infants. Ukrainian-language books were removed from school libraries and it was proposed to transfer Ukraine teachers to Great Russia. 'During cholera outbreaks, even public health notices were to be posted in Russian alone' (Reid 1997: 68).

The transmission of language in education is highly significant and many languages were demoted via educational institutions. At the beginning of the nineteenth century, Dutch was the medium of instruction in schools in Friesland and spoken Frisian was banned from the classroom. 'In a school almanac (Almanak 1816) the teachers were urgently advised not to allow the children to speak Frisian nor to speak Frisian to them themselves.' Economic reasons were forwarded for the advancement of Dutch rather than Frisian. 'And to get by in their profession as a merchant, an artisan, a bargeman or something like it they had to learn Dutch' (Feitsma 1981: 166).

There are many examples of similar situations among contested language communities. In the early 1950s there was strong institutional pressure in Kashubian regions not to hand down the Kashubian dialect to children. It was argued that the Kashubian dialect would 'interfere' with children's fluency in Polish and with their acquisition of knowledge in general. Rewards and punishment were set in place to interrupt the intergenerational transmission of Kashubian, and for a time this process succeeded (Iskierski and Latoszek 1995: 144).

With the revival of confidence in their own language and cultural heritage in recent decades, the Kashubians initiated a minority language education programme in their language and have introduced lessons in Kashubian in many elementary schools. In 1991 a Kashubian secondary school was established and a course is now offered in Kashubian at the University of Gdansk within the Polish philology degree. The primary difficulty in the past has been the lack of teaching materials, phrase books and dictionaries in Kashubian, but a two-volume Polish–Kashubian dictionary has now been issued and two translations of the New Testament into Kashubian have appeared. However, each of them is based on a different orthography which is an ongoing issue for many contested languages.

There have been some suggestions that the educational criterion should be used to prove whether Sign language should be included in a list of world languages. This is apparently necessary 'to ensure that every "home sign" system used by a lone deaf villager is not included as a Sign language'. This is essentially a quest for a 'standard form' of a language which can be used as a defining marker. Standard forms are usually those with the highest prestige and are considered to exemplify the essential features of a language. It is also the form printed in books and used in schools but it can hardly be applied to Sign as 'there are no widely used written forms of sign languages and no sign language has a body of written literature, so any "standard" form of a sign language would have a very different function from a standard spoken language with a written literature' (Woll *et al.* 2001: 19).

There is also the issue of the relative 'newness' of Sign languages, which means that they have not yet developed a tradition in the educational sector. For practical reasons, Sign languages only emerged during the last 300 years, when the development of towns served as the catalyst for the emergence of Deaf communities in different regions. Sign languages emerged when schools were set up for Deaf children, from the late eighteenth century forward in Europe. These children were able to use a single form of language in these educational institutions, developed out of signed languages that were being used by educators. Education for Deaf children has only recently begun in many regions. This in turn provides an environment in which Sign language can develop (Woll *et al.* 2001: 12).

The print context is an ongoing problem for many contested languages as languages without a standard written form rarely feature in educational circumstances and become devalued in consequence. This has been recognised by many of those struggling for full linguistic recognition. In the case of Northern Ireland, a project at Stranmillis College, Belfast, is undertaking the development of an educational programme about, rather than in, Ulster-Scots (Gilbert 2003). It is hoped that this programme will generate a lot of interest in Ulster-Scots culture among school-children and the population generally. In itself, however, this programme will not convince the general population of the viability of Ulster-Scots as an independent language.

The European context

When operating on a horizontal axis, many speakers of contested languages may convince themselves that their speech form is a language rather than a dialect, but they are usually equally keen to convince others of the significance of their form of communication. For this reason many of them seek legitimacy for their tongue at a vertical level. As linguists or laymen rarely agree on the precise criteria that constitute a language, the acquisition of language status is often a random, rather than a precise, process and is highly dependent on the political context. Until recently many languages sought linguistic status at national level. However, the establishment of organisations such as EBLUL and the increasingly widespread implementation of the ECRML have offered new processes of negotiation and ensured that language communities can receive recognition at a level higher than that of the nation state. Yet even here the process is somewhat arbitrary.

The EBLUL, for example, has a list of languages which it includes in its membership but it does not have a list of 'dialects' which are rejected. While there have been several attempts to agree criteria for language status, these have not actually succeeded and it has been recognised that many contemporary languages were considered dialects at an earlier stage in their evolution. 'No one disputes the existence of a considerable number of Romance languages. However, if one goes back in history one sees that these originated as dialects of Latin' (Ó Riagáin 2001c: 29).

Like identity, language status is fluid and may transform with evolution or with changing political contexts. While some languages are demoted and become dialects, others discard their inferior status and are raised to the status of language. In 1984, for example, Luxembourg decreed that Luxemburgish was its national language although many linguistics still regard it as a dialect of German rather than a distinct language. When Germany ratified the ECRML, it controversially accepted Niederdeutsch (Low German) as a regional language.

To a certain extent the rise of interest in regional and contested languages within the EU reflects a growing regionalisation within Europe and the emergence and revival of languages and ethnicities at regional levels generally. The 're-emphasising of identification with a relatively small group or regional culture, irrespective of political boundaries or allegiances – has led to the revival of local idioms or even the creation of new languages' (Schröder 1993: 24). The process of signature and ratification of the ECRML as outlined in Chapter 4 has proved particularly beneficial for speakers of contested languages and is perhaps now used in a manner that was not entirely envisaged by those involved in the original drawing up of the Charter.

In the UK, for example, Scots acquired a new affirmation with its inclusion in the Charter. A news release issued by the British Government in June 1998 indicated that by applying Part II of the Charter to Scots, the Government was 'recognising the distinctive nature and cultural value of the language'. Scots activists were quick to affirm this gesture. According to McClure (1997: 61), the recognition of Scots by the EBLUL was 'a major boost' to its status. He argues for greater legitimacy for this language among its speakers, suggesting that 'it would indeed be a disgrace if we ourselves, now that our language has been granted this expression of confidence by the European Community, failed to demonstrate our own belief in its value'. It appears in this instance that legitimacy for Scots already operates on a vertical axis but this affirmation is not necessarily reciprocated at a horizontal level.

Speakers of Ulster-Scots acquired some legitimacy through membership of the Northern Ireland Subcommittee of the EBLUL. This process was probably inevitable once the UK committee of EBLUL was divided into sub-committees, and branches were established in Scotland, Wales and Northern Ireland. As a representative for Scots had been present on the UK committee of EBLUL since its inception in 1993, speakers of Ulster-Scots applied for representation on the Northern Irish branch sub-committee. It was considered inappropriate to deny representation to speakers of Ulster-Scots on the Northern Irish committee when Scots had already been represented on the UK national committee for a number of years previously.

As soon as Ulster-Scots was accepted, speakers of Ullans were quick to publicise this vertical affirmation of their speech-form. Again this failed to satisfy many cultural activists, who are happy that it receives recognition in the public sphere but are opposed to its classification as a distinct language. Mac Póilin (1998) argued that it was as a variety of Scots, rather than English, that the Ulster-Scots Language Society was granted membership of the Bureau. Of course, this in itself does not imply that Ulster-Scots is a separate language. It merely suggests that it is dialect of Scots, rather than English, but Scots itself is a contested language which casts doubts on the efficacy of this classification.

Mac Póilin (1998) also pointed to the fact that membership of the EBLUL does not necessarily constitute proof that either Scots or Ulster-Scots are separate languages. In each case the national committee decides whether or not a linguistic group is accepted. But there is considerable variation in the decisions taken by national committees in different states. Mac Póilin (1998: 3) points to the case of the Spanish national committee, which has denied membership to representatives of Asturian-speakers, 'although Asturian differs at least as much from Castilian Spanish as Scots does from Standard English'.

However, this process such should not suggest that EBLUL as an organisation reinforces the role of nation state in the conferral of legitimacy on a particular speech form, or that the Bureau is necessarily nationalist in ideological terms. Committees and sub-committees are simply organised into the administrative units of the EU. Moreover, speakers of a language denied representation on a national committee of EBLUL can refer the matter to a higher level.

Here an important issue is raised – that of the authority that confers legitimacy on a cultural concept. The standing of the conferring body, in this instance, EBLUL, is vital to the legitimacy of the status which it confers on Ulster-Scots. If in the case of Northern Ireland EBLUL is considered to have low visibility or little authority in relation to national institutions, then the legitimacy that it confers on Ulster-Scots in not internalised and remains disputed. If EBLUL itself is not legitimised then it can only fail in its efforts to confer legitimacy on regional or minority languages. In other words the Bureau itself must undergo the process of legitimisation and must be able to justify its own existence in terms of other institutions that have become widely accepted or internalised. But EBLUL already derives respectability from the fact that it is an institution created by the EU and has – in the past at least – derived most of its funding from that source. Moreover the number of countries signing the ECRML is increasing, which inevitably has implications for the relevance of the body at an international level. In that context its authority as a conferring body is unquestionable as it has already received international approval.

Ulster-Scots also benefited from official recognition by other bodies and received a major boost with the publication of the Good Friday Agreement in 1998. The Agreement proposed a range of changes in the public sector in Northern Ireland and included the cultural dimension within its terms of reference. With regard to linguistic diversity in Northern Ireland, the Good Friday Agreement affirmed that 'participants recognise the importance of respect, understanding and tolerance in relation to linguistic diversity, including in Northern Ireland, the Irish language, Ulster-Scots and the languages of the various ethnic communities, all of which are part of the cultural wealth of the island of Ireland' (Government of the United Kingdom of Great Britain and Northern Ireland and Government of Ireland 1998: 22). Speakers of Ulster-Scots may have been happy with their inclusion in this statement of principle, but many opponents were quick to argue that the British Government had referred to Ulster-Scots but not 'the Ulster-Scots language', thereby failing to confer legitimacy on Ullans as a distinct language.

Ulster-Scots achieved further affirmation with its inclusion by the British Government within the terms of reference of the Charter. Originally the Government failed to nominate Ulster-Scots for inclusion within the ambit of the document, but it subsequently commissioned research to help it decide how to treat Ulster-Scots for the purposes of the Charter. In consequence of its research, the British Government affirmed that Ulster-Scots in Northern Ireland would be recognised as a minority or regional language for the purposes of Part II of the Charter.

This placed Ulster-Scots on a par with Scots language in Scotland and represented an official acknowledgement of the status of language for Ulster-Scots. Subsequently a new cross-border implementation body for language has been established in Ireland. Eight members of this official body deal with the Ulster-Scots language and matters relating to Ulster-Scots cultural issues. While this has not prevented some linguists insisting on the dialectical status of Ulster-Scots, it represents legitimacy for a language that may in time be followed by a more horizontal and widespread affirmation of its status.

Perhaps even more controversial than Ulster-Scots has been the case of BSL in the UK. Deaf people from all over the British Isles have been campaigning for many years for official Government recognition of BSL. In July 2000, great crowds marched through London protesting that BSL is one of the largest UK minority languages and should be acknowledged as such (McCullogh 2000). Despite their campaign, BSL was not actually included by the British Government within the terms of reference of the Charter. Proponents of BSL were greatly disappointed as they felt that this was the only manner in which they could ensure acceptance of their language in public settings. It would also guarantee adequate state funding for training and provision of interpreters and would 'open the doors for deaf empowerment in social and government bodies' (McCullogh 2000: 93).

The debate conducted between the Minister's advisers and the Deaf organisation at this time raised many interesting questions (Woll 2001: 76). The first of these inevitably queried the authenticity of BSL as a language, and advisers to the minister questioned whether BSL is actually a language or simply a non-verbal form of communication. While acknowledging its difference from English, Ministerial advisers suggested that the debate was really a matter for linguists. A response from the Deaf organisation suggested that linguists were in agreement about the linguistic status of BSL and referred the adviser to a series of articles.

Further discussions revolved around the question of territory which will feature strongly in the next chapter. Ministerial advisers pointed to the fact that BSL is not used within a specific territory or region of the UK. Instead it is used by a number of Deaf individuals throughout the UK, regardless of where they live. As it could not be identified with a particular region, it could hardly qualify as a regional language and is therefore not a regional or minority language for the purposes of the Charter. In response the Deaf organisation acknowledged the logic of this argument but noted that BSL does qualify as a minority (non-territorial) language. They also highlighted the fact that the Catholic Deaf community in Northern Ireland use a form of Sign language that is specific to that region within the UK.

The concept of 'traditional' language was also raised in this debate. Unlike other non-territorial languages such as Romany, BSL is relatively new and has not been transmitted inter-generationally over a number of centuries. For this reason, advisers to the minister argued that BSL could hardly qualify as a 'traditional' language. In response, the Deaf organisation pointed to historical facts regarding Sign language in the UK. As early as 1575, there were some references to the use of Sign by a Deaf person in Britain. Moreover, many descriptions and illustrations of Sign and Sign language grammar were published in the nineteenth century. Interestingly they also suggested that this Sign language had been adopted in other parts of the British Empire, inferring that the Sign languages of both Australia and New Zealand are dialects of BSL.

The apparent 'newness' of BSL, they argued, referred to the name given to the language rather than the language itself. In fact the term 'British Sign Language' was first used by Dr Mary Brennan some 25 years ago in her endeavour to formally differentiate BSL from other Sign languages. The language had existed for decades and centuries before then but was simply called 'Sign'. The late recognition of BSL as a distinct language is merely a reflection of the fact that modern linguistic research on BSL did not begin until the late 1970s.

Ultimately the British Deaf community succeeded in this quest for recognition and the British Government subsequently agreed to include BSL within the terms of reference of the Charter. Essentially this recognition of their language has proved extremely beneficial for the Deaf community as recognition of BSL as a minority language implies that those that use it are a minority with rights. European institutions have gradually come to recognise the Deaf community as a distinct cultural group, and on 19 November 1988 the European Parliament resolved that member states should 'grant their indigenous sign language equivalent status of that of national spoken language' (Hogan-Brun and Wolff 2003: 13). By 1998, several states in Europe, such as Denmark, Finland, Portugal and Sweden had given some degree of official recognition to their indigenous Sign language.

Conclusion

While the quest for recognition of full linguistic independence is motivated by cultural and emotional factors among speakers of many contested languages, the implications of such recognition often bring practical and economic benefits. Once a form of communication is officially recognised as a minority language, it is almost inevitable that the language will become visible in the public sphere, gain some entry into educational institutions and ultimately may bring some form of employment for speakers of such languages.

Moreover, the recognition of a language in one region can bring positive benefits to those speaking it in another. The inclusion of Low German by the German Government within the terms of reference of the ECRML was probably motivated by the Dutch government's recognition of Low Saxon (essentially the same language) when it ratified the document. As noted in an earlier chapter, one of the issues raised by those who developed the Charter was the significance of territory for a language which provides the focus for the next chapter.

7
Nomads, Language and Land

Cultures and languages are frequently perceived as rooted in a particular territory but this is hardly relevant for groups that have maintained nomadic rather than sedentary lifestyles over the centuries and regarded state territorial boundaries as irrelevant. Such groups 'could teach us how meaningless frontiers are: careless of boundaries, Romanies and Sinti are at home all over Europe. They are what we claim to be: born Europeans' (Grass 1992: 108).

There is a popular assumption that peoples who maintain a nomadic lifestyle are in some sense at a more backward level of existence than the settled community and the lack of conformity appears to threaten the values of the settled population. 'Pseudo-anthropology feeds the basic European nightmare: a terror of peoples who move.' This 'nightmare' has been exaggerated by what Ascherson (1996: 76) terms 'nineteenth century evolutionist intellectuals' who postulated that 'moving peoples were no longer a merely physical menace emerging from the trackless East. They now also seemed to incarnate a cosmic disorder in which the past rose out of its tomb and swarmed forward on horseback to annihilate the present.'

Although internal migration is a feature of contemporary Europe, and revisions of EU treaties, such as that which occurred at Maastricht, specifically offer protection to peoples on the move (cf. Chapter 1), this primarily applied to Europeans moving from one country to another within the EU and the potential movement of huge numbers of Eastern and non-Europeans is still generally feared. Newspapers frequently predict hoards of (foreign) migrants who will impinge on national cohesion and dilute national identity.

Strictly speaking, one should not confuse nomadic peoples such as Sinti, Roma and Sámi with immigrants such as the Turks in Germany or

West Indians in Britain or North Africans in France. While the next chapter focuses on non-Europeans and their languages in contemporary Europe, the focus in the current chapter is on traditional and contemporary lifestyles of groups who have at one point or another practised nomadism in Europe. The fact remains that 'unless a culture and an ethnic group can be identified with a territory they will rarely be tolerated for any length of time, especially if the host nationality is either under threat or seeking to extend itself' (Mundy 1997: 32). This chapter will examine the implications of the nomadic lifestyle for cultures and languages. In particular it will focus on the languages and cultures of the Roma in various European regions, the Sámi in Scandinavia and Travellers in Ireland.

Identities and lifestyles

The Sámi have traditionally maintained a nomadic lifestyle concentrating on reindeer herding in their Sápmi homeland which extends from the Kola Peninsula in Russia through the Northern parts of Finland and Sweden to the Norwegian provinces of Finnmark, Troms and Nordland and the Swedish provinces of Norrbotten, Västerbotten and Jämtland (Asp 1995: 75; Lehtola 2002: 14) (Map 7.1). Most of this territory is located to the north of the Arctic Circle and is generally known as Sápmi – the indigenous word for Sámi which is frequently applied to the area of Sápmi settlement. The numbers of Sámi depends on the way they are counted but estimates vary from 60,000 to 100,000. The majority of these live in Norway and are highly concentrated in the province of Finnmark. The smallest group live in Russia and number about 2000.

Essentially the Sámi are a minority living in four neighbouring countries with their own language and culture (Nic Craith 2004). 'During the nineteenth century there was much hostility to their way of life, particularly in Norway which, on the basis of racial theories and social Darwinism, felt that they should be either extinguished or raised to a higher level' (Alcock 2000: 174). However, their circumstances have now changed and they constitute the only ethnic group within the boundaries of the EU to be recognised as an aboriginal people.

Unlike the Sámi, the Roma/Gypsies are scattered throughout Europe and particularly in Eastern Europe. In contemporary Eastern and Southern Europe, they are largely settled and sedentary whereas those in Western Europe still cultivate the nomadic lifestyle. Their origins are usually located in migrations from India through Persia into Europe

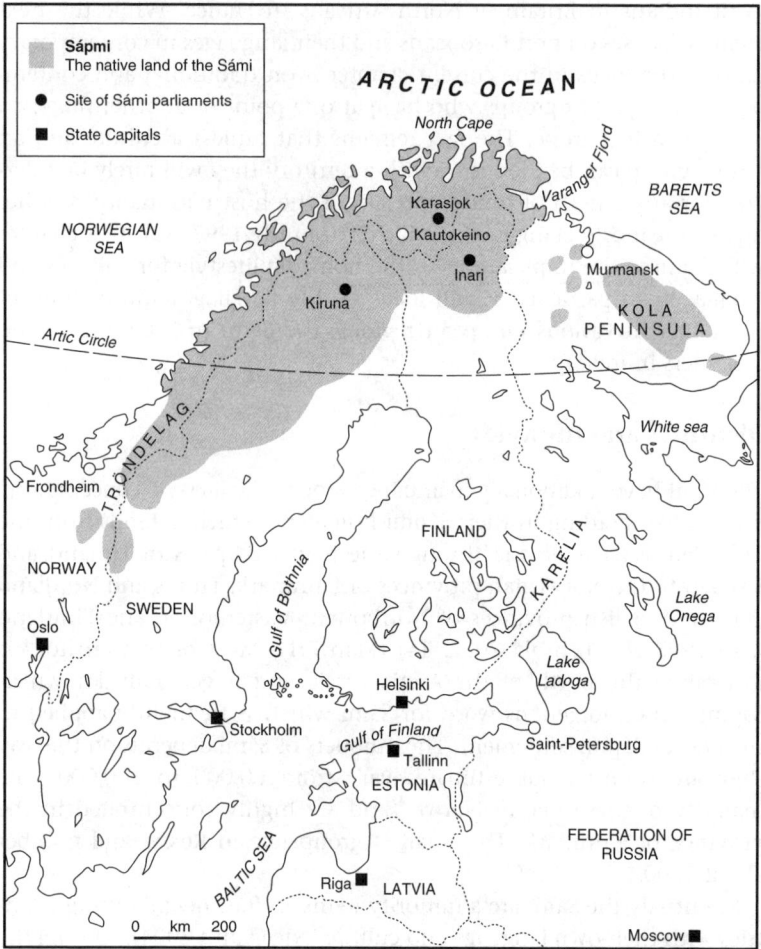

Map 7.1   The area of the Sámi people and Sámi languages. *Source*: Adapted from seurujärvi-kari *et al.* (1997).

between the fifth and the thirteenth centuries AD and they 'have been continuously present in almost all European countries for at least four and a half centuries' (Bakker 2001: 295).

Although they are frequently perceived in mono-cultural terms, that is as Gypsies, they actually constitute a multiplicity of groups including the Sinti in Germany and neighbouring countries, the Manouche in France, Belgium and Holland as well as Finnish Gypsies, and other

Yugoslav groups (Kenrick 1994: 20–1). Moreover, many such groups regard 'their own members as "real" Romanies and all others as "less real" '. This bias is rooted in history and is reflected in the variety of self-ascriptions. 'Thus a Mačvano Vlax would never call himself a Sinto or a Romanchal, and *vice versa*; not would he call a Sinto or Romanchal a *Rom.*' Generally speaking, 'greater commonality is evident among Romani groups saying what they are *not* – a Sinto may not be a Mačvano, but neither is he regarded by other Romani groups as a *gadžo*, a non-Romani' (italics original in Hancock 2003: 273).

Numbers of Gypsies/Roma in different countries are difficult to determine simply because demographic data have not always been available and there are many reasons for this. In the first instance, many Roma have not had the opportunity to register their ethnicity at official level. The 1991 census was the first occasion in the Czech Republic, for example, when Roma had the opportunity to report their ethnic identity. However, many of them did not take the opportunity to identify themselves as Roma. 'In the atmosphere of the 1990s no advantage could be gained from claiming Roma identity' (Nekvapil, and Neustupný 1998: 124–5).

In the case of the Austrian Roma and Sinti, no reliable demographic data became available until 1993 simply because these groups had not been officially categorised as minorities. It is also the case that many Roma did not wish to be viewed as a distinct minority because of the persecution they had suffered in the past. The final acquisition of official acknowledgement as a minority group in 1993 was not necessarily welcomed by many Roma and Sinti who, 'due to the traumatic experience of Nazi persecution, generally do not even want to be visible in public' (De Cillia *et al.* 1998: 27).

The context in which one identifies oneself is always relevant. Billig (1995: 69) uses the term 'pastiche personality' for the multi-faceted nature of our personalities. His social identity theory places great emphasis on the contextual nature of identity where self-categorisations act as switches, which turn social identity on and off in different situations. Even apparently objective categorisations of identity such as colour can be altered by the context or location. An individual with black-and-white ancestry is considered Black in the USA, whereas s/he is regarded as being 'of mixed race' in South Africa (Maalouf 2000: 20–1). In Ghana such a mixed-race person would be classified as White.

When interviewed in Bulgaria, for example, Gypsies tended to ascribe their ethnic belonging to different groups according to the social context. When mixing with 'outsiders', Gypsies identified themselves as Bulgarians but when among other Gypsy subgroups, they viewed themselves as Turks. This situation is not unusual even among the settled population but it leaves many questions unanswered. 'Are those individuals who are officially assigned to the Gypsy minority but self-identify as Turks, speak Turkish and follow the Muslim customs Turks or Gypsies?' (Boneva 1998: 83).

Undoubtedly, the negative perception of the Roma impacted on official statistical returns in many countries. Many Roma in Romania prefer to declare themselves as Romanian or Hungarian because of the negative implications – low social status and historical discrimination – that ensue from the categorisation 'Roma' (Jordan 1998: 197–8). A similar situation applied in Hungary where Roma/Gypsies were not regarded as an ethnic minority group in the socialist era. Instead 'the frequently discussed "Gypsy question" was perceived as a social problem which it was hoped, could be solved by means of welfare and administrative methods' (Szalai 1999: 306). In Macedonia 'there remained an unwillingness of Roma to self-identity due to the continuing stigma attached to being a Rom encapsulated in the pejorative term "cigane" by which they were and are widely known' (Poulton 1998: 60). Although it is difficult to determine the precise numbers of Roma in Europe, the Roma themselves have prepared a number of maps and statistics which is possibly the most reliable indicator to date. These statistics have been summarised in Map 7.2 which illustrates the concentration of Roma in contemporary Europe.

The terminology used to describe many nomadic groups is a sensitive issue. While at one stage, the term 'Lapp' was commonly used for nomads in the Arctic regions, the people themselves use the ethnonym Sámi which has now come to the fore. 'Rom' (singular) or 'Roma' (plural) is the preferred terminology for the Roma/Gypsies. The word 'Rom' means man and human being in Romani-Chib, their own language. Rom and Gypsy are not equivalent terms. 'The word "Gypsy" is a collective name for many different extended groups including Sinti, Rom, Calderash' (McDonagh 2000c). It is also the case that in recent years the term 'Gypsy' has lost favour and is increasingly seen as 'a pejorative term that reflects worldviews and oppression practices of the dominant population'. In contrast, the term 'Roma' 'is meant to reflect the rich heritage and cultural dignity and distinctiveness of an oppressed but also resisting people, as well as their common history and identity of interests' (Blasco 2002: 174).

In Ireland, those who practice the nomadic lifestyle are officially known as Travellers and a recent campaign has focused on the slogan

Map 7.2 Roma population in Europe. *Source*: Adapted from RomNews Society (2003).

'Citizen Traveller' (Murphy *et al.* 2000). This concept of 'Traveller' is hardly a modern invention. Instead it constitutes a literal translation of the Scottish Gaelic term *luchd siubhail*, which was freely used in Perthshire, Scotland, up to the eighteenth and nineteenth centuries (Douglas 2002: 139). Although generally Travellers do not wish to identify themselves as Gypsies, this did not apply in Scotland, where Travellers actually opted for that term since that category was officially protected by the Race Relations Act. Subsequently the term 'Travellers' was included with Gypsies for legal protection, although one Traveller suggested that this protection had not done them any favours. In fact, 'it did Travellers a lot of harm in Scotland, because people started calling us *Gypsies* or *Gypsy Travellers'* (italics original in Stewart 2002: 188).

While the term 'Traveller' generally seems acceptable, Travellers themselves make the point that the expression is insufficient as it seems to focus on the lifestyle rather than on the people. 'We're Travelling *people'* (italics original in An Anonymous Traveller 2002: 170). Travellers themselves have identified two subgroups: Cant and Gammon within the Irish Travelling community. 'If you look at the Cant group, they're darker, whereas the Gammon group is paler, with freckles, not really dark black hair, and not really dark skin – there's very much a difference there, as well' (An Anonymous Traveller 2002: 171). This internal diversity among Travelling groups in Ireland is rarely recognised. Although the 'Travelling community' in Ireland comprises several different groups from 'traditional families to new recruits to long-established speakers of Romani, there is a general tendency to use the term Traveller to represent all' (Ní Shúinéar 2004).

Whether or not Travellers constitute a distinct minority remains a matter for much debate in Ireland. Unlike other ethnic minorities, Travellers are indigenous to Ireland and are commonly regarded as being deviants in society rather than constituting a distinct ethnicity. Perhaps the fact that they have the same skin colour as the rest of the general population is a contributory factor to this limited perspective – although it should be noted that the 'yellow Tinker' is a frequent motif in Traveller stereotyping (McVeigh 1998). Despite their separate history and cultural traditions, Travellers are under constant pressure to assimilate. O'Connell (1994: 11–15) has classified the settled community's perceptions of them into five distinct models demonstrating that settled people often regard the failure of nomads to conform as either a problem requiring correction or a deficiency arising out of their perpetual poverty.

It is not the intention here to explore in depth the question of whether Travellers constitute a distinct ethnicity or not but certain factors should be taken into account. Despite the fact that the settled community may deny this minority a separate cultural identity, there is no doubt that it regards them as different. Travellers also perceive themselves as constituting a definite group, and the distinction between insiders and outsiders in this community is quite clear. Very definite boundaries separate Travellers from the settled community and it is not a simple matter to move from one community to the other.

The dispute on the origin of the Travelling community usually reflects a mono-cultural perspective. Colonial origins are often ascribed to Travellers, who are portrayed by the settled community as a people dispossessed since the time of the Great Famine in nineteenth-century Ireland. In other words, they were not originally a distinct ethnic group, and their cultural traditions have emerged from poverty and inferiority and are simply a consequence of British oppression. This version of history is rejected by many civil rights activists and Travellers who, sharing their own common myth of origin, trace the distinctiveness of their community back to pre-colonial Gaelic Ireland (McLoughlin 1994, McDonagh 2000c, Ní Shúinéar 1994).

Ní Shúinéar (2004: 17) argues strongly against what she calls the 'drop-out' historical narrative. Her objection is not related to the fact that such a theory might somehow render Traveller culture worthless or even that it is unpalatable. Instead it is grounded in falsehood and is 'blatantly motivated by a political agenda: to justify their re-assimilation into mainstream society'.

Moreover, this 'tampering' with Irish Traveller history should be set in the context of the denial of a valid historical narrative to Romani in an international context. Until now at least, Romani history has not formed part of any educational system worldwide. 'Western culture perceives "gypsies" to be a people without a history, whose church was made of cheese, and who steal (or wander) because they stole (or made) Christ's nails' (Hancock 2003: 274).

The significance of language

Although they differ on its degree of relevance, experts agree that language can play a critical role in defining nomadic groups. In Finland, Norway and Sweden, a Sámi is defined as an individual of Sámi origin who deems himself or herself to be Sámi and who either has spoken Sámi as his or her first language or has at least one parent or grandparent who speaks Sámi as his or her first language. 'What is important is ancestry, relationship to the Sámi language and through that to Sámi culture and a feeling of being Sámi' (Lehtola 2002: 10).

Asp (1995: 75) points to a variety of definitions which focus strongly on language. In the case of Finland, the principle criterion is that of 'belonging to the Lappish language group or speaking Lappish', whereas in Norway, being a Lapp implies that the language of the home is Lappish and in the Soviet Union, 'ethnological and linguistic character-istics' are particularly important.

Legislation at national levels underpins the significance of language for identity. The definition of Sámi was tied to proficiency in the Sámi language with the passing of the Norwegian Sámi Act in 1987. When the Swedish Parliament adopted legislation on the Sámi Parliament (Sámediggi) in 1992, it took a similar approach. The definition of Sámi was also linked to the native language in Finland, when the first census of the Sámi was carried out in 1962 (Seurujärvi-Kari *et al.* 1997: 3).

More than half of the Sámi speak one of the Sámi languages which belong to the Finno-Ugric language family, and the majority of these speak North Sámi. Although each group simply calls its respective language Sámi, linguists have organised the Sámi languages into two categories: Western and Eastern Sámi. The Western group is made up of the North, Lule, Pite, Ume and South Sámi languages while the Eastern group incorporates Anár, Skolt, Akkala, Kildin and Ter Sámi (Lehtola 2002: 11).

There are considerable comprehension difficulties between speakers of these different Sámi languages which cut across international state boundaries. As relationships between Sámi communities have traditionally been stronger with other Sámi to the east, 'communities on a West–East line belong to the same dialect area' (Thuen 1995: 99). Dialect differences between Northern and Southern parts of the Sápmi homeland are greater to such an extent that they are not mutually comprehensible. 'In a very real sense, then, national borders cut across the Sámi settlement area' (Thuen 1995: 99).

Like Sámi, the language of the Roma, Romani-chib or Romanès has developed in many different regions and it is now the most widespread minority language in Europe from a geographic perspective. It is the common language of the Roma, the Sinti, the Kale and other European population groups, and belongs to the Indo-Aryan branch of the Indo-European language family. In fact it is the only New-Indo-Ayran language spoken exclusively outside the Indian subcontinent (Halwachs 2003: 192).

As Romani-chib evolved in different locations, it developed in close contact with local languages and includes more than 60 dialects which are not necessarily mutually comprehensible. In the Balkans, for example, the Romani language developed during the close linguistic contact with Romanian and to a lesser extent with Hungarian and Slavonic. This has subsequently become a distinct dialect cluster within the language, called today 'Vlax' (Price 2000: 379–80).

Due to historical circumstances, contemporary Roma do not necessarily speak Romani as their first language. In many states, they lacked official support for their mother tongue. In Bulgaria, for example, Gypsies were deprived of their cultural organisations in the second half of the 1950s. The language of their newspaper was changed to Bulgarian and their theatre was attached to a Bulgarian cultural centre. Practically all Gypsy organisations were dismantled (Boneva 1998: 87–8). In 1978, a Resolution of the Secretariat of the Central Committee of the Bulgarian Communist Party sought forcible assimilative actions for the Gypsy population and emphasised 'the necessity' of preventing any possibility of opening Gypsy schools (Boneva 1998: 88).

Despite the lack of state support, many Roma throughout Europe are bi- or tri-lingual. In the case of Bulgaria, many of them seem to have little difficulty in switching to any of the three main languages spoken in Bulgaria: Bulgarian, Turkish and Gypsy. Yet the language is very important for self-definition in many instances. In the case of Hungary, for example, only the native speakers of Romani use the category 'Rom' to identify their own ethnic group and language. Native Hungarian-speaking Gypsies do not identify themselves by this name (Szalai 1999: 298).

In the case of Ireland, the Traveller language is hardly a criterion of membership but it does play an important role. 'Speaking Traveller language identifies you as a Traveller' (An Anonymous Traveller 2002: 175). 'It's not only the pride of speaking your own language. Again, it's going back to identifying – not identifying to the settler people out there, it's identifying to yourself, within oneself, of who *you* are. Of who you are yourself' (italics original in An Anonymous Traveller 2002: 176). Another suggests that he 'will speak Cant for nothing other than the sheer pride of being able to speak my own language. That's why I speak it, not to frighten or scare or impress anybody. I'm proud that I can speak another language, and that it's my language' (Power 2002: 164).

The language spoken by the 25,000 Travellers in Ireland is exclusive to the Travelling community. While academics usually call it Shelta, Travellers themselves use the terms 'Gammon' or 'Cant' which may be derived from the Irish Gaelic *caint* meaning speech. The language reflects the bilingual surroundings in which it developed and the vocabulary consists of Irish words and terms which have been changed or adapted. This vocabulary is set in a simplified English grammatical structure (Binchy 1994: 134).

Children generally acquire the language as a joint first language, along with English and are warned not to share it with outsiders. In common with Romani, Cant is ascribed a secret status which should not be shared with non-Travelling peoples and has been called the 'secret language' of Travellers (Cleeve 1983). There are several reasons for this perception. In the first instance, members of the settled community who were aware of the language assumed that its primary object was to exclude outsiders. 'It was thought at that time that the only purpose of the language was a secret code to exclude outsiders, as other occupational groups, for example, doctors and lawyers have medical, legal or other jargons which exclude lay people' (Binchy 2002: 11).

Although this perception reduces Cant to a language used simply in a single functional context and ignores other ranges of communication, it does contain an element of truth. 'That it's a secret language, only spoken in defence or spoken in the presence of country people when we don't want ye to know what we're saying – yes, that is true, our language, Cant, has been used in that way' (McDonagh 2002: 156). The element of secrecy is also considered important in the presence of the police, but some Travellers have reported the acquisition of Cant by police in areas where there are halting sites such as Ballyfermot, Rathfarnham and Clondalkin in Dublin. In consequence 'Travellers who have been arrested can't talk now because the Guards are aware of the situation, and they use it against you' (in McDonagh 2002: 159).

Knowledge of Romani or Cant is difficult to acquire outside the community partly because they have not developed standardised literary forms. Instead the language has been transmitted orally from generation to generation through the art of storytelling. The lack of a codified standard reflects the socio-political situation of Travellers and Roma who have survived in groups in different regions throughout Europe. They have neither desired nor sought to engage in empire building and have failed to build political-economic structures which would secure their share of political power (Halwachs 2003: 196).

The lack of a codified standard hinders the development of a presence for the language in print and in national systems of education. Moreover, Roma themselves avoid schools which they view as a threat to their way of life. One Rom has suggested that formal education 'requires that Roma enter the non-Romani world, which is seen as polluting and counter-cultural'. Not only are the toilet facilities unclean because they are shared with non-Roma but 'equally unacceptable would be the seating of boys and girls in the classrooms, and the topics addressed in the curricula'. Overall schools are seen as environments that 'homogenize and de-ethicize the child' (Hancock 1999).

The status of the Romani language in national systems of education differs from country to country, but there are schools where Romani is used and Romani educational material has been published for several Romani dialects in different European countries. Nevertheless the use of Romani in primary education is marginal and is even worse at second level. At university level, the language has been studied and taught in universities in Austria, Denmark, France, Germany, Italy and the UK.

Since the collapse of communism in 1989 in Eastern Europe, there has been a proliferation of publications there in the Romani language. This includes magazines such as *Patrin* (Slovakia), *Informaciaqo Lil* and *Rron po Drom* (Poland) and *Džaniben* (the Czech Republic). Poets such as Leksa Manus, Rajko Djurič and Sejdo Jašarov have been publishing works in Romani. The Romani Union has instituted a successful Romani language summer school, which is attended each year by a growing number of individuals, Roma and non-Roma, who wish to learn the language, and the Soros–Roma Foundation (Switzerland) is developing a programme to teach Romani to Roma who do not speak it (Price 2000: 381).

The Sámi languages have fared better than Romani-Chib or Cant in terms of literacy, and six of the Sámi languages have developed a literary form although many of these are quite recent. It was not until 1978, for example, that the common Nordic spelling of North Sámi, the largest of the Sámi languages was adopted. Sámis encounter an additional issue in that the most Easterly languages use the Cyrillic alphabet (Seurujärvi-Kari *et al.* 1997: 25). Moreover, the Sámi languages were remarkably absent from the system of education until recent decades. It was not until the 1990s that the Scandinavian states introduced new legislation concerning the use of Sámi in education and the position of the Sámi languages in schools stabilised. Contemporary Sámi can receive their education from the level of pre-school all the way to university in the Sámi language (Seurujärvi-Kari *et al.* 1997: 32).

Several important landmark achievements should be noted. A policy on long-term language day care centres were introduced in Finland in 1997 which were designed to enable Anár and Skolt Sámi children to acquire their own mother tongue before entering school. Such institutions were originally designed for the Maori, the aboriginal people of New Zealand, where skilled members of the community teach the language and culture to children under school age. A Sámi curriculum was introduced in Norway at this time. The school program included Sámi culture as well as language and is perceived as an important element in school support for the development of a Sámi identity (Lehtola 2002: 90).

Improvements in the education system reflect progress in legislation issues in recent decades. The first Sámi language law was passed in Norway in 1990 and Norway became officially bilingual in six of its most Northern municipalities. Sámi and Norwegian had equal status in these regions and municipal officials were required to have knowledge of the Sámi language. The improved status at official level in turn motivated parents to send their children to Sámi language day care centres and schools.

Two years later new Sámi Language Acts came into effect in Finland and Norway. The Acts stipulated that the Sámi language could be used as the administrative language in six municipalities in Norway and in four municipalities in Finland. In practical terms, this ensured that certain public notices and other documents were issued in Sámi as well as in the majority language (Seurujärvi-Kari *et al.* 1997: 25–6). In 2004 a new Act strengthening the provisions for Sámi was introduced in Finland. The purpose of the Act was to ensure the constitutional right of the Sámi to maintain and develop their own language and culture.

Romani has not yet acquired a similar status and although it is geographically the most widespread minority language in the EU, it is not an official language anywhere in Europe. Nevertheless a range of prestigious institutions at international level has expressed support for recognition of the Romani language. These include the United Nations, the European Parliament, and the CoE through its Standing Conference of Local and Regional Authorities of Europe. Since 1993, the Hungarian Act on the Rights of National and Ethnic Minorities recognises Gypsies/Roma as one of the 13 minorities in Hungary, and provides equal rights in terms of language use (Szalai 1999: 299). More recently several countries such as Austria, Finland, Germany, the Netherlands and Sweden have listed Romani as a minority language within their territorial boundaries which automatically leads to some promotion of the language and some form of financial commitment (Halwachs 2003: 205).

Cant has fared less well than either Sámi or Romani and has no official status in either Ireland or the UK. In part this is a natural consequence of the reluctance to recognise Travellers as a distinct cultural or historical group (Binchy 2002: 15). A further reason for the slow progress or lack of progress in terms of language status and legislation for all these languages is simply the mobility of the populations that speak them, which hindered the development of local powerful structures which could lobby in support of their culture and language.

Land, region and space

Although the populations that speak these languages either have been or are nomadic, the position of Sámi is quite different to others cited in this chapter in that broadly speaking Sámi is associated with specific regions in the Sápmi homeland in the Arctic Circle. However, this has generated few privileges as international state borders have divided the traditional Sápmi homeland and ensured that the Sámi are effectively a minority in four countries. Moreover, when Finland and Sweden joined the EU on 1 January 1995, a new type of 'border' was introduced into Sápmi – the border between the EU and Norway and between the EU and Russia.

The attitudes of Sámi to borders are summed up in a provocative book entitled *Terverisiä Lapista* (*Greetings from Lapland* 1971) (Valkeapää 1983: 83). The author's mother was a Norwegian Sámi from Gouvdageaidnu (Kautokeino) in the far North of Scandinavia while his father's family were based much further South in Sweden, near the Arctic Circle. Early in life, the author was subjected to the harsh realities of the nomadic lifestyle during the evacuation to the mountain regions on the Swedish side of the border. At the time of writing, the family lived in Finland (when they were not travelling around).

The author notes that when he started school he learned that he had no mother tongue. When at home, he discovered that he did not have a fatherland either. Valkeapää suggests that if asked to define his fatherland, his response 'would to a large extent follow lines on the landscape and the gaps which are to be found between different kinds of livelihood'. For him the 'mechanically drawn-up boundaries which are marked on the map are unnatural dividing lines'.

In the past, those with nomadic lifestyles were often forgotten or ignored in international covenants or charters. Communities are generally perceived to have a particular place; a 'shared location' and those who could not be identified with a particular place were hardly regarded as a community. But it would be a mistake to assume that nomadic peoples such as Travellers lack a sense of community. Instead it seems that their concept of community applies at a larger level. 'All Travellers owe allegiance to the greater "community" of Travellers' (Binchy 1994: 149–50). Travellers themselves make the point that the concept of Traveller is essentially one of community. 'To be a Traveller is to be part of a community.' When settled people focus on the concept 'Traveller', they immediately think of mobility, but that is not the essence of a Traveller.

Although being mobile is part of being a Traveller, it is not what a Traveller is. Being a Traveller means being part of a community that has a shared history, shared culture and an understanding of what it is like to be a Traveller. It's having a family with a support mechanism there. (McDonagh 2000a 28–9)

Nomadism possibly generates a sense of community that is larger on a physical scale than the immediate locality of a settled community. It 'entails a way of looking at the world, a different way of seeing things, a different attitude to accommodation, to work and to life in general' (McDonagh 2000b: 34). Travellers have a concept of mapping that is entirely different from conventional maps. They employ 'the alternative spatial languages or "tracings" of kinlines, tradelines and memory lines' and 'negotiate a separate identity and sense of place' from the settled community.

Burke (2002: 90) suggests that a Traveller's definition of the term 'country' is 'radically different from that which is understood by sedentary society'. Essentially country is understood as 'a region characterised by family or cultural unities, not necessarily coinciding with country lines and not necessarily rural'. Travellers engage with alternative mapping and would, for example, mark houses with generous owners for other Travellers by leaving rags or sticks in a particular manner called *patrin*. 'Such non-textual modes of representation challenge sedentarist assumptions of what constitutes script' (Burke 2002: 90).

The Sámi also have a special relationship with the land and nature which provided the resources for both their material and their spiritual culture. Sámi adapted their lifestyle to the yearly cycle of nature and the local natural environment and this relationship is a two-way process. 'Throughout centuries of adapting to varying natural conditions the Sámi left their "cultural mark" on the physical environment' (Lehtola 2002: 88). The relationship with the land is reflected in the Sámi language which has a particularly rich vocabulary in relation to nature and reindeer. 'Dissimilar landscapes and ways of living create different concepts.' In the case of reindeer husbandry, for example, one 'will find a rich assortment of words and expressions which have arisen from the countryside, equipment and processes related to the work involved'. For this reason, many tourists experience great difficulty in understanding the variety of Sámi place names. 'The world is full of language barriers which a large number of people never manage to surmount' (Valkeapää 1983: 78).

For many of the nomadic peoples such as the Sámi, individual ownership of the land was not an issue and they never formed institutional structures. From medieval times, the Sámi organised themselves into *siidas* or villages, each of which has its own territory. Members of different *siidas* enjoyed a complex system of rights which included grazing rights for their reindeer, fishing rights on certain sections of the river and hunting rights. These land rights were owned by the extended family or families rather than the individual. 'There were no "Private" signs or other barriers' (Drysdale 2001: 100).

It was ultimately the lack of formal ownership on the part of the Sámi that facilitated land claims by others as Sámi land rights were gradually ignored, lost or forgotten. In the early twentieth century, the Sámi in Norway were regarded as a 'landless' people who were obliged to pay taxes but no longer had any rights – especially in relation to land ownership. 'One country even adopted a law, according to which land could be owned only by citizens who both knew and used the Norwegian language' (Seurujärvi-Kari *et al.* 1997: 30).

However, this situation is being re-addressed and the special position of the Sámi is reflected in their recognition as an indigenous people acknowledging their existence in the Arctic Circle before the present international state boundaries were drawn. The concept of an indigenous people has gradually been marked in various documents to safeguard human rights as well as into national legislation in the Scandinavian states. The Norwegian government formally recognised the Sámi as an indigenous people in 1990 (Seurujärvi-Kari *et al.* 1997: 2).

Sámi themselves emphasise the concept of indigeneity in relation to language policy. They insist on the responsibility of national governments for Sámi language rights as those of an aboriginal people rather than a language minority. 'For that reason the governments have a greater responsibility for Sámi language rights than they have for such minorities whose language preservation is based on the situation in their mother country' (Lehtola 2002: 85).

Sámi are also developing links with one another in different countries (Nic Craith 2004). At the first Sámi Conference in Karasjok in 1956, the Nordic Sámi began to organise themselves when it was decided to establish a joint Nordic Sámi Council in order to safeguard the interests of the Sámi people. At its 15th conference in Helsinki in 1992, membership of the Council was officially extended to the representative organisation of the Kola Peninsula Sámi, and the name of the Nordic Sámi Council was shortened to Sámiraddi. The rules of the Sámi Council were also revised at the conference. The Council now has fifteen members: five from Norway, four from Sweden, four from Finland and two from Russia. The Nordic Sámi Council (Sámi Ráddi) works closely with each of the Sámi Parliaments on projects such as the Sámi language board (Directorate-General for Research 2002: 4).

Co-operation on an official cross-border level has been increasingly consolidated among the Sámi. On 6 February 1997, the Sámi Parliaments of Finland, Norway and Sweden entered an agreement on co-operation in Trondheim (Norway) to coincide with the celebration of the Sámi national holiday and the 80th anniversary of the first Sámi Nordic meeting which was also held in Trondheim. The Sámi Parliamentary Council was formally established on 2 March 2000 which involved the Sámi Parliaments of Norway and Finland as members and the Sámi of Russia who had observer status. The president of the Norwegian Sámi Parliament, Sven-Roald Nystö, was elected as the first president. The Swedish Sámi Parliament joined 2 years later after a decision at the plenary meeting in Kiruna.

Several symbols of the unity of the Sámi have emerged. The Sámi flag was adopted in 1986 by the 13th Sámi Conference at Åre, Sweden. The emblems on the flag derive from the symbols found on a Sámi shaman's drum and emphasise the Sámi link with nature. A blue and red circle represents both the moon and the sun. The other colours on the flag are taken from the Sámi national costumes. The choice of the sun as a national symbol comes from an epic poem written down by the Southern Sámi, Anders Fjellner (1795–1876). This poem presents the notion that the Sámi are the sons and daughters of the sun. The national anthem, 'Sámi Soga Lávila' ('The Song of the Sámi People') was written by Isak Saba (1875–1921), a teacher from Finnmark, Norway, who became the first Sámi to be elected to the Norwegian Parliament in 1906.

The anthem reflects the close relationship between the Sámi and the landscape. It suggests that the mystery of the Sápmi homeland is its 'never-ending mountain crests' as well as its everlasting lakes and moorland heights. It lauds its gushing rivers and sighing forests in which the Sámi forefathers had achieved victory over adversity. Significantly it also celebrates the importance of the indigenous language suggesting that as long as their 'golden language' and the words of their forebears are cherished, repressors will not triumph (Seurujärvi-Kari *et al.* 1997: 17).

Since 1993, the Sámi have celebrated their National Day on the 6 of February. This date, which was decided upon at the 15th Sámi conference in Helsinki in 1992, marks the first meeting by Northern and Southern Sámi from Norway and Sweden in Trondheim on 6 February 1917. On that historic day, Sámi united on a cross-border basis for the first time, in order to fight for common causes (Seurujärvi-Kari *et al.* 1997: 17).

Ultimately the goal of Sámi self-determination is simply to preserve and promote Sámi language and culture, rather than founding a new state or changing state borders. 'We are one people, despite living in different countries. We are like the Kurds spread across the Middle East, if more peaceful. But there is no desire to set up an independent Sámi state. We are also Finns, Swedes, Norwegians and Russians' (Drysdale 2001: 95).

Modern technology has further developed a sense of community and the emergence of a Sámi concept of a cross-border community was facilitated through several innovations, especially the radio which is a natural communicator across borders and overcomes distances effortlessly. The concept of a common Sámi culture and a unified community was evident in early Sámi radio productions when development of co-operation across the national borders began in the 1960s. The most concrete result was the pan-Nordic news which began broadcasting from Romsa (Tromsa) in 1964. Current affairs programmes were broadcast from Kiruna from 1973 to 1986 (Lehtola 2002: 92–3). Nowadays, Sámi radio stations constitute independent regional units which operate within the national broadcasting companies in all three Scandinavian countries. These units are located in Inari (Finland), Karasjoj (Norway) and Kinrua (Sweden). The Sámi radio stations broadcast some 35–40 hours weekly. 'Sámi radio programmes jointly produced and broadcast by the three Sámi radio stations can be heard for about four and a half hours a day' (Seurujärvi-Kari *et al.* 1997: 35). Cross-border co-operation among the Sámi has hardly been confined to technology and has practical benefits in other spheres. Sámi in Finland, for example, can travel to Norway for medical care without incurring extra expense as their medical bills revert to the Finnish authorities.

Travellers have also benefited from modern technology and suggest that the introduction of the mobile phone in particular has benefited their language which operates effectively as a boundary mechanism to exclude individuals who may use radio scanners to listen in to conversations on mobile phones. Such individuals will hardly benefit from listening to a conversation they cannot understand. The use of Cant is regarded as a very good strategy on mobile phones. 'When you're having conversations, it is to protect their business. It's not being negative, it is to protect the business of what they're talking about and their privacy' (Power 2002: 163).

With modern technology such as mobile phones or the Internet, the link between culture and a specific place may become less important, but the concept of place is still very significant in international charters such as the ECRML. The introduction to the Charter's explanatory notes focuses immediately on the fact that 'many European countries have on their territory regionally based autochthonous groups speaking a language other than that of the majority of the population'. This is explained as a 'consequence of historical processes whereby the formation of states has not taken place on purely language-related lines'. As a result small language communities have been surrounded by larger ones.

Languages covered by the Charter are primarily those which can be located in a distinct territory or region. Non-territorial languages are defined as those 'used by nationals of the State which differ from the language or languages used by the rest of the State's population, but which, although traditionally used within the territory of the State, cannot be identified with a particular area thereof'. The explanatory notes indicate that the significance of territory in this Charter is for practical reasons since most of the measures advocated in the Charter require the definition of a territorial base or geographical field which is not coterminous with the state as a whole.

The ECRML does attempt to define the concept of territory of a regional or minority language as that where a language 'is spoken to a significant extent, even if only by a minority, and which corresponds to its historical base' although it also suggests that each state could define the concept of 'regional or minority language territory' in a more precise form 'in the spirit of the charter' (CoE 1992b).

Although the Charter excludes 'non-territorial languages' from the category of regional and minority languages due to their lack of a territorial base, it does advocate that languages traditionally used on state territories by citizens of a state could be included on a limited basis within the terms of reference of the Charter and it specifically identifies Romani as such an example. While it would be complicated to apply the provisions of Part III to non-territorial languages like Romani or Cant, there should be far less difficulty in applying the principles of respect and dignity as contained in Part II.

A number of states have included Romani within the terms of reference of the Charter. In 1998, the Netherlands undertook to apply the principles enshrined in Part II of the Charter to the Romani languages. The same year, Germany designated the Romani language of the German Sinti and Roma for inclusion within its terms of reference. The German Government undertook to apply the principles enshrined in Part II of the Romani Language in the Federal Republic of Germany, but in keeping with its federal structure it made several provisions from Part III for the Romani language in individual Länder as well. It identified the application of several sections of Part III of the Charter to the Romani language in the Federal Republic and additionally in the Länder of Baden-Wüttemberg, Berlin, the Free and Hanseatic City of Hamburg,

Hesse, North-Rhine/Westphalia, Lower Saxony, Rhineland-Palatinate and Schleswig-Holstein.

In 2000, Slovenia which was not then a member of the EU suggested that it would include Romani language within the terms of reference of the Charter. The following year, another accession member, Slovakia, confirmed that it would also apply the Charter in accordance with its constitution, ensuring equality for all its citizens to promote the European language heritage without disadvantage to its own official language to several minority languages including Rom. In the instrument of ratification deposited on June 2001, Austria identified the Romani language of the Austrian Roma minority as one of those to which the Charter should apply in Burgenland. Moreover, it did not confine such recognition to Part II of the Charter and also included sections from Articles 8, 11, 12 and 14 which relate to issues in education, the media, cultural activities and facilities and economic and social life.

As might be expected, two of the Nordic countries, Finland and Sweden, included the languages of the Sámi as well as of the Roma within the terms of reference of the Charter. As early as 1994, Finland declared its intentions to apply principles of the Charter to both Roma and Sámi languages. While it applied several provisions from Part III to the latter, it confined its obligations to Roma to principles of respect, tolerance and understanding. It was 6 years later before Sweden deposited its declaration of ratification. As was the case with Finland it opted for principles of respect and tolerance for Romani-Chib, one of its non-territorial minority languages, but undertook a range of obligations to other languages including Sámi. Norway did undertake to apply several articles from Part III of the Charter to Sámi, but it did not make any provision for speakers of Romani-Chib within its territories.

Conclusion

For practical reasons it is easier to write covenants and charters for languages in a particular region, and governments can be more easily persuaded to agree to documents that limit their responsibilities to particular locations. However, the significance of territory for culture is becoming less important. 'As people move with their meanings, and as meanings find ways of travelling even when people stay put, territories cannot really contain cultures' (Hannerz 1996: 8).

The accessibility of modern technology has had significant consequences for the linking of culture or language to a particular place. With electronic mail, one can communicate effectively and immediately with individuals and groups across the globe. Television permits individuals to witness political and cultural events on the other side of the world without leaving home. Shopping can be conducted from privacy of one's bedroom. All of these inventions impact on our sense of imagined community which is being enlarged on a daily basis. In this sense, perhaps the settled population is developing a sense of community which is more akin to that of nomadic peoples.

However, traditional nomadic communities are hardly a matter of major anxiety for settled populations in contemporary Europe. Instead it appears that the increasing presence of non-Europeans is generating concern. Although some recognition on a limited basis is offered to non-Europeans who settle in Europe, it appears that their languages do not yet receive any substantial form of protection – an issue which will be examined in the next chapter.

8
The Outsiders: Non-European Languages

Although speakers of minority languages in Europe are hardly content with the political recognition they receive at either national or European levels, their position is far superior to that of speakers of immigrant, non-European languages which have, for the most part, been ignored in European charters or conventions. While there have always been speakers of non-European, migrant languages in Europe, these have only emerged as community languages in recent decades, particularly in countries such as France, Germany or Great Britain where languages such as Arabic, Turkish and Cantonese are widely spoken by millions of individuals. Although these languages are highly significant for a sense of identity among non-European immigrant groups and have recently acquired some limited recognition within various state systems of education, they are often perceived negatively by speakers of dominant languages and policy makers who view their presence 'as obstacles to integration' (Extra and Gorter 2001: 3).

Immigrants in Europe

There is a long history of non-ethnic Europeans on the continent. Africans began settling in Europe after they had served in the Roman legions. Contemporary culture in Southern Spain reflects its long association with Moorish colonisers (cf. Chapter 1). Labour shortages following the two World Wars in the twentieth century served as the catalyst for invitations to millions of non-Europeans to come and take up employment in Europe. 'After decades of discrimination and abuse they have been given little reward for their achievement, confined in almost every country to the lowest paid jobs and the most miserable of housing' (Mundy 1997: 55).

Migration to Europe in the 1960s and early 1970s was motivated primarily by economic factors. Mediterranean and non-European workers were invited into various regions on a contract basis. Initially they were expected to stay for a limited period of time. As their period of residence was extended, the pattern of economic migration was followed by a further wave of social migration when their families joined them. With time, a second generation was born to these immigrants, but the status of these families was largely unrecognised and the parents themselves were often ambivalent about whether to stay or to return to their country of origin (Extra and Gorter 2001: 12).

The pattern of immigration was not consistent throughout the continent. Some countries have a relatively long history of immigration – particularly those with a colonial past such as Great Britain, France or the Netherlands. Turkish and former Yugoslavian residents have tended to concentrate in Germany and the concept of *Gastarbeiter* (Guest worker) was particularly associated with West Germany which clearly perceived these labour immigrants as temporary residents. Although there was a possibility that such workers could overstay their welcome, there was a sense that these labour migrants would at some stage return to their country of origin and be replaced by other volunteers (Extra and Gorter 2001: 38).

For various reasons it is impossible to obtain reliable demographic data on immigrant groups in EU countries. In some instances no such data has ever been collected or if it has, it has not been updated. In other regions the data simply reflects the numbers of immigrants with legal resident status but does not extend to those who are present on an illegal or 'pre-legal' basis. It is also the case that such data is increasingly difficult to obtain for second-generation immigrants who will not be visible when criteria such as 'country of birth' or 'nationality' are applied. More significantly, most residents from former colonies have obtained the nationality of their country of immigration (Extra and Gorter 2001: 13).

Despite their period of residency in Europe, these immigrant groups are usually regarded as foreigners (*étrangers, ausländer*) who are in need of integration. The term 'non-national residents' is frequently applied in this context and various categories such as 'non-indigenous', 'non-European', 'non-territorial' or even 'non-regional' are applied to their languages. This terminology reflects the general assumption that as these people have no roots in Europe, they can hardly become 'rooted' in the continent. While they live, work and raise their families in

Europe, it is anticipated that they will maintain their loyalty solely to their country of origin.

Such assumptions either refuse to recognise the existence of multiple or transnational identities or regard them as an obstacle to national and/or European integration. Yet composite loyalties are a feature of European as well as non-European immigrants in Europe. It applies to traditional inhabitants and newcomers alike although the quality of this transnationalism may differ. Research among Turkish and Moroccan communities in Brussels concluded that while immigrants shared a social-contract type of citizenship with Belgians, they also adhered to a more communal type of long-distance citizenship in their countries of origin. A key feature of the latter centred on a close linkage of national and religious attachments (Phales and Swyngedouw 2002).

This long-distance nationalism has been further consolidated by the globalisation of communication in recent decades. Transnational travel and trade have facilitated ease of return visits to countries of origin. Telecommunications, satellite television and the Internet have assisted communication in the 'mother tongue'. Internet services have also enabled the establishment of 'web communities' and served as the catalyst for electronic discussions and the distribution of publications in the language of the home country. Internet radio services deliver local media to global audiences. There are also economic advantages to be gained by the maintenance and use of the ancestral language as they offer access to markets not just in the countries of origin or the 'ancestral home' but throughout their transnational linguistic community (Cheesman 2001: 155).

This linkage with country of origin is frequently perceived as problematic. The rise of nation states in the eighteenth and nineteenth centuries served as the catalyst for a fixation on territorial boundaries. The emergence of nation states involved the collective construction of national territory as well as of its imagined communities. The 'politics of purity' demanded the exclusion of the foreigner. 'One people, one culture, one language, one book, one goal; what does not fall under this all-encompassing "one" is ambivalent, polluting and dangerous' (Kristeva 1982: 76).

Drawing distinctions between 'self' and 'others', between 'citizens' and 'aliens' has been a central component of the process of national self-determination. Although internal migration and freedom of movement are key guarantees for contemporary EU citizens, immigration from Central and Eastern Europe as well as from countries such as Turkey, which are aiming to join the EU is perceived as strongly problematic. The boundaries separating members of the EU from their non-European counterparts have strengthened as the EU has consolidated.

Since the attack on the World Trade Centre in the USA on September 11th 2001, the presence of Islam – especially of the fundamentalist variety in Europe – has generated high levels of anxiety. Such apprehensions are not necessarily confined to the association of Islam with terrorist attacks. There is also the perceived unacceptability of Sharria Law. At the time of writing, Turkey has refused to change the law that adultery is a criminal offence. More importantly, many Westerners feel that Muslims have very different and possibly incompatible ideas on the state, society and the role of religion.

One of the major issues concerning immigrants for modern states is the question of citizenship and whether this should be linked to territory. Some states such as Germany have a tradition of refusing citizenship to immigrants unless they satisfy the principle of *jus sanguinis* (i.e. blood-line or descent). However, as noted previously (cf. Chapter 2), a change in the citizenship law on 1 January 2000 has meant that children who are born in Germany of immigrant families automatically receive German citizenship and parents with non-German passports may apply for German citizenship for any of their children under the age of seven. These new Germans may hold dual citizenship until the age of 23 when they are obliged to select their preferred citizenship.

This change in legislation should ensure that the number of bilingual or multilingual German citizens will increase enormously (Gogolin and Reich 2001: 194). However, it offers no protection to their languages. Although it is now accepted that non-European immigrants may settle in Europe in the long term, this has not yet translated into recognition that the languages of such immigrants will be spoken in Europe on a more permanent basis and represent what is effectively the 'new' languages of Europe.

These 'new' languages include some which are very large on a demographic scale, such as Arabic, Chinese, Hindi/Urdu, Malay, Russian, as well as national languages of states with varying positions in the world affairs, such as Bengali, Japanese, Korean and Somali. It also encompasses 'low-status' languages such as Kurdish which are not official in any state and diaspora languages of states in Asia and Africa which are hardly in a position to defend their language rights effectively (Cheesman 2001: 151).

All of this creates tensions in relation to the politics of language in Europe. While limited, but increasing recognition is given to marginalised 'indigenous' languages, little attention is given to non-European languages. Proponents of such a strategy usually argue that non-European languages have a motherland outside the Continent which can offer protection from a distance. Moreover such languages are hardly at risk of extinction on a global scale. Examples here would include Turkish which is Germany's second language and the Sylheti dialect of Bengali which is now Wales' third language (Cheesman 2001: 151–2). Such questions place issues of cultural survival at a global level at odds with the issue of local or national cultural recognition; a point which will be examined in the final chapter. In the meantime case studies of immigrant languages in Western Europe will be considered.

Non-European languages in Western Europe

Non-European languages have emerged strongly as community languages in Western Europe in recent decades. Some are a consequence of the link between former colonies and empires such as Arabic languages in France, Indian languages in the United Kingdom (Reynolds 2001), Congolese languages in Belgium and Surinamese languages in the Netherlands (Extra and Yagmur 2002: 30). A survey of the top 10 languages spoken in London at the turn of the millennium revealed significant numbers of speakers of Panjabi, Gujarati, Hindi/ Urdu, Bengali and Sylheti in the City. Turkish, Arabic, English Creoles, Cantonese and Yoruba also feature in the list of most widely spoken languages (Storkey 2000: 65). Afro-Asian 'community languages' are spoken by a rapidly growing number of people in Western Europe and this phenomenon has been paralleled by a process of ghettoisation (Schröder 1993: 13). A more detailed analysis of various case studies in Germany, France and Northern Ireland suggests considerable difficulties for speakers of non-European languages, not least of which relates to the lack of information on the precise proportions speaking non-European languages.

There are about 10 million individuals of non-German origin living in Germany and many of these are bilingual or multilingual in that they speak one or more languages in addition to German on an everyday basis. A considerable number of non-European languages are spoken in Germany, many of which have a group size of 100,000 or more. Examples here would include Arabic, Kurdish, Turkish and Viet- namese (Gogolin and Reich 2001: 197). Turkish is perhaps the largest of these and there are over two million Turkish passport-holders of diverse ethnicity living in Germany (Cheesman 2001: 165).

A similar situation applies in the case of France, where there are no official language figures as there is no census on mother tongues in that country and other sources must be used to arrive at some form of estimate. There are considerable numbers of non-European languages spoken in France including Berber which refers to a group of dialects or languages spoken by large populations in North Africa, especially in Algeria and Morocco. (Berber is not officially recognised in either of these countries.) Numbers of Berber-speakers in France have been estimated at over half-a-million (Chaker 1988). This calculation allows for a wide margin of error (Price 2000: 96).

Maghrebine Arabic is also widely spoken in France. Caubet (2001: 261) describes this form of Arabic as a 'traditional literary *koine*, which differs completely from Classical or Standard Arabic, and which seems to be common to the whole Maghreb'. Maghrebine Arabic is primarily transmitted by oral tradition and 'requires oral learning like any literary language'. This language/dialect is elaborate and archaic with a specific vocabulary. It is understood throughout Algeria, Morocco and Tunisia. Maghrebine Arabic is very different from Classical Arabic which is the official language of Morocco. However, Classical Arabic 'is a highly formal language which is used only in official contexts' (García and Molina 2001: 286). One of the dialects of Maghrebine Arabic, that is Maltese, has actually developed into a national language and become an official language of the EU (cf. Chapter 3).

For political and economic reasons, there has been strong immigration of speakers of Arabic into France from the three Maghreb states (Morocco, Algeria and Tunisia). Figures for January 1994 show 1,393,165 individuals originally from the Maghreb and retaining their nationality of origin while living in France (Caubet 2001: 263). However, there is no indication of the languages actually spoken by these individuals which are possibly North-African, Arabic, Berber or French. From an analysis of various sources, Caubet (2001: 264) concludes that the number of Arabophones of Algerian origin in France is around 1,200,000.

While census figures are available for numbers of Chinese in Northern Ireland, this does not imply that sources are reliable and ultimately the size of the contemporary Chinese community here is disputed. A survey by Irwin (1996) estimated their numbers at between 3000 and 5000 and almost 41 per cent of this young and growing population had settled in Belfast. Further studies by Irwin and Dunn (1997) suggested that the numbers were perhaps as high as 7000, an estimate below that of the Chinese Welfare Association, which believes it to be closer to 8000 (Watson and McKnight 1998). A recent census indicated the presence of more than 4000 Chinese in Northern Ireland representing 0.25 per cent of the population, but this figure is regarded as highly unreliable. More importantly, as indicated in Map 8.1, the numbers are unevenly distributed and there are high concentrations of Chinese in urban locations in particular. It appears that the majority of them are first-generation Chinese who are primarily engaged in the catering trade.

The presence of these non-European minorities has been motivated by different factors. Economic factors served as the catalyst for Turks in Germany and the Chinese in Northern Ireland. Most Turks in Germany are primarily *Gastarbeiter* (or their children) who were recruited in Mediterranean countries from 1955 onwards. Due to the massive world crisis caused by the spectacular rise in oil prices sparked by Lybia in 1969, then the 1973 Yom Kippur War and finally Iran and Iraq and the deposition of the Shah in 1979, recruitment was halted. Paradoxically, this had the effect of generating a rise in immigration – especially of children – because the reunion of families was still legal (Gogolin and Reich 2001: 195). The current changed position of these families in relation to citizenship laws has already been noted.

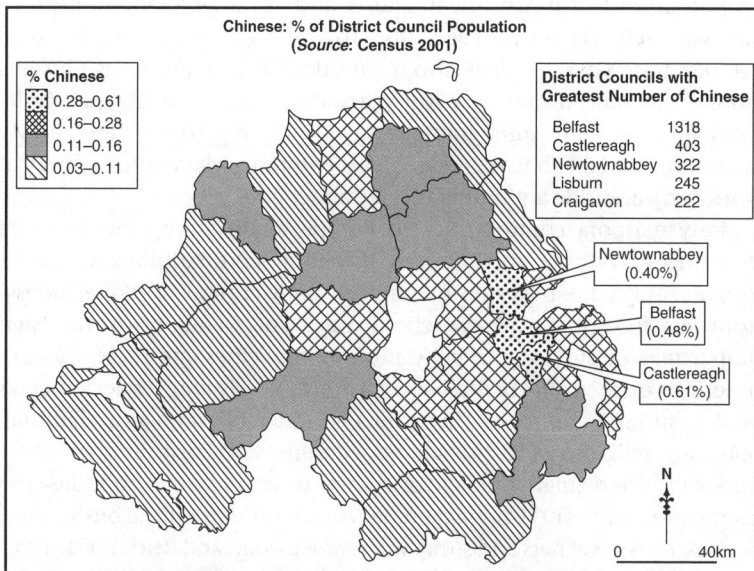

Chinese: % of District Council Population (*Source*: Census 2001)

% Chinese
- 0.28–0.61
- 0.16–0.28
- 0.11–0.16
- 0.03–0.11

District Councils with Greatest Number of Chinese

Belfast	1318
Castlereagh	403
Newtownabbey	322
Lisburn	245
Craigavon	222

Newtownabbey (0.40%)
Belfast (0.48%)
Castlereagh (0.61%)

N

0　　40km

Map 8.1　Chinese in Northern Ireland.

Chinese in Northern Ireland are also a relatively new group. They began arriving in the early 1960s and their first recorded restaurant, 'The Peacock', opened in Belfast in 1962. By 1989 their numbers in Northern Ireland had increased to 4500 and they were primarily arriving from Hong Kong (particularly the New Territories). Smaller numbers of Chinese emigrants also came from Vietnam, Mainland China, Malaysia, Singapore and Taiwan. The employment patterns of these communities seem to depend on their country of origin. While the majority of the Hong Kong community in Northern Ireland works in the catering industry, the population from Mainland China is divided largely between students/academics and refugees, although many of the latter work in the catering industry. There are smaller numbers working in other professions such as community projects, health and information technology (Holder 2003: 31).

The presence of Arabs in France is a reflection of the historic relations between France and North Africa which go back to 1830. The French Jews who arrived from Algeria and who have had French nationality since 1870 are now integrated into French society but they retain memory of their 'Maghrebinity'. Although Arabic is no longer the first language of those Arabs born in France after 1962, some of them still claim their North African heritage and culture. Jews form a strong proportion of North Africans in France and of the one million individuals who left Algeria in 1962 after the War of independence, some 140,000 were Jews. There is also a considerable proportion of Muslims among this Arab minority. Forty years after the war of Algerian independence, Muslim immigrants and Jewish repatriates 'are slowly accepting the fact that they can share emotions via a culture, that of North Africa, inside a plural France' (Caubet 2001: 263).

Many diaspora communities in Europe retain strong memories of their ancestral home, and celebrate its culture and traditions in various formats. Turks are a very visible minority in Germany. Turkish shops – from fast food to travel agencies – are found in many towns. High proportions of Turks are to be found in many cities and these communities can easily avail themselves of Turkish goods and services such as books, clothing and food. There are a considerable number of cultural, political, religious and social associations and institutions where Turkish is the regular language of communication. 'A new middle-class is emerging with Turkish entrepreneurs (not only in ethnic businesses), doctors, clerks, teachers and social workers' (Gogolin and Reich 2001: 198).

There are several bilingual sources of information available to the Turkish community in Germany. *Milliyet*, a Turkish newspaper, offers chats, general information and news in both Turkish and English. Moreover, several bilingual (mostly Turkish–German) magazines have recently come on the market. These are primarily directed at young immigrants and deal with topics relevant to that age group such as popular music. Under public law, the broadcasting services transmit programmes in Turkish. Four private stations broadcast Turkish programmes in Berlin (Gogolin and Reich 2001: 201).

The Chinese in Northern Ireland enjoy similar cultural networks although these are hardly developed to a similar level as that of the Turks in Germany. Apart from restaurants the most obvious symbol of Chinese presence in Ulster is the celebration of the Chinese New Year, which falls between mid-January and mid-February. As well as local parades and ceremonies, the Chinese Chamber of Commerce (NI) organises an annual celebratory dinner. In addition to this, the Chinese women's group in Belfast celebrates a variety of other carnivals such as that of the Dragon Boat or the Moon. These occasions are marked with the preparation of special food and other activities. Chinese festivals are also incorporated into general public festivals and a Chinese Lion Dance featured in the 2005 Saint Patrick's Day parade in Derry/Londonderry.

There are a number of Chinese community organisations in Northern Ireland, all of whom meet in a quarterly Chinese Forum convened by the Chinese Welfare Association, the largest of the groups. This association publishes *Dragon World* – a quarterly community newsletter which is distributed to members of the Chinese forum, Chinese catering establishments, as well as a further 400 individual members of the Chinese Chamber of Commerce. Radio Ulster broadcasts a 10-minute radio programme *Weh Yan Jee Sing* on a weekly basis. This monolingual programme briefs the community on the latest health and social issues.

Although these communities enjoy traditional cultural networks, one cannot assume that this automatically means they speak the language of their ancestral home, although in many instances they do. In the case of Turks in Germany, it would appear that pre-school children in Turkish quarters acquire Turkish almost to the same degree of competence as their monolingual counterparts in Turkey. Moreover language loyalty in Turkish emigrant countries appears to be above average which would indicate that overall the Turkish minority in Germany is a strong and viable ethnolinguistic group (Gogolin and Reich 2001: 198).

Arabic in France is hardly as strong linguistically as Turkish in Germany and colloquial languages or dialects such as Maghrebine Arabic are generally transmitted orally. North African dialects of

Arabic in France are frequently very conservative as emigrants continue to speak the language as it was spoken when they left their country of origin. This occurs regardless of any changes that may have occurred in the language since then in their countries of origin. Although an elaborate, archaic form of communication with specific syntactic constructions and vocabulary, Maghrebine Arabic is not necessarily a source of great pride when compared with Classical Arabic. 'More often than not, the speakers are not proud of their mother tongues, which are referred to as "dialects, patois" and the noble language, for ideological and religious reasons is Classical Arabic' (Caubet 2001: 265).

Dialects are also an issue in the case of Chinese in Northern Ireland. The high proportion of emigrants from Hong Kong means that some eighty–ninety per cent of that community speaks Cantonese. Emigrants from South China, Macao and Malaysia and a number from Vietnam who arrived in the 1970s also speak Cantonese. Some 10–20 per cent of the Chinese community in Northern Ireland speaks Mandarin and Fujianese while a small proportion (mainly elderly members) speaks Hakka. The predominance of Cantonese among the Chinese community in Northern Ireland means that the complex rather than the simplified written form of Chinese is most commonly used (Holder 2003: 31).

Only a small proportion of first-generation Chinese in Northern Ireland are proficient in spoken English but this changes considerably with the second generation. Some parents have reported receiving advice to stop speaking Chinese to their children and to switch to English instead. Such counsel is hardly helpful as many of these parents do not speak English in the first instance and, moreover, they are naturally keen to communicate with their children in their mother tongue (Watson 2000: 98).

Overall there are marginal differences in the proficiency in English between men and women and the slightly higher levels of English among Chinese males are probably a reflection of their greater participation in public life. Moreover the pattern of English profile is closely related to occupation. Levels of proficiency in English are much lower among those who are involved in the catering industry than among other Chinese who have different occupations. This may in fact indicate that language is a significant barrier to alternative employment. Chinese refugees in Northern Ireland generally have much lower levels of English than those arriving for academic purposes, and their experiences of being a refugee generally means that they are in greater need of translation and interpretation services.

Turks in Germany and Arabs in France are dealing with German and French rather than English although English is fast gaining a public presence in both countries. For both of these minorities, a central issue is the maintenance of the mother tongue rather the acquisition of the national language. In particular, there is concern that the younger members of these populations should have some opportunity to become acquainted with their ancestral tongue. In Germany, there has been a strong reliance on the country of origin to provide teachers of Turkish. Hamburg was one of the *Länder* which placed the teaching of immigrant languages in the hands of the countries of origin (Gogolin and Reich 2001: 204). France also entered on a series of bilateral agreements with different countries of origin. An agreement was reached with Tunisia in 1974, with Morocco in 1975 and with Algeria in 1981. Teachers were recruited and renumerated by the countries of origin (Caubet 2001: 267).

France has a long tradition of teaching both Classical and Colloquial Arabic. This tradition dates back to the sixteenth century in the *College des Lecteurs Royaux*. Arabic was introduced into second-level education in 1700 when it was taught by the Jesuits in what later became the prestigious *Lycée Louis le Grand*. In 1795 Napoleon Bonaparte created *L'école spéciale des language orientales*. Initially four languages including Arabic were taught there and Colloquial Arabic was part of the syllabus at the earliest stage. France subsequently became interested in the Middle East, and the introduction of North African Arabic coincided with the colonisation of Algeria from 1830 onwards (Caubet 2001: 267).

The question as to which form of Arabic should be taught within the system of education is very complex. From 1962 until recently, the only Arabic taught in secondary education in France was Classical Arabic. Initially this subject had a high prestige factor and was taught only in the best *lycées* in Paris or in the provincial capitals in Southern France. The arrival of migrants completely changed this situation. In the first instance, there was a dramatic increase in the number of pupils wishing to study Arabic. Moreover there was an impact on the geographical distribution of teaching Arabic towards the suburbs which at both social and educational levels soon transformed into ghettos.

This triggered a negative reaction on the part of many parents who stopped choosing Arabic as a language of the roots for their children, and decided instead to adopt English rather than Arabic as a language of social promotion. The negative image of the language was compounded by the difficulties in learning Classical Arabic which necessitated the acquisition of a new graphic system. In addition, it had the effect of ghettoizing the children in the classroom as Arabic was only taken by children of North African origin (Caubet 2001: 269).

Arabic in France has been taught within two different frameworks which revolve around issues of migration and return, and the ideology behind these programmes was quite different. The first of these ELCO (éducation de langue et culture d'origine) was strongly linked to migration and assumed that emigrants would at some point return to their country of origin. As these children would ultimately return 'home', it was important that they would enjoy parallel programmes with their counterparts in the country of origin. This implied that they should be taught in Classical rather than Colloquial Arabic. There was no assumption of return migration in the alternative foreign languages programme.

Questions arose as it gradually became clear that there would be little return migration, and children were hardly likely to revert to the language of their ancestral home. In those circumstances should children be taught Classical Arabic or was it more important that they acquire the Colloquial Arabic spoken in their locality? As might be expected, there was considerable opposition on the part of the authorities in the countries of origin to any rejection of Classical Arabic – particularly as they were funding the project, but in a sense the entire debate on ELCO is becoming less relevant, especially as it is increasingly clear that most Maghrebins will remain in France rather than return to Algeria.

A report to the minister of education in 1985 (Berque) recommended that children should be introduced to the *langue et culture d'apport*, rather than the language and culture of the country of origin. A more revolutionary element of the report suggested that all children in the classroom rather than those exclusively of North African origin should be involved in the programme. This would have the benefit of introducing all children at an early age to the concept of a plurality of civilisations. The idea was so radical at the time that it was not given any consideration. Fifteen years later, the debate re-emerged. On this occasion it was raised as an equality issue. Since all citizens in France were presumed to be equal (regardless of their origin), they should receive the same treatment at school and be taught the same subjects (Caubet 2001: 268).

A programme launched in 1995 introduced foreign languages into all primary schools in France with an official list of six potential choices, that is Arabic, English, German, Italian, Portuguese and Spanish. (Almost inevitably, most schools opted for English.) However, in the case of Arabic, Colloquial Arabic was officially selected by the *Inspection d'arabe* for this programme, and Moroccan Arabic was specifically chosen in Montpellier in 1996 and in Mantes-la-Jolie in 1997 (Caubet 2001: 268). In both places, secondary school teachers were seconded to carry out the teaching.

The specific programme on Moroccan Arabic subsequently received a very positive reaction. Children of North African origin were proud that their ancestral culture was recognised within the school system. This recognition had the approval of the parents generally. 'Only a few parents of French origin in Montpellier were reluctant, but most of their children had no prejudice and felt happy to learn a new language' (Caubet 2001: 268). The diversity of Arabic taught also varies at third-level education. Currently there are two chairs for Colloquial Arabic, which date back to the beginning of the twentieth century (Caubet 2001: 272).

The discourse of autochthony

Case studies such as Arabic in France or Turkish in Germany raise the question as to whether societies are required to accommodate and recognise *all* cultural differences and languages – or if any such recognition should be confined to indigenous groups? It is generally accepted that it would prove impossible to offer parity of esteem evenly to every group that asserts its difference, and issues of recognition appear to rest in the categorisation of some cultural groups as more entitled to recognition than others. A typology of minorities has been constructed by several sociologists (cf. Eriksen 1993; Kymlicka 1995; Fenton 1999; May 2001). Such typologies usually prioritise proto-national and indigenous rather than migrant minorities in a state.

This principle is reflected in the Framework Convention for the Protection of National Minorities which was opened for signature in February 1995. Although no definition of 'national minorities' is offered in this convention, the very title suggests that non-national (i.e. immigrant) groups are excluded. Article 5 is very explicit in the protection offered to national minorities 'to maintain and develop their culture, and to preserve the essential elements of their identity, namely their religion, language, traditions and cultural heritage'. However, there is a more ambiguous statement in the following Article which suggests that parties would encourage intercultural dialogue and promote mutual respect among all individuals living on a particular territory, 'irrespective of those persons' ethnic, cultural, linguistic or religious identity'. This particularly applied in the fields of culture, education and the media.

This strategy of protection for indigenous European rather than migrant non-European languages has also employed by the EBLUL which does not advocate any rights for speakers of non-European languages. An examination of language maps of Europe produced by EBLUL will feature the presence of Turkish in Greek Thrace, but will not offer any evidence of Turkish-speaking in other countries such as Germany. While the non-representation of millions of Turkish-speakers in other regions could be explained by a lack of official statistics, interviews with individual members of EBLUL revealed a strong predisposition to protest against rights for such speakers on the basis that the ancestral homeland could provide the desired recognition.

Non-European languages are also excluded from the terms of reference of the ECRML. The explanatory notes to the Charter suggest that 'specific problems of integration' arise in situations of new and often non-European languages which are spoken as a result of 'recent migration flows often arising from economic motives'. The committee of experts on regional or minority languages in Europe concluded that problems arising in such contexts 'deserved to be addressed separately, if appropriate in a specific legal instrument' (CoE 1992b).

The exclusion of non-European languages in the ECRML proved a contentious issue in France when the question of ratification of the Charter was debated. When France signed the ECRML in May 1999, it was assumed that six or seven regional, indigenous languages such as Alsatian, Basque, Breton, Catalan, Corsican, Flemish and Occitan would benefit. This enthusiasm was subsequently undermined when France's Constitutional Council made it clear that it had no intention of actually ratifying the Charter, for many reasons.

Before the signing of the Charter in May 1999, several reports on its implications for the state were commissioned by the then Prime Minister Lionel Jospin. A report on the constitutional significance of the Charter by Guy Carcassonne (1998) raised the question of the exclusion of migrant languages from the terms of reference of the Charter. Carcassonne was also concerned with the implications of the Charter for non-territorial languages as discussed in the previous chapter. He was convinced that the terms of reference of the Charter should extend to languages such as Romani, Yiddish and Berber.

Although Carcassonne suggested that Berber should be included within the terms of reference of the Charter, he specifically excluded Arabic (without a qualifier) from his report. Many would agree with such a conclusion as Arabic operates in an entirely different context from Berber in an international context. 'Since Arabic is today the sixth language spoken in the world, i.e. ahead of French, it is difficult not to see it as a foreign language, whichever criteria we use' (Caubet 2001: 274–5). Such arguments focus on Arabic as a monolithic whole, rather than as a collection of different languages or dialects. Interestingly, interviews with Estonians revealed a similar argument against the recognition of Russian within the Baltic territories. Estonians argued that Russian is very widely spoken on an international scale and can hardly be considered a 'minority' language in any context.

In December 1998, Bernard Cerquiglini, the director of the *Institut National de la Langue Française* and vice-president of the *Conseil Supérieur de la Langue Française*, was requested to list the languages that would qualify for France's signature of the Charter. His report in April 1999 identified 75 languages on French territories which should qualify for recognition within the terms of reference of the Charter. His list included several languages which were a subject of surprise including Yiddish, Romani Chib, Eastern Armenian, Colloquial Arabic and Berber. 'In doing so he was the first to give recognition to the actual mother tongue spoken in the communities from the Maghreb' (Caubet 2001: 274).

Cerquiglini's report also included disputed languages such as Gallo and Picard, which are frequently regarded as dialects of French. He concluded that all these languages – whether autochthonous, non-indigenous or contested – came under the remit of the Charter (Judge and Judge 2000). From this perspective it was unethical to offer privileges to indigenous languages such as Breton or Catalan while failing to safeguard non-indigenous and particularly non-European language groups within French boundaries.

Of course several other factors hindered the ratification of the Charter in France. The Council believed that the recognition of languages other than French in specific territories was contrary to the principles of the unity of the French people and the indivisibility of the Republic. Some expressed fears of the Charter as a political tool, which could destabilise the country and serve as the catalyst for movements for regional autonomy. As noted in earlier chapters, regional languages such as Irish in Northern Ireland or the Basque language in Spain are frequently associated with nationalism or separatism.

In the case of France, the issue of equality was also raised. Those in favour of ratification of the Charter argued that regional differences should be recognised and individuals should be permitted to operate publicly in their mother tongue, even if that were not French. Those against the Charter argued that differences of language or race were a matter of private concern. If every individual had the right to speak

French in public, then all were treated equally. These different interpretations of the notion of equality are prime examples of what Charles Taylor (1994) terms 'the politics of difference and universalism'. In the former instance, equality is achieved when group differences are recognised. For the latter, equality implied uniformity and homogeneity.

At the time of writing, France is officially a monolingual country and has failed to ratify the Charter. Yet proponents of recognition of non-European languages within the terms of reference of the Charter can be satisfied that at least the issue of exclusion has been raised – if not resolved. Moreover objections to this perspective are being increasingly voiced. 'Allocating special rights to one group of minorities and denying the same rights to other groups is hard to explain with the principle of equal human rights for everyone' (Extra and Yagmur 2002: 46).

Proponents for recognition of non-European languages argue that the principle of indigeneity as a criterion for recognition is highly dubious. As time passes migrant languages are increasingly spoken by second- or third- rather than first-generation groups and the dividing line between migrancy and indigeneity becomes less obvious. At what point do migrants become indigenous and how does one justify different treatment for such groups? A Union which offers recognition to its indigenous languages, while discriminating against the languages of more recent newcomers is becoming increasingly untenable. 'New European languages are commonly used by people who do not conform to outdated prejudices as to what a European is supposed to *look* like, as well as sound like' (italics original in Cheesman 2001: 163).

An opposing view would raise the difficulties in making such advances. How does one decide which non-indigenous languages are deserving of recognition and where does one stop? The point about indigenous languages is that there is a conclusion – that is, their territorial homelands and boundaries. However, this counter argument become increasingly dubious in the context of migration flows across the continent. There is also the matter of dialects seeking recognition as languages (cf. Chapter 6) and the number of languages – even indigenous ones in Europe – is a never-ending question.

The issue of citizenship is also crucial to this argument. In recent times, 'migrants' have taken up citizenship of the country in which they live and the dividing line between migrants and non-citizens is becoming increasingly dubious. As the status of migrant changes from that of incomer to citizen, it may be logical to ask what the implications for their languages are. The change in status may make the non-recognition of their languages increasingly untenable.

The accusation of double standards has also been raised in this context. Prior to its accession to the EU, the Republic of Slovakia was criticised on many occasions for its anti-democratic tendencies. The US State Department's human rights report of 1996 specifically singled out Slovakia for its anti-democratic policies. At the EU's summit in Spain in December of that year, the German Chancellor Helmut Kohl omitted Slovakia from the list of early entrants to the Union. The key policy issue hindering Slovakia's integration into the West was the treatment of its Hungarian minority and its reluctance to implement a language law which would recognise the status of Hungarian, particularly in the education sector, an issue which has since been addressed (Daftary and Gál 2000, 2003).

Proponents of recognition for speakers of non-European languages in Europe would query why countries such as Slovakia can be openly criticised for their lack of support for their Hungarian minority but no such criticisms are applied to European countries for their neglect of non-European languages. The counter-argument would revert to the principle of indigeneity noting that Hungarians in Slovakia are not migrants but have been living there since 1000 AD. 'Slovakia' was part of Hungary in the Austro-Hungarian Empire up until 1918. Hungarians form 10 per cent of the population (Alcock 1998: 221).

However, the situation is not entirely bleak and there have already been some improvements. In June 1996, several institutions and non-governmental organisations signed the *Universal Declaration of Linguistic Rights* in Barcelona. (The final text of the Declaration was unanimously adopted on 30 January 2000 in Oegstgeest in the Netherlands.) When focusing on language groups, this Declaration explicitly includes immigrant languages as well as regional minority languages within its terms of reference.

Article 1 adopts the case of 'a historical language community within its own territorial space' as its primary referent but qualifies this with a range of other groups, which are also deemed to constitute language communities. Article 1.4 specifically refers to nomadic peoples within their areas of migration and groups established in geographically dispersed locations as language communities. More significantly, Article 1.5 defines migrants as constituting yet another language group. Such communities are made up of 'any group of persons sharing the same language which is established in the territorial space of another language community but which does not possess historical antecedents equivalent to those of that community'. As examples of such groups it mentions immigrants, deported persons, refugees and members of diasporas.

Article 4 specifically addresses the question of integration and suggests that individuals who take up residence in the territory of another language group have both the duty and the right to maintain an attitude of integration towards the host group. This does not automatically imply any loss of the migrant culture. Instead integration is perceived as a positive rather than a negative process which offers individuals the benefits of socialisation in such a way that they may retain their original cultural characteristics while participating fully in the society in which they have settled. While maintaining their own culture, they integrate sufficiently in order to enable them to function socially with the same ease as those of the host group.

The process of integration is essentially quite different to that of assimilation which is hardly an additive process as it involves the loss of the original cultural characteristics which are replaced by those of the host society. The Declaration considers that such forms of acculturation should not be forced on any individual group. Instead assimilation should be entirely voluntary and 'must on no account be forced or induced and can only be the result of an entirely free choice'. (This is also the line taken by the Framework Convention for the Protection of National Minorities as well as OSCE instruments.) Most significantly this Declaration addresses the question of equality for languages and suggests that 'the rights of all language communities are equal and independent of the legal or political status of their languages as official, regional or minority languages'. (This is an issue which will be examined in the final chapter.)

Although specific documents on the linguistic rights of immigrant groups in Europe hardly exist, reference should also be made here to Recommendation 1383 on Linguistic Diversification, which was adopted by the Parliamentary Assembly of the CoE in September 1998. Article 5 in this document advocates greater variety in modern language teaching in the member states of the CoE, and suggests that such teaching should focus not simply on English but on other European and world languages as well as offering fluency in their own national and regional languages. Article 8i recognises the importance of 'non-native' groups in the context of language planning which could be interpreted as progress (Extra and Gorter 2001: 23).

The recognition of migrant languages has been further aided by the Migration Policy Group. In co-operation with the European Cultural Foundation in Amsterdam, this group has called for a comprehensive survey of available policy documents and developments with a view to reconciling the concepts of diversity and cohesion. A report in 2000 suggested that new and historic minorities alike had made significant contributions to Europe's cultural, ethnic and linguistic diversity. Although some European states are reluctant to recognise this diversity, it is hardly a new feature in European society which has had multi-ethnic nation states in both its distant and its recent past (Extra and Yagmur 2002: 44).

An inclusive perspective was also adopted in the UNESCO's Universal Declaration of Cultural Diversity (2002) which makes no distinction between regional and immigrant languages. Article 2 advocates policies of cultural pluralism in the world's increasingly diverse societies; suggesting that that such pluralism is essential for harmonious interactions among groups with dynamic cultural identities. It proposes that policies which encourage inclusion and participation for all citizens will serve as guarantees of social cohesion and give practical expression at policy levels to the reality of cultural diversity.

Article 4 argues that the 'defence of cultural diversity is an ethical imperative, inseparable from respect for human dignity'. This implies a commitment to human rights and fundamental freedoms of all individuals including those of aboriginals and those belonging to minorities. It stipulates that no one may invoke the principle of cultural diversity in order to infringe upon human rights as guaranteed by international law, or indeed to limit their scope.

This UNESCO Declaration explicitly links the question of cultural diversity with human rights. Moreover, an Action Plan for member states is attached to the Declaration which commits participating parties to co-operation in the achievement of a wide set of objections which include language-related issues. Article 5 of the Action Plan deals with the protection of the linguistic heritage of humanity and gives support to the 'expression, creation and dissemination in the greatest possible number of languages'. The subsequent Article encourages linguistic diversity at all levels of education, and while respecting the mother tongue it encourages the learning of several languages from an early age.

There was also an important gesture towards inclusiveness by Philip Blair, who had worked for a number of years on the preparation of the European Charter. In a paper delivered at a conference in Belfast, he acknowledged the problem of autochthony in the Charter but argued strongly that this does not imply the Charter is only concerned with indigenous languages, 'since a language that is not traditionally spoken on a given territory today may legitimately be so regarded in the future' (2003: 41). As an example, he suggested that at some stage in the future,

Turkish may come to be regarded as traditionally spoken in Berlin or Urdu in Bradford.

Finally one should also note that a 2004 publication from the European Commission on the languages of Europe acknowledged the existence of non-indigenous languages on the continent. It stated that 'a wide variety of languages from other parts of the world are spoken by immigrant communities in EU countries' and gave the following statistics: 'Turkish is spoken as a first language by an estimated 2% of the population in Belgium and the western part of Germany and by 1% in the Netherlands.' It noted that

> other widely-used migrant languages include Maghreb Arabic (mainly in France and Belgium), Urdu, Bengali and Hindi spoken by immigrants from the Indian subcontinent in the United Kingdom, while Balkan languages are spoken in many parts of the EU by migrants and refugees who have left the region as a result of recent wars and unrest there.

The document acknowledged the lack of formal status or recognition for these languages in EU countries as well as the fact that they are not covered by EU language-teaching programmes. However, it appeared to suggest that this was not entirely problematic as 'many national and local authorities provide classes to help immigrants learn the language of their adopted country and thus integrate into the workforce, the local community and national life in general'. It concluded with the statement that 'many immigrant communities in the EU have been in place for several generations now and their members are bilingual, at ease, both in the local language and in that of their community' (European Commission 2004: 9).

Conclusion

Overall the question of non-European languages in Europe has received little attention. As yet, there are many difficulties relating to regional, contested and non-territorial languages which have been prioritised by groups such as the EBLUL. Moreover there is a view that non-European languages should not drain the limited resources available to other language groups who may be in great difficulty, but seek whatever recognition and support they desire from their country of origin.

There are also other matters emerging in the new Europe. As the EU expands, the presence of English has become increasingly prevalent.

Although theoretically the EU is a multilingual institution, at a practical level all languages other than English are becoming minoritised in relation to this global language. Recognition and status are issues for all languages albeit at different levels. In the quest for recognition there is little sympathy for languages such as Arabic or Turkish which are perceived as operating in global rather than European contexts. Moreover, there is the issue, not dealt with yet, of the association of such languages with terrorist activities.

Languages in Europe are currently arranged in a somewhat hierarchical manner with global, official, state languages at the top of the pyramid and non-European languages at the bottom. Yet in an increasingly democratic society, questions must be raised about the future of such arrangements and whether it is time to review policies and politics of recognition.

9
Europe and the Politics of Belonging

Throughout this book, various aspects of language policy in Europe have been considered, ranging from EU policy towards official languages to the neglect of languages of non-European, migrant communities. This final chapter will set out an overall evaluation of EU language policy; beginning with the political question of Europe itself and then proceeding to the concept of 'European languages'. The hierarchisation of languages within the EU has been a constant theme in the book and this final chapter will query the notion of equality and its implications for different categories of languages. In conclusion a series of recommendations will be proposed, which could address some of the anomalies and inequalities inherent in current EU policies and point the way towards a more equitable system.

Europe and its languages

The initial chapter addressed the changing concept of Europe over many centuries and challenged the notion of Europe as a historical entity. Whether or not one agrees that the concept of Europe has been with us for centuries, there is no doubt that for many people, Europe has now become coterminous with the EU and the terminology has often become confused. Part of the confusion may derive from the fact that the EU as a political entity has set the objective of building a single Union 'reflecting the will of the citizens and States of Europe to build a common future'. The preamble to the Treaty establishing a constitution for Europe suggests that 'while remaining proud of their own national identities and history, the peoples of Europe are determined to transcend their former divisions and, united ever more closely, to forge a common destiny'. This single political polity has been identified by many a lay person with historical Europe.

A European history or cultural identity was hardly a priority for the EEC in its early stages of development, but this changed somewhat with the revision of the Treaty in Maastricht, which gave EU institutions some competence in the area of culture and cultural policy. Article 128.1 of that Treaty suggests that 'the Community shall contribute to the flowering of the cultures of the Member States while respecting their national and regional diversity and at the same time bringing the common cultural heritage to the fore'. It also encouraged co-operation between member states in the 'improvement of the knowledge and dissemination of the culture and history of the European peoples' as well as the 'conservation and safeguarding of cultural heritage of European significance'. These principles were reinforced in the revisions of the Treaty in Amsterdam and in Nice.

Since then a constitution has been published which postulates that Europe is 'united in diversity'. The constitution suggests that having been 'reunited after bitter experiences; Europe intends to continue along the path of civilisation, progress and prosperity, for the good of all its inhabitants'. Moreover it desires to remain 'open to culture, learning and social progress'. As well as this 'it wishes to deepen the democratic and transparent nature of its public life, and to strive for peace, justice and solidarity throughout the world'.

Despite these assurances the concept of a collective EU civilisation or culture appears vague (Kostakopoulou 2001: 14). Although there have been some attempts to engender a sense of collective identity, the EU is hardly certain whether what has emerged is its 'true' identity or culture. There are several reasons for this sense of ambiguity, not least of which is its uncertain history and the presence of several 'Europes' which were not necessarily coterminous: the Europe of Greek mythology, the Holy Roman Empire, the Europe of the Enlightenment and so on (Kostakopoulou 2001: 26).

Even with the predominance of English, the EU lacks a common *lingua franca*, and has no uniform system of education or mass media. There have been some endeavours to develop a set of EU symbols such as the EC anthem, emblem and flag, harmonised EU passports and car number-plates, but these have failed to inspire individual citizens. There have also been EC-funded initiatives that have had local rather than international impact such as the European City of Culture, the European Woman of the Year Award and the Jean Monnet awards for universities.

The problem of a lack of commitment to the concept of the EU on the part of its citizens has been identified in some European publications. Fontaine (1993: 17) suggests that 'common citizenship is forged over time, through shared experience and the *affectio societatis* which unites individuals and gives them a sense of belonging to a collective identity'. Apparently the lack of commitment to this collective identity would be solved once 'people had a clearer idea of the real issues in the political date at European level'.

To date it seems that a collective EU identity is perceived simply as the sum of its diverse national and regional units and there are many instances of the appropriation and re-interpretation of national cultural icons as the indices of a unified European history (Shore 2000: 54). In 1996, Jacques Santer, the then President of the EC suggested that Europe was made up of several distinct cultural identities, languages and schools of thought. He regarded this multicultural heritage as the context in which contemporary Europeans viewed society at large. Santer identified the common cultural heritage of Europe as that of Shakespeare, Cervantes, Rimbaud and Mozart; but interestingly he also included Russian cultural icons such as Tolstoy and Moussorgski. His conclusion was that one can speak of 'a common cultural heritage' which is 'reflected in the diversity of Europe's individual cultures' (Santer 1996, cited in Julios 2002: 186).

The development of a concept of EU cultural identity usually refers to a collection of national icons and identities. The Preamble to the Charter of Fundamental Rights (The European Convention 2003: 75) suggests that the 'Union contributes to the preservation and to the development of these common values while respecting the diversity of the cultures and traditions of the peoples of Europe as well as the national identities of the Member States.' Inevitably, there are tensions inherent in this process. Cultural elements such as shared language, memory and history which give unity to identities at national levels tend to divide them at European level (Shore 2000: 18).

The overarching principle of unity in diversity has proved very difficult to establish. 'Diversity is a wild and chameleonic animal with thousands of heads that can hardly be kept imprisoned in the case of one legal principle' (Toggenburg 2004: 18). The slogan 'unity in diversity' could be interpreted in several different ways. On the one hand, it could be perceived as an acknowledgement and celebration of the diversity of European (national) identities or the diversity of European cultures, including Europe's regional and minority cultures. On the other hand, it could be regarded as an appropriation of power to the centre – as if

'Europe's "mosaic of cultures" was but a multiplicity of smaller units in a greater European design.' From that perspective European culture is defined as the 'over-arching, encapsulating and transcendent composite of national cultures; a whole greater than the sum of its discordant parts' (Shore 2000: 54).

Nowhere are tensions between European versus national identity more perceptible than in the context of Europe's languages. While Europe's linguistic pluralism is frequently lauded, it also poses serious challenges for EU policy makers. Chapters 2 and 3 focused on the promotion of specific languages to the status of national languages during the development of nation states. They also examined EU support for official, national languages. The enhancement of a small number of languages at official EU level can alienate the millions of citizens who speak a different mother tongue and distance them from the decision-making process. This *de facto* exclusion can generate lack of confidence in the community-building objective.

While speakers of minority languages complain of the limited recognition afforded to their languages, there are more significant implications for those who are perceived to speak a language that is 'non-European'. From a political perspective it can be very difficult to decide what makes a language European. In the *Encyclopaedia of the Languages of Europe*, Glanville Price argues powerfully that Arabic is a European language. He supports the case with three reasons. In the first instance, Arabs occupied extensive territories in Southern Europe, sometimes for lengthy periods and especially during the Middle Ages. Price also points to the existence of a long-standing Arabic-speaking people in Cyprus. He also notes the presence of large numbers of Arabic-speakers in contemporary Western Europe and especially France (Price 2000: 11). One could also add that Maltese, which is historically a dialect of Arabic has achieved the status of official language of the EU.

Price also extends the umbrella term 'languages of Europe' to the community (immigrant) languages spoken in Britain, France and the Netherlands. Here the term 'community language' is used to refer to the languages of 'reasonably settled communities of (in most cases recent) incomers from areas such as Asia, Africa or the Caribbean'. Price argues that if these languages 'are not, in the usual sense of the term, "European languages", it seems difficult not to recognise them as having achieved the status of "languages of Europe"'.

The classification of certain languages as belonging to Europe can prove very arbitrary – particularly from a political perspective. The distribution of different languages in contemporary Europe simply reflects the interplay of linguistic, geographic, cultural and political criteria over time. Some critics might suggest that here one should rely on linguistic factors, but the entire book has approached language as a political rather than a linguistic concept. Moreover to rely on a linguistic criterion 'in defining what is essentially European, would clearly not help, as all European languages other than Basque are related to languages in Asia' (Phillipson 2003: 35).

Overall it seems that EU language policy has been underpinned by the concept of territory. With the emergence of the nation-state model, certain languages became associated with the national territory. These national languages were subsequently privileged within the EU polity and, in most instances, were given the status of official, working languages. Several chapters examined the marginalisation of those languages which were confined to specific regions and considered peripheral to the national territory. Nevertheless as noted in Chapters 4 to 6, there has been some limited recognition of such languages in varying degrees. Nomads have also received limited acknowledgement of their languages because of their historical residence in Europe.

Emigrants from countries outside Europe have suffered an almost total lack of recognition for their languages. In some sense they are perceived as 'not belonging' to the political entity and undeserving of recognition within the public space. The concept of indigeneity has been explored in the previous chapter where it has been argued that the 'indigenousness' of any specific location is always relative to more recent arrivals. In the twenty-first century, when migration is occurring on a global scale, the promotion of certain imagined communities and heritages because they somehow belong to the political entity and the lack of acknowledgement for others who are perceived not to belong requires further debate.

In a colonial era the degradation of the indigenous population who lived on the native soil was regular practice. Indigeneity was equated with inferiority and, in some instances, natives were deprived of access to power structures. (This was not entirely uniform practice as the British left Rajahs in control of their territory in India, and tribal chiefs were left in control of their tribes in Africa.) In most places, however, the British ruled, taxed and controlled foreign policy, but they did not interfere with local traditions (except to eliminate suttee) or local rule.

The historical process of limiting access to power to the indigenous population is seen as unacceptable nowadays. However, the privileging of some language communities over others primarily because of their historical link to a particular territory could also be regarded as the same process in reverse and is possibly equally unjustifiable. As noted in several chapters in this book, the remit of the ECRML applies solely to what are deemed to be autochthonous languages, and interviews with several individuals involved in EBLUL have strongly reinforced this perspective.

The rhetoric of indigeneity has been identified by Gupta (2002) as a recent trend which emphasises the European and the Judaeo-Christian tradition. In many European countries it has served to enhance electoral success. She points to the example of the Netherlands which attempted to impose a Dutch language on mosques. There is also the case of David Blunkett, a former British Minister, who regretted the fact that English was not the language of the home in 30 per cent of British Asian families.

How does one define the languages of Europe? Arabic, Bengali, Chinese (Mandarin, Cantonese etc.), Hindi and Urdu, and many other languages are chiefly spoken outside the geographical or political European entity. Yet this is hardly to deny that they are important languages within contemporary Europe. 'They are languages of transnational and local communities with increasingly rich *European* cultural heritages: press and other media production, literature, performance and other arts, cultural, educational and other institutions' (italics original in Cheesman 2001: 153).

The answer seems to lie in the premise that these are languages in but not of Europe, that is they do not belong here. One of the key arguments against the protection of such languages is in fact that they belong elsewhere. Arabic, for example, is predominantly spoken outside Europe rather than within the political entity of the EU. It is argued that languages such as these can be maintained from their home base. This position ignores the fact that all languages are fluid and subject to constant change. Non-European languages spoken over generations in Europe will inevitably develop European characteristics and will gradually develop elements that differ from the language spoken in the country of origin.

A similar argument suggests that the communities speaking such languages are essentially committed to their ancestral homelands and could hardly develop a sense of loyalty to Europe. Why then should the EU commit its resources to languages spoken by individuals and communities that will inevitably return 'home'? Evidence to date has proved that this is hardly the case and it is now time to accept that many of these communities are here to stay. To counteract this it has been suggested in other interviews with members of the EBLUL that non-Europeans should form their own forum, but this strategy is effectively a form of linguistic apartheid and denies them their place in European affairs – both historically and in contemporary times.

Many speakers of marginalised European languages feel greatly threatened by the notion that non-European languages should also be included within the terms of reference of various charters and frameworks. It is argued that the strategy of exclusion is very important for the protection of those languages that do belong to Europe. However, such 'indigenous' European languages are under far greater threat from the predominance of English and possibly French, than from Berber in France or Arabic in Germany. Sometimes such points of view derive from an economic perspective. If more language communities benefit from the same resources, this inevitably implies less financial assistance for indigenous language community. However, speakers of non-European languages also contribute to the finances of the country in which they work and should be entitled to a return on their resources.

The implications of equality

All of this raises the question of equality for different languages in Europe and this is an issue that has become increasingly significant in the past decade. The *Universal Declaration of Linguistic Rights* adopted in Barcelona in 1996 was 'based on the principle that the rights of all language communities are equal'. Such rights were entirely 'independent of the legal or political status of their languages as official, regional or minority languages'. The principle of equality for all languages was reinforced in Article 10.1 which reiterated the statement that 'all language communities have equal rights'.

Furthermore, the Declaration suggested that discrimination against language communities should be inadmissible, 'whether it be based on their degree of political sovereignty, their situation defined in social, economic or other terms, the extent to which their languages have been codified, updated or modernised, or on any other criterion'. It emphasised that 'all necessary steps must be taken in order to implement this principle of equality and to render it effective'.

This principle of equality (albeit with certain modifications) was reinforced some years later by the Council of Ministers of the EU. On 14 February 2002, a Council Resolution on the Promotion of Linguistic Diversity and Language Learning suggested that 'all European languages are equal in value and dignity from the cultural point of view and form an integral part of European culture and civilisation' (European

Commission 2002: C50/1). While this resolution may appear satisfactory on the surface, it raises more questions than answers. The clause 'from the cultural point of view' is ambiguous and overall the resolution appears to imply inequalities among languages at other, possibly more important levels.

The focus on equality for languages in Europe acquired a new significance with the process of drafting the new Constitutional Treaty for the EU. Many language groups endeavoured to take advantage of the opportunities for discussion offered by this process and to influence the draft text. One suggestion by EBLUL was that a specific article on linguistic diversity should be introduced into the constitution which would build on Article II-82 of the Charter of Fundamental Rights of The European Union. That article had stipulated that the 'Union shall respect cultural, religious and linguistic diversity.'

This suggestion of a specific article was supported by Mr Neil MacCormick who submitted a contribution on 24 September 2002 arguing for the equality of all languages in the EU. MacCormick suggested that 'the linguistic diversity of the European Union must be protected'. All languages should be recognised as an integral element of the rich heritage of the Union, and 'all languages and cultures should have equal rights' as outlined in the *Universal Declaration of Linguistic Rights*. Moreover, he argued that 'all official languages in the territory of the European Union must be given proper status at European level' (in Warasin 2003).

In addition to a specific article on linguistic diversity, EBLUL suggested that Article 13 of the Maastricht Treaty on European Union which advocated non-discrimination in relation to sex, racial or ethnic origin, religion or belief, disability, age or sexual orientation should be amended to include a language criterion. Members of EBLUL believed that the absence of specific language protection could in turn generate indirect discrimination against speakers of minority languages and in particular against those groups which define themselves primarily in terms of language. In conjunction with Members of the European Parliament, EBLUL contacted several prominent individuals in order to raise awareness of this issue. Although the principle was rejected initially in several quarters, EBLUL received some support from others. Some of this support was grounded in the principle of equality.

In a speech delivered at the Danish Parliament on 5 November 2002, the High Commissioner on National Minorities of the OSCE, Mr Rolph Ekeus, argued against the lack of status of languages such as Catalan, Romani and Russian which were spoken internationally in several countries by several millions of speakers and yet are categorised within the EU polity as 'lesser-used languages'. He also noted that Article 13 of the EC Treaty which deals with discrimination failed to include language within its remit. Ekeus suggested that 'this conspicuous short-coming needs to be addressed to ensure that, in a transformed Union, all Europeans will enjoy full equality'. He endorsed the maintenance of the full extent of Europe's rich linguistic diversity 'which is both an essential part of European identity and a tremendous human resource' (Ekeus 2002). Ultimately EBLUL's proposals to the Convention on the Future of the European Union were supported in writing by many prominent individuals. As well as Mr Rolph Ekeus, these included Prof. Patrick Thornberry, UN-rapporteur of the Committee on the Elimination of Racial Discrimination and Mr Fèlix Martí, from UNESCO's Linguapax Institute.

The quest for equality for all languages received further attention in February 2003 at a meeting of the European Parliament's Intergroup for Regional and Minority Languages in Strasbourg. The meeting was addressed by Mrs Viviane Reding, the EU Commissioner for Education and Culture. As she outlined the Commission's new Action Plan on Language Learning and Linguistic Diversity, she emphasised the importance of protecting and promoting linguistic diversity in the EU. The principle of protection was extended to official and lesser-used languages alike as 'all languages are equal, no matter if they are big or small' (Warasin 2003).

The success of EBLUL's efforts became apparent with the publication of the constitution in 2003. The principle of equality was reinforced in Part 1, Title VI, Article 1–45, which suggested that 'in all its activities, the Union shall observe the principle of the equality of its citizens, who shall receive equal attention from its institutions, bodies, offices and agencies'. The article on non-discrimination in Part 2, Title III of the Charter of the Fundamental Rights of the Union, Article II-21, suggested that 'any discrimination based on any ground such as sex, race, colour, ethnic or social origin, genetic features, language, religion or belief, political or any other opinion, membership of national minority, property, birth, disability, age or sexual orientation shall be prohibited'.

While the principle of equality for all languages has gained increasing significance, there is some uncertainty as to its precise implications. Does it imply that all languages should be treated in exactly the same manner – or does it infer some positive discrimination in favour of 'smaller' languages? The previous chapter referred to Charles Taylor's work which draws attention to two alternative approaches to the concept of equality, which he terms the politics of universalism and the politics of difference. While the politics of universalism requires that every citizen has identical rights, the alternative approach focuses on the distinctiveness of each individual and encourages positive discriminatory practices in order to ensure equality. 'With the politics of equal dignity, what is established is meant to be universally the same, an identical basket of rights and immunities; with the politics of difference, what we are asked to recognize is the unique identity of this individual or group, their distinctness from everyone else' (Taylor 1994: 38).

Proponents of the politics of universalism seek non-discrimination so that every individual receives similar treatment. They 'seek to protect against harm caused by prejudice and discrimination, and therefore to restore and maintain a level playing field' (Packer 1999: 259). This process is perceived as essentially neutral and could be regarded as 'colour-blind' or 'culture-blind'. In contrast, advocates of the politics of difference seek positive or reverse discrimination for collectivities in order to ensure that no one suffers discrimination. Their concern is 'to facilitate the equal opportunity for persons belonging to minorities to maintain and develop their identity/ies' (Packer 1999: 259).

Proponents of the politics of universalism do not believe in the concept of positive discrimination. They argue that the politics of difference focuses on variations between groups and encourages instability in society.

> The 'politics of difference' is a formula for manufacturing conflict, because it rewards the groups that can most effectively mobilise to make claims on the polity, or at any rate it rewards ethnocultural political entrepreneurs who can exploit its potential for their own ends by mobilizing a constituency around a set of sectional demands. (Barry 2000: 21)

Supporters of the politics of difference argue that the politics of universalism forces people to be homogenous. Groups in this context incur the damage of mis-recognition and their culture may be mis-interpreted or homogenised.

Different processes of recognition are at the heart of many crisis points. In 1933, for example, the Albanian government abolished all private schools including those of the Greek minority. When the Greeks reacted against this decision, the Albanians argued that every individual was receiving equal treatment and that the Greeks could hardly have greater expectations than the Albanian majority. Two years later the case was brought before the Permanent Court of International Justice, which ruled that there was a difference between equality *de jure* and equality *de facto*. While the former might preclude discrimination of any kind, the latter might require some differential treatment in order to establish equilibrium between different situations (Alcock 2000).

A more immediate example can be found with reference to the case of Irish in Northern Ireland. Irish-medium education in Northern Ireland is a relatively recent and successful phenomenon (Peover 2001, 2002; Ó Coinn 2002; 2003). At the time of writing almost 3000 children are taught through the medium of Irish in 32 primary and 3 post-primary schools across the Province. The growth of Irish-medium education at primary level in the 1970s and 1980s inevitably generated a demand for second-level immersion education which proved to be a long and arduous task. While initial negotiations between parents and the Department of Education Northern Ireland (DENI) were positive, several difficulties arose in relation to the viability criteria for *Meánscoil Feirste* (Belfast Secondary School). Although the DENI reduced the number of pupils required for formal recognition and financial support from 80 to 60 pupils, the lack of funding compelled the school to restrict its own intake, creating an impossible situation. As long as the school curtailed its intake of pupils on the basis of lack of funding, it would fail to meet the government target of projected enrolment, thereby ensuring it could never achieve formal recognition.

By 1993, relations between parents and the DENI were strained and the school took the parents' case to the European Court of Human Rights. Parents of pupils in this school argued for parity of esteem for Irish-medium and Welsh-medium education and for similar viability criteria for both. During this campaign there was a great emphasis on Irish-speakers as a community. Initially they had portrayed themselves as a 'risen people' (O'Reilly 1999: 129) and emphasised the wealth of their cultural heritage, but when they failed to gain funding, they focused on themselves as a victimised community suffering discrimination at the hands of the DENI.

As the campaign progressed, parents drew increasingly on the issues of equality and parity of esteem for Irish- and English-medium education. One parent complained that the failure to fund Irish-medium education at second level was 'a clear signal to all concerned that the idea of equality and parity of esteem for all traditions has not yet been embraced' by the government (in O'Reilly 1999: 130). The head of the primary school *Bunscoil Phobal Feirste* argued that 'the principle of recognizing both traditions [British and Irish] lies at the heart of all aspirations in our community'.

The Irish government then intervened, drawing on a discourse of rights and John Bruton, the then Taoiseach, requested John Major, British Prime Minister at the time, to reverse the DENI's decision to withhold funding from the school. Bruton argued that such a move would demonstrate parity of esteem for both the British and the Irish communities in Northern Ireland at a practical level, but this raised the question of the meaning of parity of esteem. While nationalists regarded the funding of Irish-medium schools as demonstrating equality of esteem for Irish culture, Michael Ancram, the then Minister for Education, viewed it in a different context. He did not believe that Irish-medium education should receive any special concession. Instead they should be treated in a similar fashion to schools using the majority language, that is English.

Herein lies a practical example of the debate between the politics of universalism and the politics of difference. Should minority language schools receive special funding in order to ensure that they can operate effectively or should they be treated on exactly the same basis as schools in the majority language? From a nationalist perspective in Northern Ireland, the answer was obvious: 'parity of esteem in any field needs special funding to enable it to be visible and functioning. You have to pay for a diverse culture.' The unionist ministry adopted a contrary position. Basically Ancram felt that parity of esteem meant parity of financial aid (in O'Reilly 1999: 133).

This hardly seemed fair and equitable to nationalists. 'Because everyone is NOT the same in a divided society, he should be providing extra money to enable parity of esteem AND to compensate for the anti-Irish discrimination his department practiced for decades.... As it is, funding will come by the back door. That's parity of esteem NIO style' (caps original in O'Reilly 1999: 133). Ultimately the second-level school received official recognition and funding in 1996, but the campaign had drawn heavily on different interpretations of concepts of equality.

Incompatible interpretations of the concept of equality can cause immense difficulties in any context. A report by the European Commission's Directorate-General for Research in 2002 agued that the principle of linguistic diversity which is so often iterated by the EU and the CoE is inherently ambiguous and unclear. 'Linguistic diversity does not define *per se* which languages are to be protected.' On occasions this principle has been taken to refer to a principle of equality for those languages that are official in the member states. In the Directorate-General's view, it should also apply 'to all indigenous European languages' (italics original in Directorate-General for Research 2002: 54). However, the Directorate interprets this stance from the perspective of the politics of difference and argues that respect for minority languages must imply the provision of a policy basis for 'a specific, active policy in the field of promoting diversity' (Directorate-General for Research 2002: 51).

In an EBLUL report on Convention on the Future of the European Union, Markus Warasin, the then Secretary-General of EBLUL, adopted a politics of difference approach to the concept of equality. From his perspective the concept of respect as outlined in Article 13 of the Maastricht Treaty 'includes affirmative actions for such languages'. Clearly the idea of respect was being interpreted in the form of positive interventions. Warasin (2003) emphasises the principle of equality inherent in the notion of respect. 'To respect linguistic diversity also contains the recognition that all European languages are equal, whether they are widely or lesser-used.'

The concept of equality for all languages has also been incorporated into discourses on human rights. Ferdinand de Varennes (1996: 117) argues that 'respect of the language principles of individuals, where appropriate and reasonable, flows from a fundamental right and is not some special concession or privileged treatment. Simply put, it is the right to be treated equally without discrimination, to which everyone is entitled.' This argument is endorsed by May (2003: 224) who suggests that where there are 'a sufficient number of other language speakers, these speakers should be allowed to use that language as part of the exercise of their individual rights as citizens. That is, they should have the opportunity to use their first language if they so choose' (May 2003: 224).

Arguments for equality in the context of languages in Europe usually refer to the lack of positive discrimination for minority languages while recognising the continued importance of majority languages. The explanatory notes to the ECRML reinforce this point. These point out that 'the charter does not conceive the relationship between official and regional or minority languages in terms of competition or antagonism'. Instead 'it deliberately adopts an intercultural and multilingual approach in which each category of language has its proper place'. Supporters of the principle of equality for minority languages point out that 'advocacy of minority language rights is not about replacing a majority language with a minority one'. Instead it is simply 'about questioning and contesting why the promotion of a majority (national) language would necessarily be at the expense of all others' (May 2003: 224).

Moreover, proponents of equality for minority languages argue that the principle of multilingualism which theoretically applies to inter-state languages in an EU context should also be applied to intrastate languages within the EU. 'If the Netherlands can argue that Dutch has a right to be represented as a working language of the EU, then, by impli-cation Frisian has a right to be represented as a working language of the Netherlands. After all, it is clearly a working language of the Netherlands' (May 2003: 223).

This argument gains a new significance when one considers the increasing prevalence of English within the EU polity. The spread of English as a world language means that the principle of equality becomes increasingly important for all other languages in the EU including those that are currently privileged as nation-state languages and as official, working languages. Although at the time of writing, 19 nation-state languages are theoretically equal to English within the context of the EU, the fact remains that an ever-increasing number speaks English while the proportions of those speaking even official languages such as French and German is in decline.

A special Eurobarometer survey which was held in December 2000 highlighted the growing significance of English in the pre-2004 member states of the EU. In addition to their mother tongue, 41 per cent of people surveyed in those states knew English whereas the figures for French and German were 19 per cent and 10 per cent respectively. Overall the language most frequently spoken as a first foreign language in Europe was English (32 per cent) followed by French (9.5 per cent). Moreover, English was the language most likely to be spoken on an occasional basis on trips abroad or in the company of foreign visitors. Most significantly, while 71 per cent of Europeans at that time consid-ered that everyone in the EU should be able to speak one European language in addition to their mother tongue, almost the same proportion of respondents suggested that this should be English (Special Euroba-rometer 'Europeans and Languages').

The predominance of English is now a matter of concern for many in the EU and also contains many contradictions. The EU actively promotes the concept of multilingual education. Its Action Plan for 2004–2006 warns against the dominance of English in different systems of education and suggests that trends to teach English in non-Anglophone countries 'may have unforeseen consequences on the vitality of the national language'. It recommends that 'university language policies should therefore include explicit actions to promote the national or regional language' (Commission of the European Communities 2003: 8). At the same time English is widely used throughout official meetings. 'Whether in the academic, commercial, political, bureaucratic or social areas, English certainly dominates every aspect of the Union's life. Even at the core of Europe's multilingual information machine, English has become a dominant presence' (Julios 2002: 198).

Revising language policies in Europe

It is easy to criticise various aspects of EU policy in relation to the languages of its citizens, migrants and outsiders but far more difficult to suggest viable alternatives. With every enlargement, the diversity of languages spoken in the EU will increase and the personnel required to deal with such issues will also rise. In 2004 the proportion of countries within the EU increased by 66 per cent; the number of EU citizens by 20 per cent and that of official languages by 82 per cent. Enlargement entailed 6300 new posts in the European institutions between 2004 and 2006. Of these, 2070 were posts for linguists.

There are major differences in the various ideologies underpinning the role of language in different states. For Germans, the Herderian concept of language is dominant. In the case of France, there is greater emphasis on the notion of a civic republican tradition. Moreover, many countries differ quite widely on the level of awareness of the significance of language policy. Finland and Greece, for example, give priority to language questions whereas such issues are considered less significant in the case of Denmark and England. The basis of a common language policy would be significantly improved by a greater understanding of these major differences in ideologies (Phillipson 2002). There needs to be far greater investment in such issues at university level. To date the field of language planning at all levels has received insufficient academic attention.

Enlargement of the EU has focused attention particularly on the number of official languages. There is a real need to revisit the debate on the status of official languages within the EU but such discussion should focus on reality as well as rhetoric. This applies equally to the context of global as well as regional languages. If we are operating in the context of a multilingual Europe, it is necessary to establish the meaning of multilingualism. Should it be understood as the acquisition of several languages or is it the case that one is really operating in the context of English plus another tongue?

Does the EU aim to produce 'multilingual citizens per se' or should it focus on the generation of 'English-speaking multilingual Europeans'? Julios (2002: 201) is strongly in favour of the latter arguing that 'bilingualism with English is already fast becoming a fact of life for the citizens of Europe, as habitual use of English within the Union is found to be necessary or potentially necessary'. Moreover, she suggests that 'it would be reasonable to suggest that in order to partake in Europe . . . it is desirable to master the English language'.

Many would react with anxiety to such an argument but debates on official policy should focus on reality as well as aspiration. Such complexities apply equally to other 'global' languages spoken within the EU. If German is the second language of the Union why is it not spoken consistently at meetings when French (the EU's third language) is preferred? This is one of the many unresolved paradoxes. Although Germany is demographically and economically a dominant force, it is progressively marginalised within the workings of the Union. As French is now being displaced by English, should French-speakers champion the cause of other official languages and argue that languages other than English (and French) are used? The question of a reduction in the number of official languages has generated considerable debate. While those in favour of linguistic diversity would hesitate to concur with such a principle, it could possibly be conceded solely on the basis that no one is permitted to use his or her mother tongue. Then everyone would gain an understanding of the difficulties generated when communicating in a second rather than a first language.

The EU institutions should reconsider the rhetoric of equality for official, working languages. At the moment there is no formalised distinction between 'working' and 'official' language but common practice is for EU institutions to work through a reduced number of languages, primarily French and English and occasionally German. Moreover it is patently obvious that such languages are not treated equally. While there may be a formal equality between these languages, there remains 'a pecking order of states and languages, currently visible in the shift from French to English as the primary working language of EU institutions' (Phillipson 2002: 273). The issue of 'real working languages' ought to be seriously addressed and reconsidered so that a mutually satisfactory situation can evolve.

It will also be important to review the terminology used to qualify languages as many of those currently in vogue are impractical. Consider the notion of 'global language' for example. The concept actually refers to the written rather than to the spoken word. In print, English is a global language. At a spoken level, there are many different kinds of English worldwide and these are not always mutually comprehensible. McArthur has attempted to organise the idealised formal World Standard English into regional varieties which have a standard usage or are developing one (in Mazumdar *et al.* 2005: 65). These are outlined in Table 9.1. All of these categories are further subdivided illustrating the fragmentation of English at a global level. The subdivisions of British and Irish Standard English illustrate the case in Table 9.2. (Many would not agree with the inclusion of Scots and Ulster-Scots here.)

Although we all speak of English as a global language, the fact remains that English is being shaped in an entirely new fashion in different locations. 'New Englishes are mushrooming the globe over, ranging from "Englog", the Taglog-infused English spoken in the Phillipines, to "Japlish", the cryptic English poetry beloved of Japanese

Table 9.1   Regional varieties of World Standard English

British and Irish Standard English
American Standard English
Canadian Standard English
Caribbean Standard English
West, East and South(ern) African Standard(ising) English
South Asian Standard(ising) English
East Asian Standardizing English

Table 9.2   Freely evolving regional dialects of British and Irish Standard English

Regional varieties of English with standard usage	Freely evolving regional dialects
British English	
	BBC English
	English English
	Scottish English
	Scots
	Norn
	Welsh English
	Ulster-Scots
Hiberno English	
Irish English	

copywriters . . ., to "Hinglish", the mix of Hindi and English' (Mazumdar *et al.* 2005: 64). In the post-apartheid era of South Africa, many Blacks have shaped their own version of English which is laced with indigenous words, as a 'sign of freedom'. This seems a preferable option to Afrikaans which is associated with past oppression.

Although all these groups speak very different Englishes, the print language is largely the same. For this reason we think of English as a global world language. This principle of diversification also applies to the German language. Austrians, Swiss and Germans all use the same print language but their spoken language is quite different. Reference has also been made earlier in this book to the case of Chinese which contains many dialects that are mutually incomprehensible but are unified at the level of print. Perhaps one of the reasons that minority languages have become marginalised is their insistence on distinctive print languages. If, for example, the six Celtic languages had a common spoken form, would they be considered endangered?

Official languages are simply those that have maintained unity at print level, have had access to state power and enjoyed the benefits of decades and centuries of state planning while minority languages are simply those that are now gaining access to power structures. They have not had the advantage of historical state support. Ultimately speakers of minority languages have lacked 'the political, institutional and ideological structures which can guarantee the relevance of those languages for the everyday life of members of such groups' (Nelde *et al.* 1996: 1).

Terminology in relation to regional languages needs to be revisited. Currently, there is an infinite variety of terms sometimes with partly overlapping meanings. Concepts such as 'lesser-taught languages', 'least-taught languages', 'lesser-used languages' and regional or minority languages need to be reconsidered. Instead one should direct the focus on speakers rather than on languages and, where possible, use concepts such as monolinguals, bilinguals and so on.

The focus on speakers rather than languages and the concept of community development was strongly reinforced in the *Euromosaic* study. Minority language communities frequently operate in the context of economic as well as geographic disadvantage. 'Most stateless, minority language groups are unfavourably located vis a vis economic advantage' (Nelde *et al.* 1996: 9). Yet they usually manage to develop their own dynamic. For many of these the EU context offers opportunities that are unavailable within the framework of the nation state and it may well be the case that the EU should adopt a multicentric language policy that would support 'the further development of these communities as autonomous systems against the background of local, regional and global challenges' (Directorate-General for Research 2002: 167).

The EU policy for languages spoken in the regions of Europe could focus on the advancement of the community as whole and offer support in different sectors such as economy, media and legislation. This is particularly relevant among groups that share languages with a neighbouring state. In such instances, the EU could support transfrontier co-operation in fields such as education, training, cultural production, broadcasting, information technology and so on. It is vital that those who wish to speak such regional languages are given the opportunity to survive economically in this context. By involving language planning experts in informing and training representatives of these communities, EU policy could ultimately aim at 'a greater self-sustainment for the communities in question' (Directorate-General for Research 2002: 167).

There may also be a case for extending the mechanisms which currently permit Irish and Catalan to be used in occasional plenary sessions of the Parliament so that other minority languages can be spoken on a sporadic basis. Such a gesture would have great symbolic significance as it would acknowledge the presence of these languages at official sessions and would not incur undue practical problems – although it might mean extra interpreters and cabins (Directorate-General for Research 2002: 68).

Ultimately the Union needs to reconsider its language policies to take stock of different ethnolinguistic language groups. *Euromosaic* has already pointed to different concepts for language policy within Europe. In the case of Southern (Mediterranean, Romance) countries, there appears to be a preference for legislation which recognises, protects and maintains language communities. Northern countries tend to support local rather than central measures and have a distinct preference for self-generated protective structures, specifically tailored to local needs. Language policy for nomadic communities should recognise their different systems of mapping and their diverse senses of place. 'The desiderata of language groups in Europe are so heterogeneous that *one* language policy cannot satisfy all ethnolinguistic groups and all minority speakers in the same way' (italics original in Nelde 2000: 445).

Conclusion

The focus of this book has been on language as a political rather than a linguistic concept and on the exploration of the link between language and various political entities. The implications of this study are to show that while some languages in the twenty-first century are infinitely more privileged than others, this is no indication of any inherent quality in the languages themselves. It is merely an inevitable consequence of state planning for languages and access to power.

Currently the EU places great emphasis on the importance of language skills for all its citizens. It suggests that 'building a common home in which to live, work and trade together means acquiring the skills to communicate with one another effectively and to understand one another better'. Moreover 'learning and speaking other languages encourages us to become more open to others, their cultures and outlooks' (Commission of the European Communities 2003: 3). The EU Action Plan is genuinely inclusive and citizens are encouraged to focus on 'smaller' as well as 'larger', migrant as well as autochthonous languages.

Overall the Action Plan appears to focus on the significance of language for economic reasons. Proficiency in language enables citizens to take advantage of the freedom to work in another member state. European companies with good intercultural and language skills will thrive in the global market-place. While economics is the key to language survival I would argue for a different emphasis. If we wish to maintain and promote linguistic diversity in contemporary Europe, it will be necessary to ensure that people can survive economically in their preferred language. This will require a shift of focus from the language itself to those that speak the language and will involve the development of a multicentric language policy that will cater to the settled, nomadic and migrant lifestyles that are a feature of contemporary society.

Select Bibliography

Accession Partnership and NPAA Priority (2001) *Promotion of Integration of Society in Latvia*, http://europa.eu.int/comm/enlargement/pas/phare/programme/national/latvia/2001/le0101–01-promotion-integration-society.pdf.

Adams, Gerry (1986) *Free Ireland: Towards a Lasting Peace*. Dingle: Brandon Books.

Adamson, Ian (1991) [1982] *The Identity of Ulster: The Land, The Language and The People*. Bangor: Pretani Press.

Ager, Dennis (1999) *Identity, Insecurity and Image: France and Language*. Clevedon: Multilingual Matters.

——(2003) *Ideology and Image: Britain and Language*. Clevedon: Multilingual Matters.

Aitken, A. J. and McArthur, Tom (eds) (1979) *Languages of Scotland*. Edinburgh: W & R Chambers.

Alcock, Antony (1998) *A Short History of Europe from the Greeks and Romans to the Present Day*. Basingstoke, New York: Macmillan.

——(2000) *A History of the Protection of Regional Cultural Minorities in Europe from the Edict of Nantes to the Present Day*. Basingstoke, New York: Macmillan.

An Anonymous Traveller (2002) 'Who We Really Are: Language and Identity' in John Kirk and Dónall Ó Baoill (eds), *Travellers and their Language*. Belfast: Cló Ollscoile na Banríona, pp. 169–79.

Anderson, Benedict (1991) [1983] *Imagined Communities: Reflections on the Origin and Spread of Nationalism*. London, New York: Verso.

Anonymous (2002a) 'Think Local: Cultural Imperialism Doesn't Sell', *The Economist*, 13 April, 12–14.

——(2002b) 'Europe's Muslims', *The Economist*, 10 August, 9–10.

——(2004a) 'Charlemagne: Real Politics at Last', *The Economist*, 30 October, 52.

——(2004b) 'Special Report: Turkey and the EU', *The Economist*, 18 September, 31–4.

Ascherson, Neal (1996) *Black Sea: The Birthplace of Civilisation and Barbarism*. London: Vintage.

Asp, Erkki (1995) 'The Lapps as a Minority Group in Finland' in Brunon Synak (ed.), *The Ethnic Identities of European Minorities: Theory and Case Studies*. Gdańsk: Wydawnictwo Uniwersytetu Gdańskiego, pp. 75–94.

Assembly of European Border Regions (1995) [1981] *European Charter of Border and Cross-Border Regions*, http://www.aebr.net/profil/pdfs/charta.en.pdf.

Bainbridge, Timothy and Teasdale, Anthony (1995) *The Penguin Companion to European Union*. Harmondsworth: Penguin.

Bakker, Peter (2001) 'Romani in Europe' in Guus Extra and Durk Gorter (eds), *The Other Languages of Europe: Demographic, Sociolinguistic and Educational Perspectives*. Clevedon: Multilingual Matters, pp. 293–313.

Bakker, Peter and Johan Häggman (2002) *Linguistic Diversity in Greece*. Brussels: European Bureau for Lesser Used Languages.

Balibar, Étienne (2004) *We, the People of Europe? Reflections on Transnational Citizenship*. Princeton and Oxford: Princeton University Press.

Barbour, Stephen (1996) 'Language and National Identity in Europe: Theoretical and Practical Problems' in Charlotte Hoffman (ed.), *Language, Culture and Communication in Contemporary Europe*. Clevedon: Multilingual Matters, pp. 28–45.

Barry, Brian (2000) *Culture and Equality: An Egalitarian Critique of Multiculturalism*. Cambridge: Polity Press.

Batchelor, Richard (2000) *What You Need to Know about Marketing English Language Courses*. London: British Council.

Bauman, Zigmunt (1998) *Globalization: The Human Consequences*. Cambridge: Polity Press.

Beardsmore, H. (1982) *Bilingualism: Basic Principles*. Clevedon: Multilingual Matters.

Bélinki, Karemla (2003) 'Yiddish in the Baltic and Nordic Countries', Unpublished paper at *Partnership for Diversity Network*, Helsinki.

Belt, Don (2004) 'Europe's Big Gamble', *National Geographic*, May, 54–65.

Berger, P. and Luckmann, T. (1991) *The Social Construction of Reality: A Treatise in the Sociology of Knowledge*. London: Penguin.

Berque, J. (1985) *L'immigration à l'école de la République. Rapport au Ministre de l'Éducation Nationale*. CNDP: La Documentation Française.

Bilaniuk, Laada (2003) 'Gender, language attitudes, and language status in Ukraine', *Language in Society*, 32, 47–78.

Billig, Michael (1995) *Banal Nationalism*. London: Sage.

Binchy, Alice (1994) 'Travellers' Language: a Sociolinguistic Perspective' in May McCann, May, Séamus Ó Síocháin, and Joseph Ruane (eds) (1994) *Irish Travellers: Culture and Ethnicity*. Belfast: Institute of Irish Studies, pp. 134–54.

——(2002) 'Travellers' Use of Shelta' in John Kirk and Dónall Ó Baoill (eds), *Travellers and their Language*. Belfast: Cló Ollscoile na Banríona, pp. 11–16.

Blair, Philip (2003) 'The European Charter for Regional or Minority Languages' in Dónall Ó Riagáin (ed.), *Language and Law in Northern Ireland*. Belfast: Cló Ollscoil na Banríona, pp. 38–44.

Blanke, Richard (1999) ' "Polish-speaking Germans" Language and National Identity among the Masurians', *Nationalities*, 27(3), 429–53.

Blaschke, Karlheinz, Toni Bruk, Ludmila Budar, Detlef Kobjela, Manfred Ladush, Maria Mirtschin, John Petrik and Detrich Scholze (1998) *The Sorbs in Germany*. Görlitz: Založba za serbski lud.

Blasco, Paloma Gay, Y. (2002) 'Gypsy/Roma Diasporas. A Comparative Perspective', *Social Anthropology*, 10(2), 173–88.

Blister-Broosen, Helga (2002) 'Alsace', *Journal of Multilingual and Multicultural Development*, 23(1/2), 98–111.

Bloomaert, Jan (1996) 'Language and Nationalism: Comparing Flanders and Tanzania', *Nations and Nationalism*, 2(2), 235–56.

Boelens, K. (1990) [1987] *The Frisian Language*. Leeuwarden: Provincial Government of Friesland.

Boneva, Bonka (1998) 'Ethnicity and the Nation: The Bulgarian Dilemma' in Christina Bratt Paulston and Donald Peckham (eds), *Linguistic Minorities in Central and Eastern Europe*. Clevedon: Multilingual Matters, pp. 80–97.

Borzyzkowski, Józef (1995) 'Lusatian Sorbs and the Kashubes: Similarities of History and Community of Existence' in Brunon Synak (ed.), *The Ethnic Identities of European Minorities: Theory and Case Studies*. Gdańsk: Wydawnictwo Uniwersytetu Gdańskiego, pp. 167–78.

Borzysykowski, Jósef (1996) Opening Address at Sixth International Conference on Minority Languages, Gdańsk University.

Bourdieu, Pierre (1977) *Outline of a Theory of Practice*. Cambridge: University Press.

——(1984) *Distinction: A Social Critique of the Judgement of Taste*. London: Routledge and Kegan Paul.

——(1990) *In Other Words*. Cambridge: Polity Press.

——(1991) *Language and Symbolic Power*. Cambridge: Polity Press.

——(1994) *Raisons Pratiques: Sur la Théorie de l' Action*. Paris: Éditions du Seuil.

Boyd, Sally (2001) 'Immigrant Languages in Sweden' in Guus Extra and Durk Gorter (eds), *The Other Languages of Europe: Demographic, Sociolinguistic and Educational Perspectives*. Clevedon: Multilingual Matters, pp. 177–92.

Brassloff, Audrey (1996) 'Centre-Periphery Communication in Spain: The Politics of Language and the Language of Politics' in Charlotte Hoffman (ed.), *Language, Culture and Communication in Contemporary Europe*. Clevedon: Multilingual Matters, pp. 111–31.

Breeillat, Dominique (2001) 'The European Charter for Regional or Minority Languages: the French Case', in the Organisation Board of the Coimbra Group (ed.), *Migration, Minorities, Compensation: Issues of Cultural Identity in Europe*. Brussels: The Coimbra Groups Working Party for Folklore and European Ethnology, pp. 19–29.

Brezigar, Bojan (1996) *Between Alps and Adriatic: The Slovenes in the European Union*. Brussels: European Bureau for Lesser Used Languages.

——(2004a) 'EBLUL out of the crisis by decentralisation' http://yeni.bitwise.it/default.php?s = events&p = news/newsitem.php&id = 196&m = &l = english.

——(2004b) 'The Role of the European Bureau for Lesser Used Languages within the EU Policy for Regional and Minority Languages', *Europa Ethnica*, 61(1), 52–5.

Broadbridge, Judith (1998) 'The Ethnolinguistic Vitality of Alsatian-speakers in Southern Alsace, in Stefan Wolff (ed.), *German Minorities in Europe: Ethnic Identity and Cultural Belonging*. Oxford: New York: Berghahn, pp. 47–62.

Broeder, Peter and Extra, Guus (1999) *Language, Ethnicity and Education: Case Studies of Immigrant Minority Groups and Immigrant Minority Languages*. Clevedon: Multilingual Matters.

Burgarsksi, R. (1995) *Jezik od mira do rata* [Language from Peace to War]. Belgrade: Slovograf.

Burgess, Adam (1997) *Divided Europe: The New Domination of the East*. London: Pluto Press.

Burke, Mary (2002) 'Hidden like a Religious Arcanum: Irish Writing and Shelta's Secret History' in John Kirk and Dónall Ó Baoill (eds), *Travellers and their Language*. Belfast: Cló Ollscoile na Banríona, pp. 79–100.

Busch, Brigitta (1997) *Slovenian: The Slovenian Language in Education in Austria*. Ljouwert/Leeuwarden: Mercator-Education.

——(2001) 'Slovenian in Carintha' in Guus Extra and Durk Gorter (eds), *The Other Languages of Europe: Demographic, Sociolinguistic and Educational Perspectives*. Clevedon: Multilingual Matters, pp. 119–36.

Carcassonne, G. (1987) *Etude sur la Compatibilité entre la Charte Européene des Languages Régionales ou Minoritaires et la Constitution. La Documentation Francaise*, 8 Septembre 1998, http://www.admifrance.gouv.fr.

Cassar, Carmel (2001) 'Malta: Language, Literacy and Identity in a Mediterranean Island Society', *National Identities*, 3(3), 257–75.

Caubet, Dominique (2001) 'Maghrebine Arabic in France' in Guus Extra and Durk Gorter (eds), *The Other Languages of Europe: Demographic, Sociolinguistic and Educational Perspectives*. Clevedon: Multilingual Matters, pp. 260–77.

Cenoz, Jasone (2001) 'Basque in Spain and France' in Guus Extra and Durk Gorter (eds), *The Other Languages of Europe: Demographic, Sociolinguistic and Educational Perspectives*. Clevedon: Multilingual Matters, pp. 45–57.

Cerquiglini, B. (1999) Les Language de la France. Site de la Délégation à la Langue Française, http://dglf.culture.fr.

Chaker, S. (1988) 'Le Berbère' in Geneviève Vermes (ed.), *Ving-cinq Communautés Linguistiques de la France, Vol 2. Les Language Immigrées*. Paris: L'harmattm, pp. 145–64.

Cheesman, Tom (2001) ' "Old" and "New" Lesser-Used Languages of Europe: Common Cause' in Camille O'Reilly (ed.), *Language, Ethnicity and the State: Vol 1: Minority Languages in the European Union*. Basingstoke: Palgrave, pp. 147–68.

Christiansen, P. (1996) 'Culture and Politics in a Historical Europe', *Ethnologia Europaea*, 26(2), 137–46.

CIEMEN (Centre International Eacarré per a les Minories Étniques I les Nacions) (2002) *The European Union and Lesser-Used Languages*. Luxembourg: European Parliament.

Cleeve, Brian (1983) 'The Secret Language', *Studies*, 287, 252–61.

Cohen, M. (1971) *Materiaux pour une Sociologie du Language* 1. Paris Maspero.

Commission of the European Communities (2002) Report from the Commission to the Council, the European Parliament, The Economic and Social Committee and the Committee of the Regions: The Implementation and Results of the European Year of Languages 2001. Brussels: European Commission.

——(2003) *Promoting Language Learning and Linguistic Diversity: An Action Plan 2004–2006*. Brussels: European Commission.

Committee of the Regions (2001) *Opinion on the Promotion and Safeguard of Regional and Minority Languages*. Brussels: European Union.

Conference of the Representatives of the Governments of the Member States (2004) *Consolidated Version of the Treaty Establishing the European Community*, http://www.europa.eu.int/eur-lex/en/treaties/dat/C_2002325EN.003301. html#anArt152.

Conversi, Daniele (1990) 'Language or Race', *Ethnic and Racial Studies*, 13(1), 50–70.

——(1997) *The Basques, the Catalans and Spain: Alternative Routes to Nationalist Mobilisation*. London: Hurst.

Council of Europe (1992a) *European Charter for Regional or Minority languages*, ETS, No.158, http://conventions.coe.int/Treaty/EN/Treaties/Html/148.htm.

——(1992b) *European Charter for Regional or Minority languages: Explanatory Report*, http://conventions.coe.int/Treaty/en/Reports/Html/148.htm.

——(1995) *Framework Convention for the Protection of National Minorities*, http://conventions.coe.int/Treaty/EN/Treaties/Html/157.htm.

Crawley Quinn, Josephine (2002) 'Ancient Rome' in John Stevenson (ed.), *The History of Europe*. London: Octopus Publishing Group, pp. 54–89.

Crystal, David (1997a) *English as a Global Language*. Cambridge: Cambridge University Press.

——(1997b) *The Cambridge Encyclopaedia of Language*. Cambridge: Cambridge University Press.

——(1999a) 'The Death of Language', *Prospect*, November, 56–9.

——(1999b) 'Death Sentence', *Guardian*, 25 October, G2, 2–3.

——(2000) *Language Death*. Cambridge: Cambridge University Press.

Cunningham, Kristina (2001) 'Translating for a Larger Union', http://europa.eu.int/comm/translation/reading/articles/.

Cussans, Thomas, Philip Parker, Barry Winkleman, Oliver Cicely and Jane Cheverton (eds) (1998) *The Times Atlas of European History*. London: Times Books.

Daftary, Farimah and François Grin (eds) (2003) *Nation-Building, Ethnicity and Language Politics in Transition Countries*. Flensburg: European Centre for Minority Issues.

Daftary, Farimah and Gál Kinga (2000) *The New Slovak Language Law: Internal or External Politics?* Flensburg: European Centre for Minority Issues.

——(2003) 'The 1999 Slovak Minority Language Law: Internal or Eternal Politics?' in Farmiah Daftary and François Grin (eds), *Nation-Building, Ethnicity and Language Politics in Transition Countries*. Flensburg: European Centre for Minority Issues, pp. 31–71.

Dáil Éireann (1999) *An Bille um Chomhaontú na Breataine-na hÉireann: British-Irish Agreement Bill*. Dublin: Government Publications Office.

Dalby, Andrew (2003) *Language in Danger*. London: Penguin.

Davies, Norman (1997) *Europe – A History*. London: Pimlico.

Dawood, N. trans. (1999) [1956] *The Koran*. London: Penguin.

De Cillia, Menz Rudolf, Dressler Florian, Wolfgang and Petra Cech (1998) 'Linguistic Minorities in Austria', in Christina Bratt Paulston and Donald Peckham (eds), *Linguistic Minorities in Central and Eastern Europe*. Clevedon: Multilingual Matters, pp. 18–36.

Delanty, Gerard (1995) *Inventing Europe*. Basingstoke: Macmillan.

Demirdirek, H. (1998) *Re-claiming Nationhood through Re-nativization of Language: The Gagauz in Moldova*, paper presented at the workshop 'The Politics of Language Diversity and National Identity across Europe', 5th EASA Conference, Frankfurt am Main, 4–7 September 1990.

Department of Health and Social Services (1993) *The Northern Ireland Census 1991: Irish Language Report*. Belfast: HMSO.

Der Avoird, Tim Van, Peter Broeder and Guus Extra (2001) 'Immigrant Minority Languages in the Netherlands' in Guus Extra and Durk Gorter (eds), *The Other Languages of Europe: Demographic, Sociolinguistic and Educational Perspectives*. Clevedon: Multilingual Matters, pp. 215–42.

Deutsch, Karl (1968) 'The Trend of European Nationalism – the Language Aspect' in Joshua A. Fishman (ed.), *Readings in the Sociology of Language*, pp. 598–606.

de Varennes, Ferdinand (1996) *Language, Minorities and Human Rights*. The Hague: Kluwer Law International.

DiGiacomo, Susan (2001) ' "Catalan is Everyone's Thing": Normalizing a Nation', in Camille O'Reilly (ed.), *Language, Ethnicity and the State: Vol 1: Minority Languages in the European Union*. Basingstoke: Palgrave, pp. 56–77.

Directorate-General for Research (2002) *The European Union and Lesser-Used Languages*, Luxembourg: European Parliament.

Dobson, John (2001) 'Ethnic Discrimination in Latvia' in Camille O'Reilly (ed.), *Language, Ethnicity and the State: Vol. 2: Minority Languages in Eastern Europe post 1989*. Basingstoke: Palgrave, pp. 155–87.

Douglas, Sheila (2002) 'Travellers' Cant in Scotland' in John Kirk and Dónall Ó Baoill (eds), *Travellers and their Language*. Belfast: Cló Ollscoile na Banríona, pp. 155–60.

Douglas, Sheila (2002) 'Unblocking the Right Nostril' in John M. Kirk and Dónall Ó Baoill, *Language Planning and Education: Linguistic Issues in Northern Ireland, the Republic of Ireland, and Scotland*. Belfast: Cló Ollscoile na Banríona, pp. 192–7.

Drakulic, Slavenka (1996) *Café Europa: Life After Communism*. New York, London: Penguin.

Druviete, Ina (1998) 'Republic of Latvia' in Christina Bratt Paulston and Donald Peckham (eds), *Linguistic Minorities in Central and Eastern Europe*. Clevedon: Multilingual Matters, pp. 160–83.

——(1999) 'Language Policy in a Changing Society: Problematic Issues in the Implementation of International Linguistic Human Rights Standards' in Miklós Kontra, Robert Phillipson, Tove Skutnabb-Kangas and Tibor Várady (eds), *Language: A Right and a Resource: Approaching Linguistic Human Rights*. Budapest: Central European University Press, pp. 263–76.

Drysdale, Helen (2001) *Mother Tongues: Travels through Tribal Europe*. London: Picador.

Dunkerley, David, Lesley Hodgson, Stanislaw Konopacki, Tony Spybey and Andrew Thompson (2002) *Changing Europe: Identities, Nations and Citizens*. London and New York: Routledge.

Durand, Jacques (1996) 'Linguistic Purification, the French Nation-State and the Linguist' in Charlotte Hoffman (ed.), *Language, Culture and Communication in Contemporary Europe*. Clevedon: Multilingual Matters, pp. 75–92.

Durkacz, Victor (1983) *The Decline of the Celtic Languages: A Study of Linguistic and Cultural Conflict in Scotland, Wales and Ireland from the Reformation to the Twentieth Century*. Edinburgh: John Donald Publishers Ltd.

EBLUL (2004) Recommendations for the IGC on the Draft Treaty of the European Constitution, http://ww2.eblul.org:8080/eblul/Public/le_bureau/press_releases/eblul.recommendation/view.

Edmund, John (2002) 'Ulster-Scots Language and Culture' in John M. Kirk and Dónall Ó Baoill, *Language Planning and Education: Linguistic Issues in Northern Ireland, the Republic of Ireland, and Scotland*. Belfast: Cló Ollscoile na Banríona, pp. 175–82.

Edmundson, Ricca and Níall Ó Murchadha (2002) 'Collecting the Cant' in John Kirk and Dónall Ó Baoill (eds), *Travellers and their Language*. Belfast: Cló Ollscoile na Banríona, pp. 113–24.

Edwards, John (1985) *Language, Society and Identity*. Oxford: Blackwell.

——(1990) 'Notes for a Minority-Language Typology: Procedures and Justification', *Journal of Multilingual and Multicultural Development*, 11(1, 2), 137–51.

Edwards, Vivian (2001) 'Community Languages in the United Kingdom' in Guus Extra and Durk Gorter (eds), *The Other Languages of Europe: Demographic, Sociolinguistic and Educational Perspectives*. Clevedon: Multilingual Matters, pp. 243–60.

Eichinger, Ludwig (2002) 'South-Tyrol: German and Italian in a Changing World', *Journal of Multilingual and Multicultural Development*, 23(1, 2), 137–49.

Ekeus, Rolph (2002) *From the Copenhagen Criteria to the Copenhagen Summit: The Protection of National Minorities in an Enlarging Europe*, http://www.osce.org/hcnm/documents/speeches/2002/hcnmspeech2002-6.pdf.

Eliasson, Yvonne (2003) 'The Present Situation of the Swedish Language on Åland' unpublished paper at third international conference of Partnership for Diversity Network, Helsinki.

Eriksen, Thomas Hylland (1993) *Ethnicity and Nationalism: Anthropological Perspectives*. London: Pluto.

European Bureau for Lesser Used Languages (1997) *Lesser Used Languages in Austria, Finland and Sweden*. Luxembourg: European Parliament.

——(2001) Charleroi-Declaration, First Contribution by EBLUL to the Debate on the Future of the European Union, http://ww2.eblul.org:8080/eblul/Public/ le_bureau/final_document/charleroi-declaratio/view.

——(2002) Ljouwert-Declaration, Declaration on Linguistic Diversity and the Future of the European Union, http://ww2.eblul.org:8080/eblul/Public/ le_bureau/final_document/ljouwert-declaration/view.

European Commission (ed.) (1981) 'European Parliament Resolution on a Community Charter of Regional Languages and Cultures and on a Charter Rights of Rights of Ethnic Minorities by Gaetano Arfé', *Official Journal of the European Communities*, C 287, 9 November, 106.

——(ed.), (1983) 'European Parliament Resolution on Measures in Favour of Minority Languages and Cultures, by Gaetano Arfé', *Official Journal of the European Communities*, C 068, 14 March, 103.

——(ed.) (1987) 'European Parliament Resolution on the Languages and Cultures of Regional and Ethnic Minorities in the European Community, by Willy Kuijpers', *Official Journal of the European Communities*, C 318, 30 November 1987, 160.

——(ed.) (1991) 'European Parliament Resolution on the Situation of Languages of the Community and the Catalan language, by Vivianne Reding', *Official Journal of the European Communities*, C 019, 28 January 1991, 42, 110.

——(ed.) (1994) 'European Parliament Resolution on Linguistic and Cultural Minorities in the European Community, by Mark Killilea', *Official Journal of the European Communities*, C 061, 28 February 1994.

——(ed.) (2001) 'European Parliament Resolution on the Promotion of Linguistic Diversity and Language Learning in the Framework of the Implementation of the Objectives of the European Year of Languages 2001, by Eluned Morgan', *Official Journal of the European Communities*, C 177, 25 July, 334.

——(ed.) (2002) 'Council Resolution on the Promotion of Linguistic Diversity and Language Learning in the Framework of the Implementation of the Objectives of the European Year of Languages', *Official Journal of the European Communities*, C 50/1, 23 February.

——(2004) *Many Tongues, One Family: Languages in the European Union*. Luxembourg: Office for Official Publications of the European Communities.

European Parliament (2002) *The European Union and Lesser-Used Languages*, working paper, EDUC 108 N. Brussels.

Executive Summary (2001) *Eurobarometer Report 54: Europeans and Languages*, http://europa.eu.int/comm/public_opinion/artchives/eb/ ebs_147_summ_en_pdf.

Extra, Guus (2002) 'The Other Languages of Multicultural Europe: Perceptions, Facts and Educational Bodies' in S. Baker (ed.), *Language Policy: Lessons from Global Models*, Monteray, Monteray Institute of International Studies, pp. 130–51.

Extra, Guus and Gorter, Durk (2001) 'Comparative Perspectives on Regional and Immigrant Minority Languages in Multicultural Europe' in Guus Extra and Durk Gorter (eds), *The Other Languages of Europe: Demographic, Sociolinguistic and Educational Perspectives*. Clevedon: Multilingual Matters, pp. 1–41.

Extra, Guus and Yagmur, Kutlay (2002) *Language Diversity in Multicultural Europe: Comparative Perspectives on Immigrant Minority Languages at Home and at School*, MOST Discussion 63. Paris: UNESCO.

Extra, Guus and Yagmur, Kutlay (2002) *Language Diversity in Multicultural Europe: Comparative Perspectives on Immigrant Minority Languages at Home and at School*. Paris: MOST Programme.

Faulks, Keith (2000) *Citizenship*. London and New York: Routledge.

Favell, Adrian and Hansen, Randall (2002) 'Markets against Politics: Migration, EU Enlargement and the Idea of Europe', *Journal of Ethnic and Migration Studies*, 28(4), 581–601.

Feitsma, A. (1981) 'Why and How do the Frisian Language and Identity Continue', in Einer Haugen, J. Derrick McClure and Derrick Thomson (eds), *Minority Languages Today*. Edinburgh: Edinburgh University Press, pp. 163–82.

Fernández-Armesto, Felipe (1994) *The Times Guide to the Peoples of Europe*. London: Times Books, HarperCollins.

Fenton, Steve (1999) *Ethnicity: Racism, Class and Culture*. Basingstoke: Macmillan.

Fenyvesi, Anna (1998) 'Linguistic Minorities in Hungary' in Christina Bratt Paulston and Donald Peckham (eds), *Linguistic Minorities in Central and Eastern Europe*. Clevedon: Multilingual Matters, pp. 135–59.

Field, Heather (n.d.) 'EU Cultural Policy and the Creation of a Common European Identity', http://www.pols.canterbury.ac/nz/ECSANZ/papers/Field.htm.

Fischer, Andreas (2001) 'Language and Politics in Switzerland' in John, M. Kirk and Dónall Ó Baoill (2001) *Linguistic Politics: Language Policies for Northern Ireland, the Republic of Ireland, and Scotland*. Belfast: Cló Ollscoile na Banríona, pp. 105–22.

Fishman, Joshua (1980: 87) 'Social Theory and Ethnography: Language and Ethnicity in Eastern Europe' in P. Sugar (ed.), *Ethnic Diversity and Conflict in Eastern Europe*. Santa Barbara California: ABC-Clio, pp. 69–99.

——(1991) *Reversing Language Shift: Theoretical and Empirical Foundations of Assistance to Threatened Languages*. Clevedon: Multilingual Matters.

Foley, Nadette (2000) 'Language, Discrimination and the Good Friday Agreement: the Case of Ethnic Minority Languages' in John, M. Kirk and Dónall Ó Baoill (eds), *Language and Politics: Northern Ireland, the Republic of Ireland, and Scotland*. Belfast: Cló Óllscoile na Banríona, pp. 101–5.

Føllesdal, Andreas (1999) 'Third Country Nationals as European Citizens: The Case Defended', *The Sociological Review*, 104–22.

Fontaine, Pascal (1993) *A Citizen's Europe*. Luxemburg: Office for Official Publications of the European Communities.

Fontana, Gino (2003) 'Bilingualism and Protection of the Minorities in Trentino-South Tyrol' unpublished paper at third international conference of Partnership for Diversity Network, Helsinki.

Foras na Gaeilge (n.d.) *Foras na Gaeilge: Ré Nua don Teanga*, Dublin: Foras na Gaeilge.

Foucault, Michel (1979) *Discipline and Punish: The Birth of the Prison*. Translated by Alan Sheridan. New York: Vintage Books.

Frank, Robert (2002) 'The Meanings of Europe in French National Discourse: A French Europe or an Europeanized France' in Malmborg, Mikael af and Stråth, Bo (eds), *The Meaning of Europe: Variety and Contention within and among Nations*. Oxford, New York: Berg, pp. 311–26.

Fraser Gupta, Anthea (2002) 'Privileging Indigeneity' in John M. Kirk and Dónall Ó Baoill, *Language Planning and Education: Linguistic Issues in Northern Ireland, the Republic of Ireland, and Scotland*. Belfast: Cló Ollscoile na Banríona, pp. 290–99.

García, Bernabé Lópes and Molina, Laura Mijares (2001) 'Moroccan Children and Arabic in Spanish Schools' in Guus Extra and Durk Gorter (eds), *The Other Languages of Europe: Demographic, Sociolinguistic and Educational Perspectives*. Clevedon: Multilingual Matters, pp. 279–91.

Gardner, Nick (2000) *Basque: The Basque Language in Education in Spain*. Ljouwert/Leeuwarden: Mercator-Education.

Gilbert, Andrea (2003) 'Ulster-Scots in Education in Northern Ireland: The History of the Language' in Dónall Ó Riagáin (ed.), *Language and Law in Northern Ireland*. Belfast: Cló Ollscoile na Banríona, pp. 78–87.

Giddens, Anthony (1991) [1990] *The Consequences of Modernity*. Cambridge: Polity Press.

Glenny, Misha (1992) *The Fall of Yugoslavia: The Third Balkan War*. London: Penguin.

Gogolin, Ingrid and Reich, Hans (2001) 'Immigrant Languages in Federal Germany' in Guus Extra and Durk Gorter (eds), *The Other Languages of Europe: Demographic, Sociolinguistic and Educational Perspectives*. Clevedon: Multilingual Matters, pp. 193–214.

Goodwin, Jason (1999) *Lords of the Horizons: A History of the Ottoman Empire*. London: Vintage.

Görlach, Manfred (2001) 'Frisian and Low German: Minority Languages in Hiding' in John, M. Kirk and Dónall Ó Baoill (eds), *Linguistic Politics: Language Policies for Northern Ireland, the Republic of Ireland, and Scotland*. Belfast: Cló Ollscoile na Banríona, pp. 67–87.

Gorter, Durk (1989) 'Dutch State Policy Towards the Frisian Language', *Ethnic Studies Report*, VIII(1), 36–47.

Gorter, Durk, Alex Riemersma, and Jehannes Ytsma (2001) 'Frisian in the Netherlands' in Guus Extra and Durk Gorter (eds), *The Other Languages of Europe: Demographic, Sociolinguistic and Educational Perspectives*. Clevedon: Multilingual Matters, pp. 103–18.

Government of the United Kingdom of Great Britain and Northern Ireland and Government of Ireland (1998) *Agreement Reached in the Multi-Party Negotiations*. Belfast.

Graddol, David (1997) *The Future of English? A Guide to Forecasting the Popularity of the English Language in the 21st Century*. London: The British Council.

Graham, Brian (1998) 'Modern Europe: Fractures and Faults' in Brian Graham (ed.), *Modern Europe: Place, Culture, Identity*. London, Sydney and Auckland: Arnold Press, pp. 1–15.

Grant, Richard (1998) 'The Political Geography of European Integration' in Brian Graham (ed.), *Modern Europe: Place, Culture, Identity*. London, Sydney and Auckland: Arnold Press, pp. 145–63.

Grass, Günter (1992) 'Losses', *Granta*, 42, 97–108.

Greenberg, Robert (1999) 'In the Aftermath of Yugoslavia's Collapse: The Politics of Language Death and Language Birth', *International Politics*, 36, 141–58.

——(2001) 'Language, Nationalism and the Yugoslav Successor States' in Camille O'Reilly (ed.), *Language, Ethnicity and the State: Vol. 2: Minority Languages in Eastern Europe post 1989*. Basingstoke: Palgrave, pp. 17–43.

Gregory Campbell, F. (1975) *Confrontation in Eastern Europe: Weimar Germany and Czechoslovakia*. Chicago: University of Chicago Press.

Grillo, Ralph (1989) *Dominant Languages: Language and Hierarchy in Britain and France*. Cambridge: Cambridge University Press.

Grimes, B. (2000) *Ethnologue: Languages of the World*, Vol. 1, 14th Edition. Texas: US Summer School of Linguistics.

Grin, François (1991) 'The Estonian Language Law: Presentation with Comments', *Language Problems and Language Planning*, 15(2), 191–201.

——(2000) *Evaluating Policy Measures for Minority Languages in Europe: Towards Effective, Cost-effective and Democratic Implementation*. Flensburg: European Centre for Minority Issues.

——(2003) *Language Policy Evaluation and the European Charter for Regional or Minority Languages*. Basingstoke: Palgrave/Macmillan.

Grin, François and Moring, Tom (2002) *Final Report: Support for Minority Languages in Europe*. Brussels: European Bureau for Lesser Used Languages.

Grin, François and Vaillancourt, François (1999) The *Cost-effectiveness Evaluation of Minority Language Policies: Case Studies on Wales, Ireland and the Basque Country*. Flensburg: European Centre for Minority Issues.

Guerrina, R. (2002). *Europe: History, Ideas, Ideologies*. London: Arnold.

Gutmann, Amy (1994) 'Introduction', in Charles Taylor (ed.), *Multiculturalism: Examining the Politics of Recognition*. Princeton: Princeton University Press, pp. 3–24.

Haarmann, Harald (1998) 'Multilingual Russia and its Soviet Heritage' in Christina Bratt Paulston and Donald Peckham (eds), *Linguistic Minorities in Central and Eastern Europe*. Clevedon: Multilingual Matters, pp. 224–54.

Habermas, Júrgen (2001) 'A Constitution for Europe?', *New Left Review*, 11, 5–26.

Hale, John (1993) 'The Renaissance Idea of Europe' in Soledad García (ed.), *European Identity and the Search for Legitimacy*. London and New York: Pinter Publishers, pp. 46–63.

Halwachs, Dieter (2003) 'The Changing Status of Romani in Europe' in Gabrielle Hogan-Brun and Stefan Wolff (eds), *Minority Languages in Europe: Frameworks, Status, Prospects*. Basingstoke: Palgrave/Macmillan, pp. 192–207.

Hancock, Ian (1999) 'The Schooling of Romani Americans: An Overview', keynote paper at the Second International Conference on Psycholinguistic and Sociolinguistic Problems of Roma Children's Education in Europe, http://www.geocities.com/Paris/5121/schooling.htm.

——(2003) 'Language Corpus and Language Politics: The Case of the Standardization of Romani' in Farmiah Daftary and François Grin (eds), *Nation-Building, Ethnicity and Language Politics in Transition Countries*. Flensburg: European Centre for Minority Issues, pp. 269–86.

Hannerz, Ulf (1996) *Transnational Connections: Culture, People, Places*. London and New York: Routledge.

Hansson, Ulf (2002) 'The Latvian Language Legislation and the Involvement of the OSCE-HCNM: The Developments 2000–2002', *The Global Review of Ethnopolitics*, 2(1), 17–28.

Hardie, Kim (1996) 'Lowland Scots: Issues in Nationalism and Identity' in Charlotte Hoffman (ed.), *Language, Culture and Communication in Contemporary Europe*. Clevedon: Multilingual Matters, pp. 61–74.

Hastings, Adrian (1997) *The Construction of Nationhood: Ethnicity, Religion and Nationalism*. Cambridge: University Press.

Haugen, Einar (1966) 'Dialect, Language, Nation', *American Anthropologist*, 68(4), 922–36.

Hemminga, Piet (2001) *Sorbian: The Sorbian Language in Education in Germany*. Ljouwert/Leeuwarden: Mercator-Education.

Henderson, Tracy (1996) 'Language and Identity in Galicia: the Current Orthographic Debate' in Clare Mar-Molinero and Angel Smith (eds), *Nationalism and the Nation in the Iberian Peninsula: Competing and Conflicting Identities*. Oxford, Washington DC: Berg, pp. 237–51.

Henrad, Kristin (2003) 'Devising an Adequate System of Minority Protection in the Area of Language Rights' in Gabrielle Hogan-Brun and Stefan Wolff (eds), *Minority Languages in Europe: Frameworks, Status, Prospects*. Basingstoke: Palgrave/Macmillan, pp. 37–55.

Hobsbawm, Eric (1990) *Nations and Nationalism since 1780*. Cambridge: Cambridge University Press.

——(1992) 'Ethnicity and Nationalism in Europe Today', *Anthropology Today*, 8(1), 3–8.

Hobsbawm, Eric and Ranger, Trevor (eds) (1983) *The Invention of Tradition*. Cambridge: University Press.

Hogan-Brun, Gabrielle (2003) 'Baltic National Minorities in a Transitional Setting' in Gabrielle Hogan-Brun and Stefan Wolff (eds), *Minority Languages in Europe: Frameworks, Status, Prospects*. Basingstoke: Palgrave/Macmillan, pp. 120–37.

——(2004) 'Baltic Language and Integration Network: Second Workshop on "Baltic Language Policies in and Enlarged EU" ', www.blain-online.org.

Hogan-Brun, Gabrielle and Ramonienè, Meilutè (2003) 'Emerging Language and Education Policies in Lithuania', *Language Policy*, 2, 27–45.

Hogan-Brun, Gabrielle and Wolff, Stefan (2003) 'Minority Languages in Europe: An Introduction to the Current Debate' in Gabrielle Hogan-Brun and Stefan Wolff (eds), *Minority Languages in Europe: Frameworks, Status, Prospects*. Basingstoke: Palgrave/Macmillan, pp. 3–15

Hogan-Brun, Gabrielle and Ramonienè, Meilutè (2004) 'Changing Levels of Bilingualism across the Baltic', *Bilingual Education and Bilingualism*, 7(1), 62–77.

Hogan-Brun, Gabrielle and Ramonienè, Meilutè (2005) 'Perspectives on Language Attitudes and Use in Lithuania's Multilingual Setting', *Journal of Multilingual and Multicultural Development* 26(5), forthcoming.

Holder, Daniel (2003) *In Other Words? Mapping Minority Ethnic Languages in Northern Ireland*. Belfast: Multi-Cultural Resource Centre.

Horowitz, Donald L. (1985) *Ethnic Groups in Conflict*. Berkeley: University of California Press.

Huss, Leena (2001) 'The National Minority Languages in Sweden', in Guus Extra and Durk Gorter (eds), *The Other Languages of Europe: Demographic, Sociolinguistic and Educational Perspectives*. Clevedon: Multilingual Matters, pp. 137–57.

Ignatieff, Michael (1994) *Blood and Belonging: Journeys into the New Nationalism*. London: BBC Books Chatto and Windus.

Irwin, Greg (1996) *Ethnic Minorities in Northern Ireland*. Coleraine: University of Ulster.

Irwin, Greg and Dunn, Séamus (eds) (1997) *Ethnic Minorities in Northern Ireland*. Coleraine: University of Ulster.

Iskierski, Jnausz and Latoszek, Marek (1995) 'The Kashubian Ethnic Group in the Prologue to Change: Local and Regional Perspectives' in Brunon Synak (ed.),

The Ethnic Identities of European Minorities: Theory and Case Studies. Gdańsk: Wydawnictwo Uniwersytetu Gdańskiego, pp. 95–116.

Jacobson, D. (1996) *Right across Borders: Immigration and the Decline of Citizenship.* Baltimore: John Hopkins University Press.

Jaffe, Alexandra (2001) 'State Language Ideology and the Shifting Nature of Minority Language Planning on Corsica' in Camille O'Reilly (ed.), *Language, Ethnicity and the State: Vol 1: Minority Languages in the European Union.* Basingstoke: Palgrave/Macmillan, pp. 40–55.

James, Simon (1999) The *Atlantic Celts: Ancient People or Modern Invention.* London: British Museum Press.

Jansen, Thomas (1999) 'European Identity and/or the Identity of the European Union' in Thomas Jansen (ed.), *Reflections on European Identity*, Working Paper, European Commission, Forward Studies Unit, http:/europa.eu.int/comm./cdp/working-paper/European_identity_en.pdf.

Järve, Priit (2003) 'Language Battles in the Baltic States: 1989 to 2002' in Farmiah Daftary and François Grin (eds), *Nation-Building, Ethnicity and Language Politics in Transition Countries.* Flensburg: European Centre for Minority Issues, pp. 75–105.

Jenkins, Richard (2002) *Pierre Bourdieu.* London and New York: Routledge.

Jordan, Petper (1998) 'Romania' in Christina Bratt Paulston and Donald Peckham (eds), *Linguistic Minorities in Central and Eastern Europe.* Clevedon: Multilingual Matters, pp. 184–23.

Judge, A. and Judge, S. (2000) 'Linguistic Policies in France and Contemporary Issues: The Signing of the Charter for Regional and Minority Languages', *International Journal of Francophone Studies*, 3(2), 106–27.

Julios, Christina (2002) 'Towards a European Common Language Policy' in Mary Farrell, Stefano Fella and Michael Newman (eds), *European Integration in the 21st Century, Unity in Diversity?* London: Sage, pp. 184–201.

Kaivola-Bregenhøj, Annikki (2001) 'Finns in Sweden: Snapshots of Dalarna' in the Organisation Board of the Coimbra Group (ed.), *Migration, Minorities, Compensation: Issues of Cultural Identity in Europe.* Brussels: The Coimbra Group's Working Party for Folklore and European Ethnology, pp. 121–42.

Kamusella, Tomasz (2001) 'Language as an Instrument of Nationalism in Central Europe', *Nations and Nationalism*, 7(2), 235–51.

Kaplan, Robert (1994) *Balkan Ghosts: A Journey Through History.* New York: First Vintage Departures.

Katičić;, Radoslav (1972) 'Identitiet Jezika' (the Identity of Language), *Suvremena Lingvistika*, 5–6, 5–14.

Kay, Billy (1986*) Scots: The Mither Tongue.* Ayrshire: Alloway Publishing Ltd.

Kedourie, Eli (1966) *Nationalism.* London: Hurst.

Kennedy, Frances (1998) 'Italians Ask: "What Did the Romans Ever Do for Us?" ', *Sunday Independent*, 15 November, p. 19.

Kenrick, Donald (1994) 'Irish Travellers – A Unique Phenomenon in Europe?' in May McCann, Seamus Ó Síocháin, and Joseph Ruane (eds), *Irish Travellers: Culture and Ethnicity.* Belfast: Institute of Irish Studies, pp. 20–33.

Kivisto, Peter (2002) *Multiculturalism in a Global Society.* London: Blackwell.

Kockel, Ullrich (1999) *Borderline Cases: The Ethnic Frontiers of European Integration.* Liverpool: Liverpool University Press.

——(2003) 'EuroVisions: Journeys to the Heart of a Lost Continent', *Journal of Contemporary European Studies*, 11(1), 53–66.

Kofos, Evangelos (1989) 'National Heritage and National Identity in Nineteenth-and Twentieth-Century Macedonia', *European Historical Quarterly*, 19, 229–67.

Kohn, Hans (1967) *Prelude to Nation States: The French and German Experience 1789–1915*. New York: Van Nostrand.

Kostakopoulou, T. (2001) *Citizenship, Identity and Immigration in the European Union: Between Past and Future*. Manchester and New York: Manchester University Press.

Köstlin, Konrad (1988) 'Die Erfahrung des Fremden' in Ina Greverus, Konrad Köstlin, and Holga Schilling (eds), *Kultur-kontact, Kulturfonflikt: zur Erfahrung des Fremden*, Frankfurt am Main: *Institut für Kulturanthropologie und Europäische Ethnologie der Universität am Main*, pp. 17–26.

Kristeva, Julia (1982) *Powers of Horror: An Essay on Abjection*, translated by Leon S. Roudiez. New York: Columbia Press.

Kymlicka, Will (ed.) (1995) *The Rights of Minority Cultures*. Oxford: University Press.

Kymlicka, Will and Grin, François (2003) 'Assessing the Politics of Diversity in Transition Countries' in Farmiah Daftary and François Grin (eds), *Nation-Building, Ethnicity and Language Politics in Transition Countries*. Flensburg: European Centre for Minority Issues, pp. 5–27.

Lainio, Jarmo (2001) *Meänkieli and Swedish Finnish: The Finnic Languages in Education in Sweden*. Ljouwert/Leeuwarden: Mercator-Education.

Laitin, David (1996) 'Language Planning in the Former Soviet Union: The Case of Estonia', *International Journal of the Sociology of Language*, 118, 43–61.

Lehning, P. (1999) 'European Citizenship: Towards a European Identity?', University of Wisconsin Madison, Working Papers Series, European Studies, 2(3), http://polyglot.lss.wisc.edu/eur/.

Lehtola, Veli-Pekka (2002) *The Sámi People: Traditions in Transition*. Aanaa – Inari: Kustannus-Puntsi.

Leprêtre, Marc (1992) *The Catalan Language Today*. Barcelona: Departament de Cultura.

Lepschy, Giulio (1994) 'How Many Languages does Europe Need?', in M.M. Parry, W.V. Davies and R.A.M. Temple (eds), *The Changing Voices of Europe: Social and Political Changes and their Linguistic Repercussions, Past, Present and Future*. Cardiff: University of Wales Press.

Lindgren, Anna-Rütta (1998) 'Finnish in Sweden' in Ailbhe Ó Corráin and Séamus Mac Mathúna (eds), *Minority Languages in Scandinavia, Britain and Ireland*. Stockholm: Uppsala University, pp. 119–33.

Lindsay, Martin (1996) [1900] *Martin Luther: The Man who Started the Reformation*. Ross-Shire: Great Focus.

Lipset, M.S. (1963) *Political Man*. London: Mercury Books.

Llobera, Josep R. (1993) 'The Role of the State and the Nation in Europe' in Soledad García (ed.), *European Identity and the Search for Legitimacy*. London and New York: Pinter Publishers, pp. 64–80.

——(1996) 'The Role of Commemorations in (Ethno) Nation-Building. The Case of Catalonia' in Clare Mar-Molinero and Angel Smith (eds), *Nationalism and the Nation in the Iberian Peninsula: Competing and Conflicting Identities*. Oxford, Washington DC: Berg, pp. 191–206.

Ludlow, Piers (2002) 'Us or Them? The Meaning of Europe in British Political Discourse' in Malmborg, Mikael af and Stråth, Bo (eds), *The Meaning of Europe:*

Variety and Contention within and among Nations. Oxford, New York: Berg, pp. 101–24.

Lull, James (2000) *Media, Communication, Culture: A Global Approach.* Cambridge: Polity Press.

Maalouf, Amin (2000) *On Identity,* London: Harvill Press.

MacClancy, Jeremy (1996) 'Bilingualism and Multinationalism in the Basque Country' in Clare Mar-Molinero and Angel Smith (eds), *Nationalism and the Nation in the Iberian Peninsula: Competing and Conflicting Identities.* Oxford, Washington DC: Berg, pp. 207–20.

MacDonagh, Oliver (1983) *States of Mind: A Study of the Anglo-Irish Conflict 1780–1980.* London: HarperCollins.

Mac Giolla Chríost, Diarmait (2003) *Language, Identity and Conflict: A Comparative Study of Language in Ethnic Conflict in Europe and Eurasia.* London and New York: Routledge.

Mackiewicz, Wolfgang (2003) 'Multilingualism: A Major Role or a Minor Role', http://europa.ey.iny/comm/scic/interpreter/2003/mackiewicz.pdf.

Macleod, Iseabail and MacNeacail, Aonghas (1995) *Scotland: A Linguistic Double Helix.* Brussels: European Bureau for Lesser Used Languages.

Mac Póilin, Aodán (1996) 'Aspects of the Irish language Movement in Northern Ireland' in Máiréad Nic Craith ed., *Watching One's Tongue: Aspects of Romance and Celtic Languages.* Liverpool: Liverpool University Press, pp. 137–62.

——(1998) *The Linguistic Status of Ulster Scots.* Submission to the City Hall, Belfast.

Mac Póilin, Aodán and Ní Bhaoill, Róise (2004) *Irish: The Irish Language in Northern Ireland* (2nd edition). Ljouwert/Leeuwarden: Mercator-Education.

Magga, Ole Henrik (1995) 'The Sami Language Act' in Tove Skutnabb-Kangas and Robert Phillipson in collaboration with Mart Rannut (eds), *Linguistic Human Rights: Overcoming Linguistic Discrimination.* Berlin, New York: Mouton de Gruyter, pp. 219–33.

Maguire, Gabrielle (1991) *Our Own Language: An Irish Initiative.* Clevedon, Philadelphia, Adelaide: Multilingual Matters.

Malmborg, Mikael af (2002) 'The Dual Appeal of "Europe" in Italy' in Malmborg, Mikael af and Stråth, Bo (eds), *The Meaning of Europe: Variety and Contention within and among Nations.* Oxford, New York: Berg, pp. 51–76.

Malmborg, Mikael af and Stråth, Bo (eds) (2002) *The Meaning of Europe: Variety and Contention within and among Nations.* Oxford, New York: Berg.

Mandal, Ruth (1994) ' "Fortress Europe" and the Foreigners Within: Germany's Turks' in Victoria A. Goddard, Josep R. Llobera and Cris Shore (eds), *The Anthropology of Europe: Identity and Boundaries in Conflict.* Oxford and Washington DC: Berg, pp. 113–24.

Mar-Molinero, Clare (1994) 'Linguistic Nationalism and Minority Language Groups in the "New" Europe', *Journal of Multilingual and Multicultural Development,* 15(4), 319–28.

Mar-Molinero, Clare (1996) 'The Role of Language in Spanish Nation-Building', in Clare Mar-Molinero and Angel Smith (eds), *Nationalism and the Nation in the Iberian Peninsula: Competing and Conflicting Identities.* Oxford, Washington DC: Berg, pp. 69–87.

Mar-Molinero, Clare (2000) *The Politics of Language in the Spanish-Speaking World: From Colonisation to Globalisation.* London, New York: Routledge.

May, Stephen (2001) *Language and Minority Rights: Ethnicity, Nationalism and the Politics of Language*. Essex: Longman.

May, Stephen (2003) 'Language, Nationalism and Democracy in Europe' in Gabrielle Hogan-Brun and Stefan Wolff (eds), *Minority Languages in Europe: Frameworks, Status, Prospects*. Basingstoke: Palgrave/Macmillan, pp. 211–32.

Mazower, Mark (2001) *The Balkans: From the End of Byzantium to the Present Day*. London: Phoenix.

Mazumdar, Supir, Hindol Sengupta, Paul Mooney, Katka Krosnar, Emily Flynn, Marie Valla, B.J. Lee, Tracy Mcnicoll, Stephen Theil, Henk Rossouw, Amparo Lasso Rossouw, Maria and Jaime Cunningham (2005) 'Not the Queen's English', *Newsweek*, 7 March, 63–7.

McCafferty, Kevin (2001) 'Norway: Consensus and Diversity' in John, M. Kirk and Dónall Ó Baoill (eds), *Linguistic Politics: Language Policies for Northern Ireland, the Republic of Ireland, and Scotland*. Belfast: Cló Ollscoile na Banríona, pp. 89–103.

McCann, Eamonn (1974) *War and an Irish Town*. London: Penguin.

McCloskey, Brian (2001) 'Respecting Multilingualism in the Enlargement of the European Union – the Organisational Challenge', http://europe.eu.int/comm/translation/reading/articles/pdf/2001_06_07_vienna-mccluskey.pdf.

McClure, J. Derrick (1997) [1988] *Why Scots Matters*. Edinburgh: The Saltire Society.

——(2002) 'Developing Scots: How Far Have We Still To Go' in John M. Kirk and Dónall Ó Baoill (eds), *Language Planning and Education: Linguistic Issues in Northern Ireland, the Republic of Ireland, and Scotland*. Belfast: Cló Ollscoile na Banríona, pp. 186–91.

McCullogh, Bob (2000) 'Language, Discrimination and the Good Friday Agreement: the Case of Sign' in John, M. Kirk and Dónall Ó Baoill (eds), *Language and Politics: Northern Ireland, the Republic of Ireland, and Scotland*. Belfast: Cló Ollscoile na Banríona, pp. 91–5.

McDonagh, Ellen (2002) 'Cant: An Irish Traveller's Perspective' in John Kirk and Dónall Ó Baoill (eds), *Travellers and their Language*. Belfast: Cló Ollscoile na Banríona, pp. 155–60.

McDonagh, Michael (2000a) 'Ethnicity and Culture' in Frank Murphy, Cathleen McDonagh and Erica Sheehan (eds), *Travellers: Citizens of Ireland. Our Challenge to an Intercultural Irish Society in the 21st Century*. Dublin: The Parish of the Travelling People, pp. 26–31.

——(2000b) 'Nomadism' in Frank Murphy, Cathleen McDonagh and Erica Sheehan (eds), *Travellers: Citizens of Ireland. Our Challenge to an Intercultural Irish Society in the 21st Century*. Dublin: The Parish of the Travelling People, pp. 33–45.

——(2000c) 'Origins of the Travelling People' in Frank Murphy, Cathleen McDonagh and Erica Sheehan (eds), *Travellers: Citizens of Ireland. Our Challenge to an Intercultural Irish Society in the 21st Century*. Dublin: The Parish of the Travelling People, pp. 21–5.

McDonald, Maryon (1989) *We are not French! Language, Culture and Identity in Brittany*. London and New York: Routledge.

McGugan, Irene (2001) 'Scots in the Twenty-first Century' in John M. Kirk and Dónall Ó Baoill (eds), *Linguistic Politics: Language Policies for Northern*

Ireland, the Republic of Ireland, and Scotland. Belfast: Cló Ollscoile na Banríona, pp. 29–35.

McGugan, Irene (2002) 'More Progress for Scots in the Twenty-first Century' in John M. Kirk and Dónall Ó Baoill (eds), *Language Planning and Education: Linguistic Issues in Northern Ireland, the Republic of Ireland, and Scotland.* Belfast: Cló Ollscoile na Banríona, pp. 23–6.

McKee, Vincent (1994) *Politics of the Gaelic Language in Northern Ireland and the Scottish Hebrides: A Focus for Contrast,* Occasional Paper, 3. London: South Bank University.

McKeown, Laurence (1996) 'Jailteacht/Gaeltacht', *Cascando,* 5/6, pp. 42–9.

McLoughlin, Dympna (1994) 'Ethnicity and Irish Travellers: Reflections on Ní Shúinéar' in May McCann, Séamus Ó Síocháin and Joseph Ruane (eds), *Irish Travellers: Culture and Ethnicity.* Belfast: Institute of Irish Studies, pp. 54–77.

McWhorter, John (2002) *The Power of Babel: A Natural History of Language.* London: William Heinemann.

McVeigh, Robbie (1998) ' "There's no Racism because there's No Black People Here": Racism and Anti-Racism in Northern Ireland' in Paul Hainsworth (ed.), *Divided Society: Ethnic Minorities in Northern Ireland.* London: Pluto Press, pp. 11–32.

Meier_Braun, K. (1993) Die neue Völkerwanderung: Wenn Menschen nicht mehr wissen, warum sie bleiben sollen' in *Deutschland. Zeitschrift für Politik, Kultur, Wirtschaft und Wissenschaft,* 3, 44–9.

Memmi, Albert (1965) *The Colonizer and the Colonized.* New York: Orion Press.

Metzeltin, M. (1997) *Der Andere und der Fremde,* Eigenverlag 3 Eidechsen.

Montaña, Benjamin Tejerina (1996) 'Language and Basque Nationalism: Collective Identity, Social Conflict and Institutionalisation' in Clare Mar-Molinero and Angel Smith (eds), *Nationalism and the Nation in the Iberian Peninsula: Competing and Conflicting Identities.* Oxford, Washington DC: Berg, pp. 221–36.

Mugnaini Fabio and Giorgio Solinas (2001) 'Minority a Qualitative Concept?' in the Organisation Board of the Coimbra Group (ed.), *Migration, Minorities, Compensation: Issues of Cultural Identity in Europe.* Brussels: The Coimbra Groups Working Party for Folklore and European Ethnology, pp. 73–83.

Mundy, Simon (1997) *Making it Home: Europe and the Politics of Culture.* Amsterdam: European Cultural Foundation.

Murphy, Frank, McDonagh, Cathleen and Sheehan, Erica (eds) (2000) *Travellers: Citizens of Ireland. Our Challenge to an Intercultural Irish Society in the 21st Century.* Dublin: The Parish of the Travelling People.

Muzsnai, István (1999) 'The Recognition of Sign Language: A Threat or the Way to a Solution?' in Miklós Kontra, Robert Phillipson, Tove Skutnabb-Kangas and Tibor Várady (eds), *Language: A Right and a Resource: Approaching Linguistic Human Rights.* Budapest: Central European University Press, pp. 279–96.

Nelde, Peter (2000) 'Prerequisites for a New Language Policy', *Journal of Multilingual and Multicultural Development,* 21(5), 442–50.

Nelde, Peter, Strubell, Miguel and Williams, Glyn (1996) *Euromosaic: The Production and Reproduction of the Minority Language Groups in the European Union.* Luxembourg: Office for Official Publications of the European Communities.

Nekvapil, J. and Neustupný, J.V. (1998) 'Linguistic Communities in the Czech Republic' in Christina Bratt Paulston and Donald Peckham (eds), *Linguistic Minorities in Central and Eastern Europe.* Clevedon: Multilingual Matters, pp. 116–34.

Neven, Liz (2002) *Scots: The Scots Language in Education in Scotland*. Ljouwert/ Leeuwarden: Mercator-Education.

Nic Craith, Máiréad (1993) *Malartú Teanga: Meath na Gaeilge i gCorcaigh sa Naóú hAois Déag*. Bremen: European Society for Irish Studies.

——(1994) 'The Irish Language in a Comparative Context', *Oideas*, 42, 52–67.

——(1999) 'Irish Speakers in Northern Ireland, and the Good Friday Agreement', *Journal of Multilingual and Multicultural Development*, 20(6), 494–507.

——(2000a) 'Contested Identities and the Quest for Legitimacy', *Journal of Multilingual and Multicultural Development*, 21(5), 399–413.

——(2000b) 'Irish' in Jan Wirrer (ed.), *Minderheiten-und Regionalsprachen in Europa*. Wiesbaden: Westdeutscher Verlag, pp. 34–45.

——(2001) *Cultural Diversity in Northern Ireland and the Good Friday Agreement*. Dublin: Institute for British/Irish Studies.

——(2002a) *Plural Identities, Singular Narratives: The Case of Northern Ireland*. New York: Berghahn.

——(2002b) 'The Tiger No Longer Speaks Celtic: Economic Conditioning and the Irish Language' in Ullrich Kockel (ed.), *Culture and Economy: Contemporary Perspectives*. Hampshire: Ashgate, pp. 175–95.

——(2003a) *Culture and Identity Politics in Northern Ireland*. Basingstoke: Palgrave.

——(2003b) 'Facilitating or Generating Linguistic Diversity: The European Charter for Regional or Minority Languages' in Gabrielle Hogan-Brun and Stefan Wolff (eds), *Minority Languages in Europe: Frameworks, Status, Prospects*. Basingstoke: Palgrave/Macmillan, pp. 56–72.

——(2004) *Transfrontier Co-Operation and Cross-Border Languages in Europe*. Report submitted to EBLUL.

Nic Craith, Máiréad and Shuttleworth, Ian (1996) 'Irish in Northern Ireland: The 1991 Census' in Máiréad Nic Craith (ed.), *Watching One's Tongue: Aspects of Romance and Celtic Languages*. Liverpool: Liverpool University Press, pp. 163–75.

Nic Shuibhne, Niamh (2002) *EC Law and Minority Language Policy: Culture, Citizenship and Fundamental Rights*. The Hague, London, New York: Kluwer Law.

Nic Shuibhne, Niamh (2003) 'European Community Law and Minority Languages' in Dónall Ó Riagáin (ed.), *Language and Law in Northern Ireland*. Belfast: Cló Ollscoile na Banríona, pp. 122–37.

Ní Shúinéar, Sinéad (1994) 'Irish Travellers, Ethnicity and the Origins Question' in May McCann, Séamus Ó Síocháin and Joseph Ruane (eds), *Irish Travellers: Culture and Ethnicity*. Belfast: Institute of Irish Studies, pp. 54–77.

——(2002) 'The Curious Case of Shelta' in John Kirk and Dónall Ó Baoill (eds), *Travellers and their Language*. Belfast: Cló Ollscoile na Banríona, pp. 21–41.

——(2004) 'Apocrypha to Canon: Inventing Traveller History', *History Ireland*, 12(2), 15–19.

Niven, Liz (2002) 'Nae Chiels: Scots Language in Scotland' in John M. Kirk and Dónall Ó Baoill (eds), *Language Planning and Education: Linguistic Issues in Northern Ireland, the Republic of Ireland, and Scotland*. Belfast: Cló Ollscoile na Banríona, pp. 198–202.

Novitsky, Eugen (2003) 'The Russian Language in Finland and the Baltic Area', unpublished paper at third international conference of Partnership for Diversity Network, Helsinki.

Núñez Astrain, Luis (1997) *The Basques: Their Struggle for Independence*, translated from the French by Meic Stephens, Wales: Welsh Academic Press.

Oakes, L. (2001) *Language and National Identity: Comparing France and Sweden.* Amsterdam/Philadelphia: John Benjamens.

Ó Coinn, Seán (2002) 'Struchtúir na Gaelscolaíochta i dTuaisceart Éireann' in John M. Kirk and Dónall Ó Baoill (eds), *Language Planning and Education: Linguistic Issues in Northern Ireland, the Republic of Ireland, and Scotland.* Belfast: Cló Ollscoile na Banríona, pp. 52–5.

——(2003) 'An Ghaeilge agus Cúrsaí Oideachais i dTuaisceart Éireann' in Dónall Ó Riagáin (ed.), *Language and Law in Northern Ireland.* Belfast: Cló Ollscoile na Banríona, pp. 59–64.

O'Connell, John (1994) 'Ethnicity and Irish Travellers', in May McCann, Séamus Ó Síocháin and Joseph Ruane (eds), *Irish Travellers: Culture and Ethnicity.* Belfast: Institute of Irish Studies, pp. 110–20.

O'Dowd, Liam (2002) 'Transnational Integration and Cross-Border Regions in the European Union' in James Anderson (ed.), *Transnational Democracy: Political Spaces and Border Crossings.* London and New York: Routledge, pp. 111–28.

Ó hAdhmaill, Felim (1990) *The Function and Dynamics of the Ghetto: A Study of Nationalist West Belfast,* unpublished PhD thesis, University of Ulster.

Ó hAodha, Mícheál (2002) 'Travellers' Language: Some Irish Language Perspectives', in John Kirk and Dónall Ó Baoill (eds), *Travellers and their Language.* Belfast: Cló Ollscoile na Banríona, pp. 47–64.

Ommo Wilts, Kiel and Fort, Marron (1996) *North Frisia and Saterland: Frisian between Marsh and Moor.* Brussels: European Bureau for Lesser Used Languages.

O'Leary, S. (1996) *European Union Citizenship. The Options for Reform.* London: IPPR.

Ó Murchú, Máirtín (1992) 'The Irish Language' in Glanville Price (ed.), *The Celtic Connection.* Buckinghamshire: Princess Grace Irish Library, pp. 30–64.

——(2002) *Ag Dul Ó Chion? Cás na Gaeilge 1952–2002.* Dublin: an Aimsir Óg.

O' Reilly, Camille (1999) *The Irish Language in Northern Ireland: The Politics of Culture and Identity.* Basingstoke: Palgrave/Macmillan.

——(2001a) 'Introduction: Minority Languages, Ethnicity and the State in the European Union' in Camille O'Reilly (ed.), *Language, Ethnicity and the State: Vol 1: Minority Languages in the European Union.* Basingstoke: Palgrave, pp. 1–19.

O'Reilly, Camille (2001b) 'Irish Language, Irish Identity: Northern Ireland and the Republic of Ireland in the European Union' in Camille O'Reilly (ed.), *Language, Ethnicity and the State: Vol 1: Minority Languages in the European Union.* Basingstoke: Palgrave, pp. 78–103.

Ó Riagáin, Dónall (2000) *The Role of Non-Governmental Organisations in the Protection of Regional or Minority Languages,* Paper delivered at a seminar on the European Charter for Regional or Minority Languages in the Ministry of the Affairs of the Federation and of the Nationalities of the Russian Federation, Moscow, 19 May.

——(2001a) 'Language in Everyday Life' in Maurna Crozier and Richard Froggart (eds), *Cultural Traditions in Northern Ireland: Cultural Diversity in Contemporary Europe.* Belfast: Institute of Irish Studies, pp. 100–6.

——(2001b) 'Language Rights/Human Rights in Northern Ireland and the Role of the European Charter for Regional or Minority Languages' in John, M. Kirk and Dónall Ó Baoill (eds) (2001) *Linguistic Politics: Language Policies for Northern Ireland, the Republic of Ireland, and Scotland.* Belfast: Cló Ollscoile na Banríona, pp. 43–54.

——(2001c) 'Many Tongues but One Voice: A Personal Overview of the Role of the European Bureau for Lesser Used Languages in Promoting Europe's Regional and Minority Languages' in Camille O'Reilly (ed.), *Language, Ethnicity and the State: Vol 1: Minority Languages in the European Union.* Basingstoke: Palgrave, pp. 20–39.

——(2001d) 'The European Union and Lesser Used Languages', *MOST Journal on Multicultural Societies,* 3(1), http://www.unesco.org/most/vl3n1ria.htm.

——(2004) 'Irish a Step Closer to Becoming and EU Official Language', Eurolang, 11/27, http://www.eurolang.net/news.asp?id + 4828.

O'Rourke, P.J. (1994) *All the Trouble in the World.* London: Picador.

O'Sullivan, Dolores (2000) 'What is Culture?' in Frank Murphy, Cathleen McDonagh and Erica Sheehan (eds), *Travellers: Citizens of Ireland. Our Challenge to an Intercultural Irish Society in the 21st Century.* Dublin: The Parish of the Travelling People, pp. 14–20.

O'Toole, Fintan (2004) 'Have We Finished Drawing our Borders in Blood', *The Irish Times: The New Europe,* 11 May, p. 1.

Ozolins, Uldis (1999) 'Separating Language from Ethnicity: The Paradoxes of Strict Language Policies and Increasing Social Harmony in the Baltic States' in Miklós Kontra, Robert Phillipson, Tove Skutnabb-Kangas and Tibor Várady (eds), *Language: A Right and a Resource: Approaching Linguistic Human Rights.* Budapest: Central European University Press, pp. 245–62.

Packer, John (1999) 'Problems in Defining Minorities', in D. Fottrell and B. Bowring (eds), *Minority and Group Rights in the New Millennium,* The Hague: Kluwer Law International, pp. 223–74.

Painter, Joe (2002) 'Multi-level Citizenship, Identity and Regions in Contemporary Europe' in James Anderson (ed.), *Transnational Democracy: Political Spaces and Border Crossings.* London: Routledge, pp. 93–110.

Parsley, Ian J. (2002) 'Two Ulster Scotses – Authentic versus Synthetic' in John M. Kirk and Dónall Ó Baoill (eds), *Language Planning and Education: Linguistic Issues in Northern Ireland, the Republic of Ireland, and Scotland.* Belfast: Cló Ollscoile na Banríona, pp. 183–5.

Peura, Markku (2003) 'The Finnish Language in Sweden', unpublished paper at third international conference of Partnership for Diversity Network, Helsinki.

Poster, Mark (1990) *The Mode of Information.* Cambridge: Polity Press.

Pedersen, Karne Margrethe (1998) 'German in Denmark' in Ailbhe Ó Corráin and Séamus Mac Mathúna (eds), *Minority Languages in Scandinavia, Britain and Ireland.* Stockholm: Uppsala University, pp. 133–50.

Peover, Stephen (2001) 'Encouragement and Facilitation: A New Paradigm for Minority Language Education' in John, M. Kirk and Dónall Ó Baoill (eds), *Linguistic Politics: Language Policies for Northern Ireland, the Republic of Ireland, and Scotland.* Belfast: Cló Ollscoile na Banríona, pp. 195–204.

——(2002) 'The Current State of Irish-medium Education in Northern Ireland' in John M. Kirk and Dónall Ó Baoill (eds), *Language Planning and Education: Linguistic Issues in Northern Ireland, the Republic of Ireland, and Scotland.* Belfast: Cló Ollscoile na Banríona, pp. 124–30.

Permanent Representative of the Russian Federation to the United Nations (1996) *Human Rights Questions: Human Rights Situations and Reports of Special Rapporteurs and Representatives,* United Nations, http://www.un.org/documents/ga/docs/51/c3/ac351-1.3htm.

Pettegree, Andres (2002) 'The Dawn of Modern Europe' in John Stevenson (ed.), *The History of Europe*. London: Octopus Publishing Group, pp. 186–223.

Phales, K. and Swyngedouw, M. (2002) *National Identities and Representations of Citizenship. A Comparison of Turks, Moroccans and Working-class Belgians in Brussels*. Brussels: Centre for Interdisciplinary Studies.

Phillipson, Robert (1992) *Linguistic Imperialism*. Oxford: Oxford University Press.

——(1999) 'International Languages and International Human Rights' in Miklós Kontra, Robert Phillipson, Tove Skutnabb-Kangas and Tibor Várady (eds), *Language: A Right and a Resource: Approaching Linguistic Human Rights*. Budapest: Central European University Press, pp. 47–80.

——(2002) 'English for Emerging or Submerging Multiple European Identities' in John M. Kirk and Dónall Ó Baoill (eds), *Language Planning and Education: Linguistic Issues in Northern Ireland, the Republic of Ireland, and Scotland*. Belfast: Cló Ollscoile na Banríona, pp. 267–78.

——(2003) *English-Only Europe: Challenging Language Policy*. London and New York: Routledge.

Poleshchuk, Vadim (2001) 'The Limits of the Law. Estonia, Latvia and the European Commission: Changes in Language Regulation in 1999–2001', http://www.eumap.org/articles/content/40/402.

Porębski, Andrzej (1995) 'The Kashubes and Selected European Ethnic Groups in Change' in Brunon Synak (ed.), *The Ethnic Identities of European Minorities: Theory and Case Studies*. Gdansk: Wydawnictwo Uniwersytetu Gdańskiego, pp. 179–86.

Poulton, Hugh (1998) 'Linguistic Minorities in the Balkans (Albania, Greece and the Successor States of Former Yugoslavia)', in Christina Bratt Paulston and Donald Peckham (eds), *Linguistic Minorities in Central and Eastern Europe*. Clevedon: Multilingual Matters, pp. 37–79.

Power, Jimmy (2002) 'Cant: An Irish Traveller's Perspective' in John Kirk and Dónall Ó Baoill (eds), *Travellers and their Language*. Belfast: Cló Ollscoile na Banríona, pp. 161–8.

Price, Glanville (ed.) (2000) *Encyclopedia of the Languages of Europe*. Oxford: Blackwell.

Priestly, Tom (2000) 'Slovene in Austria' in Jan Wirrer (ed.), *Minderheiten-und Regionalsprachen in Europa*. Wiesbaden: Westdeutscher Verlag, pp. 222–34.

Pupavac, Vanessa (2001) 'Politics and Language Rights: A Case Study of School Grammars in Croatia' in Gabrielle Hogan-Brun and Stefan Wolff (eds), *Minority Languages in Europe: Frameworks, Status, Prospects*. Basingstoke: Palgrave/Macmillan, pp. 138–56.

Pupavac, Vanessa (2003) 'Politics and Language Rights: A Case Study of Language Politics in Croatia' in Gabrielle Hogan-Brun and Stefan Wolff (eds), *Minority Languages in Europe: Frameworks – Status – Prospects*, 138–55.

Rajendran, Charlene (1999) *Performing Identity: A Stage for Multilingual English and Multicultural Englishness*. Paper delivered at Looking into England, conference hosted by the British Council and the Centre for British and Comparative Cultural Studies at the University of Warwick, 12–18 December.

Reid, Anna (1997) *Borderland: A Journey through the History of Ukraine*. London: Phoenix.

Rex, John (1991) *Ethnic Identity and Ethnic Mobilisation in Britain*. Centre for Research in Ethnic Relations, Coventry: University of Warwick.

Reynolds, Mike (2001) 'Punjabi/Urdu in Sheffield: A Case Study of Language Maintenance and Language Loss' in Jane Cotterill and Anne Ife (eds), *Language Across Boundaries*. London, New York: British Association for Applied Linguistics in association with Continuum, pp. 99–118.

Riermersma, Alex (1998) *Implementing the Charter: The Netherlands Model*, Paper presented at conference on Our Language Heritage in Europe, City Hall, Belfast, 23 October.

Rogers, Carl (1997) 'Explorations in Terra Incognita', *American Anthropologist*, 99(4), 717–19.

Romaine, Suzanne (2002) 'The Impact of Language Policy in Endangered Languages', *MOST Journal on Multicultural Societies*, 4(2), 1–28, http://www.unesco.org/most/vl14nromaine.pdf.

RomNews Society (2003) *Facts on Roma in Europe*. Hamburg: RomNews Society.

Rowe, W. and Schelling, V. (1991) *Memory and Modernity: Popular Culture in Latin America*. London: Verso.

Said, Edward (1978) *Orientalism*. Harmondsworth: Penguin.

Sammallahti, Peeka (2000) 'Saami' in Jan Wirrer (ed.), *Minderheiten-und Regionalsprachen in Europa*. Wiesbaden: Westdeutscher Verlag, pp. 11–22.

Sampson, Anthony (1997) *The Scholar Gypsy: The Quest for a Family Secret*. London: John Murray.

Sands, Bobby (1982) *Skylark Sing Your Lonely Song – An Anthology of the Writings of Bobby Sands*. Dublin/Cork: Mercier Press.

Santer, Jacques (1996) Speech by the President of the European Commission at the Centre Européan de l'Alliance Française, Brussels, 25 June.

Schiller, Nina Glick and Fouron, Georges (2002) 'Long Distance Nationalism Defined' in Joan Vincent (ed.), *The Anthropology of Politics: A Reader in Ethnography, Theory, and Critique*. Oxford, Mass. USA: Blackwell, pp. 356–65.

Schröder, Konrad (1993) 'Languages' in Monica Shelley and Margaret Winck (eds), *Aspects of European Cultural Diversity*. London and New York: Routledge, pp. 13–64.

Sekulic, Dusko (1997) 'The Creation and Dissolution of the Multinational State: The Case of Yugoslavia', *Nations and Nationalism*, 3(2), 165–79.

Senelle, Robert (1996) 'The New Cultural Policy of the European Union' in Leonce Bekemans (ed.), *Culture: Building Stones for Europe 2002*. Brussels: College of Europe, European Interuniversity Press, pp. 63–98.

Seurujärvi-Kari, Irja and Pedersen, Steiner and Hirvoonen, Vuokko (1997) *The Sámi: The Indigenous People of Northernmost Europe*. Brussels: European Bureau for Lesser Used Languages.

Shaw, Denis (1998) ' "The Chickens of Versailles": The New Central and Eastern Europe' in Brian Graham (ed.), *Modern Europe: Place, Culture, Identity*. London, Sydney and Auckland: Arnold Press, pp. 121–40.

Shore, Cris (2000) *Building Europe: The Cultural Politics of European Integration*. London and New York: Routledge.

Shore, Cris and Black Annabel (1994) 'Citizens' Europe and the Construction of European Identity', in Victoria A. Goddard, Josep R. Llobera and Cris Shore (eds), *The Anthropology of Europe: Identity and Boundaries in Conflict*. Oxford and Washington DC: Berg, pp. 275–97.

Siddle, David (1992) 'Urbanisation, Population Mobility and the Evolution of Cultural Prejudice: Some Speculations on the Geography of Ignorance and the Growth of National Identity', *Geografiska Annaler*, 74B(3), pp. 155–66.

Škiljan, Dubraviko (2000) 'From Croato-Serbian to Croatian: Croatian Linguistic Identity', *Multilingua*, 19(1/2), 3–20.

Skutnabb-Kangas, Tove (1988) 'Multilingualism and the Education of Minority Children' in T. Skutnabb-Kangas and Jim Cummins (eds), *Minority Education: From Shame to Struggle*. Clevedon: Multilingual Matters, pp. 9–44.

——(1999) 'Linguistic Diversity, Human Rights and the "Free" Market' in Miklós Kontra, Robert Phillipson, Tove Skutnabb-Kangas and Tibor Várady (eds), *Language: A Right and a Resource: Approaching Linguistic Human Rights*. Budapest: Central European Press, pp. 187–222.

——(2000) *Linguistic Genocide in Education – or Worldwide Diversity and Human Rights?* Mahwah, NJ: Lawrence Erlbaum.

Skutnabb-Kangas, Tove, and Phillipson, Robert (1995) *Linguistic Human Rights: Overcoming Linguistic Discrimination*. Berlin, New York: Mouton de Gruyter.

Smith, Anthony (1981) *The Ethnic Revival*. Cambridge: Cambridge University Press.

——(1993) 'The Nation: Invented, Imagined, Reconstructed' in Marjorie Ringrose and Adam Lerner (eds), *Reimagining the Nation*. Buckingham, Philadelphia: Open University Press, pp. 9–28.

Smith, Dennis and Wright, Sue (1999) 'The Turn towards Democracy' in Dennis Smith and Sue Wright (eds), *Whose Europe? The Turn towards Democracy*. Oxford: Blackwell, pp. 1–18.

Smith, Len (2002) 'English Romani Language: Some Personal Thoughts' in John Kirk and Dónall Ó Baoill (eds), *Travellers and their Language*. Belfast: Cló Ollscoile na Banríona, pp. 192–6.

Smith, William (1994) 'The Irish Language and the Unionist Tradition' in P. Mistéil (ed.), *The Irish Language and the Unionist Tradition*. Belfast: The Ulster People's College, Ultach Trust, pp. 17–23.

Spires, Scott (1999) 'Lithuanian Linguistic Nationalism and the Cult of Antiquity', *Nations and Nationalism*, 5(4), 485–500.

Spohn, Willfried (2002) 'Continuities and Changes of Europe in German National Identity' in Mikael af Malmborg, and Bo Stråth (eds), *The Meaning of Europe: Variety and Contention within and among Nations*. Oxford, New York: Berg, pp. 285–310.

Stacul, Jaro (2001) 'When Language Does Not Matter: Regional Identity Formation in Northern Italy' in Camille O'Reilly (ed.), *Language, Ethnicity and the State: Vol 1: Minority Languages in the European Union*. Basingstoke: Palgrave, pp. 128–45.

Stepanenko, Viktor (2003) 'Identities and Language Policies in Ukraine: The Challenge of Nation-State Building' in Farmiah Daftary and François Grin (eds), *Nation-Building, Ethnicity and Language Politics in Transition Countries*. Flensburg: European Centre for Minority Issues, pp. 107–35.

Stevenson, John (2002) 'The Age of Revolution' in John Stevenson (ed.), *The History of Europe*. London: Octopus Publishing Group, pp. 224–279.

Stewart, Sheila (2002) 'Cant: an Irish Traveller's Perspective' in John Kirk and Dónall Ó Baoill (eds), *Travellers and their Language*. Belfast: Cló Ollscoile na Banríona, pp. 188–91.

Storkey, M. (2000) 'Using the School's Language Data to Estimate the Total Numbers of Speakers of London's Top 40 Languages' in P. Barker and J. Eversley (ed.), *Multilingual Capital: The Languages of London's Schoolchildren and their*

Relevance to Economic, Social and Educational Policies. London: Battlebridge Publications, pp. 63–6.

Stråth, Bo (2002) 'The Swedish Demarcation to Europe' in Malmborg, Mikael af and Stråth, Bo (eds), *The Meaning of Europe: Variety and Contention within and among Nations.* Oxford, New York: Berg, pp. 125–48.

Stuijt, Mark, Garay, Maido, Basmoreau, Mme and Del Bel, Thierry (1998) *Basque: The Basque Language in Education in France.* Ljouwert/Leeuwarden: Mercator-Education.

Suleiman, Yasir (2003) *The Arabic Language and National Identity.* Edinburgh: Edinburgh University Press.

Sundback, Barbro (1998) *The Åland Islands: A Success Story*, Paper presented at the Culture, Nation and Region in Europe conference, University of Cardiff, 10–11 September.

Svonni, Mikael (1998) 'Sami' in Ailbhe Ó Corráin and Séamus Mac Mathúna (eds), *Minority Languages in Scandinavia, Britain and Ireland.* Stockholm: Uppsala University, pp. 21–49.

Sweeney, K. (1988) *The Irish Language in Northern Ireland 1987, Preliminary Report of a Survey of Knowledge, Interest and Ability.* Belfast: Policy Planning and Research Unit.

Synak, Brunon (1995) 'The Kashubes' Ethnic Identity: Continuity and Change' in Brunon Synak (ed.), *The Ethnic Identities of European Minorities: Theory and Case Studies.* Gdansk: Wydawnictwo Uniwersytetu Gdańskiego, pp. 155–66.

Szalai, Andrea (1999) 'Linguistic Human Rights Problems among Romani and Boyash Speakers in Hungary with Special Attention to Education' in Miklós Kontra, Robert Phillipson, Tove Skutnabb-Kangas and Tibor Várady (eds), *Language: A Right and a Resource: Approaching Linguistic Human Rights.* Budapest: Central European University Press, pp. 297–315.

Tan, Dursan and Waldhoff, Hans-Peter (1996) 'Turkish Everyday Culture in Germany and its Prospects' in David Horrocks and Eva Kolinsky (eds), *Turkish Culture in German Society Today.* Oxford: Berghahn Books, pp. 137–56.

Tandefelt, Marika (1998) 'Swedish in Finland' in Ailbhe Ó Corráin and Séamus Mac Mathúna (eds), *Minority Languages in Scandinavia, Britain and Ireland.* Stockholm: Uppsala University, pp. 103–18.

Taylor, Charles (1994) 'The Politics of Recognition' in Charles Taylor (ed.), *Multiculturalism: Examining the Politics of Recognition.* Princeton: University Press, pp. 25–73.

Tejerina, Benjamin (2001) 'Protest Cycle, Political Violence and Social Movements in the Basque Country', *Nations and Nationalism*, 7(1), 39–57.

Theiler, Tobias (1999) *The 'Identity Policies' of the European Union.* Unpublished D. Phil thesis, University of Oxford.

The European Commission, Languages in Europe, http://europa.eu.int/comm/education/langauges/lang/europeanlanguages.html.

The European Convention (2003) *Draft Treaty Establishing a Constitution for Europe*, submitted to the European Council Meeting in Thessaloniki. Luxembourg: Office for Official Publications of the European Communities.

The Foundation on Inter-Ethnic Relations (1998) *The Oslo Recommendations regarding the Linguistic Rights of National Minorities and Explanatory Notes.* The Hague: The Foundation on Inter-Ethnic Relations.

The Swedish Assembly of Finland (n.d.) *Swedish in Finland: La Finlande Suédophone.* Helsinki: The Swedish Assembly of Finland.

Thuen, Trond (1995) 'Saami Peoplehood and Ethnopolitics in Norway' in Brunon Synak (ed.), *The Ethnic Identities of European Minorities: Theory and Case Studies*. Gdansk: Wydawnictwo Uniwersytetu Gdańskiego, pp. 95–116.

Timm, Lenora (2001) 'Ethnic Identity and Minority Language Survival in Brittany' in Camille O'Reilly (ed.), *Language, Ethnicity and the State: Vol 1: Minority Languages in the European Union*. Basingstoke: Palgrave, pp. 104–27.

Toggenburg, Gabriel (2004) 'United in Diversity', *Academia*, 35, 18–19.

Tonra, B. and Dunne, D. (1996) 'A European Cultural Identity: Myth, Reality or Aspiration?', http://www.ucd.ie/~dei/.

Traynor, Ian (2003) 'Gypsy Leaders Demand Better Deal in Europe', *The Guardian*, 1 July, p. 12.

Treaty of Amsterdam (1997) Amending The Treaty On European Union, The Treaties Establishing The European Communities And Related Acts, *Official Journal* C 340, 10 November 1997, http://europa.eu.int/eur-lex/en/treaties/dat/amsterdam.html#0145010077.

Treaty on European Union (1992) *Official Journal*, C 191, 29 July 1992, http://europa.eu.int/eur-lex/en/treaties/dat/EU_treaty.html.

Tsilevich, Boris (2001) 'Development of the Language Legislation in the Baltic States', *MOST Journal on Multicultural Societies*, 3(2), http://www.unesco.org/most/vl3n2tsilevich.htm.

Tsitselikis, Konstantinos, Giorgis Mavrommatis and Domenico Morelli (2003) *Turkish: The Turkish Language in Education in Greece*. Ljouwert/Leeuwarden: Mercator-Education.

Tsoukalas, Constantine (2002) 'The Irony of Symbolic Reciprocities – the Greek Meaning of "Europe" as a Historical Inversion of the European Meaning of "Greece"' in Malmborg, Mikael af and Stråth, Bo (eds), *The Meaning of Europe: Variety and Contention within and among Nations*. Oxford, New York: Berg, pp. 27–50.

Turner, Brian (1988) *Status*. Milton Keynes: Open University Press.

Turner, Graham (2003) 'On Policies and Prospects for British Sign Language' in Gabrielle Hogan-Brun and Stefan Wolff (eds), *Minority Languages in Europe: Frameworks, Status, Prospects*. Basingstoke: Palgrave/Macmillan, pp. 192–210.

ULTACH Trust/Iontaobhas ULTACH (1994) *Second Report/an Dara Tuairisc 1991–93*. Belfast: ULTACH Trust.

UNESCO (2002) *Universal Declaration of Cultural Diversity*, http://www.unesco.org/culture/pluralism/diversity.

Valkeapää, Nils-Aslak (1983) *Greetings from Lappland: The Sami – Europe's Forgotten People*. London: Totowa, NJ, USA: Zed Press.

Van Langevelde, AB (1993) 'Migration and Language in Friesland', *Journal of Multilingual and Multicultural Development*, 5, 393–409.

——(1994) 'Language and Economy in Friesland: A First Step towards Development of a Theory', *Journal of Social and Economic Geography*, 85(1), 67–77.

Volf, Miroslav (1996) *Exclusion and Embrace: A Theological Exploration of Identity, Otherness and Reconciliation*. Nashville: Abingdon Press.

Votruba, Martin (1998) 'Linguistic Minorities in Slovakia' in Christina Bratt Paulston and Donald Peckham (eds), *Linguistic Minorities in Central and Eastern Europe*. Clevedon: Multilingual Matters, pp. 255–79.

Vuorela, Katri and Borin, Lars (1998) 'Finnish Romani' in Ailbhe Ó Corráin and Séamus Mac Mathúna (eds), *Minority Languages in Scandinavia, Britain and Ireland*. Stockholm: Uppsala University, pp. 77–101.

Wacquant, L.D. (1989) 'Towards a Reflexive Sociology: A Workshop with Pierre Bourdieu', *Sociological Theory*, 7(1), 26–63.

Wadham-Smith, Nick and Clift, Naomi (eds) (2000) *Looking Into England: British Studies Now*, 13. London: British Council.

Warasin, Markus (2003) *SG Report on the EU Convention*. Brussels: European Bureau for Lesser-Used Languages.

Watson, Anna Man-Wah (2000) 'Language, Discrimination and the Good Friday Agreement: The Case of Cantonese' in John, M. Kirk and Dónall Ó Baoill (eds), *Language and Politics: Northern Ireland, the Republic of Ireland, and Scotland*. Belfast: Cló Ollscoile na Banríona, pp. 97–9.

Watson, Anna Manwah and McKnight, Eleanor (1998) 'Race and Ethnicity in Northern Ireland: the Chinese Community' in Paul Hainsworth (ed.), *Divided Society: Ethnic Minorities and Racism in Northern Ireland*. London: Pluto Press, pp. 127–52.

Watson, Rory (2003) 'Toned-down Constitution "Still Open to Change" ', *The Times*, 27 May, p. 4.

Webster, Jason (2005) *Andalus: Unlocking the Secrets of Moorish Spain*. London: Black Swan.

Weinstock, Nathan, Haïm-Vidal Sephiha and Anita Barrera-Schoonheere (1997) *Yiddish and Judeo-Spanish: A European Heritage*. Brussels: European Bureau for Lesser Used Languages.

Welsh Assembly Government (2003) *Iaith Pawb: A National Action Plan for a Bilingual Wales*. Cardiff: Welsh Assembly Government.

Weil, Simone (2002) [1952] *The Need for Roots: Prelude to a Declaration of Duties towards Mankind*. London and New York: Routledge.

Whorf, Benjamin (1956) *Language, Thought and Reality: Selected Writings of B. L. Whorf* (ed.), J. Carroll. New York: John Wiley & Sons.

Wicherkiewicz, Tomasz (2000) 'Kashubian' in Jan Wirrer (ed.), *Minderheiten-und Regionalsprachen in Europa*. Wiesbaden: Westdeutscher Verlag, pp. 213–21.

——(2004) *Kashubian: The Kashubian Language in Poland*. Ljouwert/Leeuwarden: Mercator-Education.

Wieviorka, M. (1995) *The Arena of Racism*. Thousand Oaks, CA: Sage.

Williams, Colin H. (1984) 'More than Tongue can Tell: Linguistic Factors in Ethnic Separatism' in John Edwards (ed.), *Linguistic Minorities, Policies and Pluralism*. London: Academic Press, pp. 179–219.

——(1991) 'The Cultural Rights of Minorities: Recognition and Implementation...' in Jana Plichtová (ed.), *Minorities in Politics. Cultural and Languages Rights*. Bratislava: Czechoslovak Committee of European Cultural Foundation, pp. 107–20.

——(1998) *Community Language Planning: the Welsh Experience*. Paper presented at conference on Our Language Heritage in Europe, City Hall, Belfast, 23 October.

Withers, Charles (1984) *Gaelic in Scotland 1618–1981: The Geographical History of a Language*. Edinburgh: John Donald Publishers Ltd.

Wmffre, Iwan (2001) 'Is Societal Bilingualism Sustainable?: Reflections and Indications from the Celtic Countries' in the Organisation Board of the Coimbra Group (ed.), *Migration, Minorities, Compensation: Issues of Cultural Identity in Europe*. Brussels: The Coimbra Group's Working Party for Folklore and European Ethnology, pp. 121–42.

Wolff, Stefan (2000) *German Minorities in Europe: Ethnic Identity and Cultural Belonging*. New York, Oxford: Berghahn.

Wolf-Knits, Ulrika (2001) 'The Finland Swedes: A Compensating Minority' in the Organisation Board of the Coimbra Group (ed.), *Migration, Minorities, Compensation: Issues of Cultural Identity in Europe*. Brussels: The Coimbra Group's Working Party for Folklore and European Ethnology, pp. 143–51.

Woll, Bencie (2001) 'Exploring Language, Culture and Identity: Insights from Sign Language and the Deaf Community' in Jane Cotterill and Anne Ife (eds), *Language Across Boundaries*. London, New York: British Association for Applied Linguistics in association with Continuum; pp. 65–80.

Woll, Bencie, Rachel Sutton-Spence and Frances Elton (2001) 'Multilingualism: The Global Approach to Sign Languages', in Ceil Lucas (ed.), *The Sociolinguistics of Sign Languages*. Cambridge: University Press, pp. 8–32.

Wright, Sue (2000a) *Community and Communication: The Role of Language in Nation-State Building and European Integration*. Clevedon: Multilingual Matters.

Wrights, Sue (2000b) 'Jacobins, Regionalists and the Council of Europe's Charter for Regional and Minority Languages', *Journal of Multilingual and Multicultural Development*, 21(5), 414–24.

Journals

Contact Bulletin
Ogmios: Foundation for Endangered Langauges
The Economist

Newspapers

The Irish Times
The Times
The Guardian

Selection of relevant websites

Charter of Fundamental Rights of The European Union
    http://www.europarl.eu.int/charter/pdf/text_en.pdf.
Charter of the United Nations
    http://www.un.org/aboutun/charter/index.html.
Consolidated Version of the Treaty Establishing the European Community (Nice)
    http://europa.eu.int/eur-lex/lex/en/treaties/dat/12002E/pdf/12002E_EN.pdf.
Demoak (Works but no English Version)
    http://www.demoak.ht.st.
Ethnologue
    http://www.ethnologue.com/.
Eurolang
    http://www.eurolang.net/.

Euromosaic
   http://www.uoc.es/euromosaic/.
European Bureau for Lesser Used Languages
   http://www.eblul.org/.
European Centre for Minority Issues (Flensburg, Germany)
   http://www.ecmi.de/.
European Charter for Regional or Minority Languages
   http://conventions.coe.int/treaty/en/Treaties/Html/148.htm.
European Language Council/Conseil Européen pour les Langues
   http://www.fu-berlin.de/elc/.
European Research Centre on Migration and Ethnic Relations
   http://www.ercomer.org.
Framework Convention for the Protection of National Minorities
   http://conventions.coe.int/Treaty/EN/Treaties/Html/157.htm.
Good Friday Agreement
   http://cain.ulst.ac.uk/events/peace/docs/agreement.htm.
International Covenant on Civil and Political Rights
   http://www.unhchr.ch/html/menu3/b/a_ccpr.htm.
Interreg 3
   http://www.interreg3.com/.
Languages in Europe
   http://europa.eu.int/comm/education/languages/lang/europeanlan-
   guages.html.
Mercator-Education
   http://www.mercator-education.org.
Mercator-Legislation
   http://www.troc.es/ciemen/mercator/index-gb.htm.
Mercator-Media
   http://www.aber.ac.uk/~merwww/.
Minorities at Risk Project
   http://www.geocities.com/~patrin/marp.htm.
Minority Language Links
   http://biblioteca.udg.es/fl/aucoc/min_link.htm.
Northern Ireland Census (2001)
   www.nisra.gov.uk/census/Census2001Output/CASTables/cas_tables.html.
Roma Gypsies
   http://www.coe.int/T/DG3/RomaTravellers/Default_en.asp.
Special Eurobarometer 'Europeans and Languages'
   http://europa.eu.int/comm/education/policies/lang/languages/eurobarometer54_
   en.html.
Sønderjylland/Schleswig Region
   http://www.region.dk.
The Foundation for Endangered Languages. University of Bristol
   http://www.bris.ac.uk/Depts/Philosophy/CTLL/FEL/.
The Oslo Recommendations Regarding the Linguistic Rights of National Minorities
   http://www.osce.org/hcnm/documents/recommendations/oslo/index.php3.
Treaty of Amsterdam
   http://europa.eu.int/eur-lex/lex/en/treaties/dat/11997D/htm/11997D.html.
Treaty on European Union (Maastricht)
   http://europa.eu.int/en/record/mt/top.html.

Treaty establishing a Constitution for Europe
  http://europa.eu.int/eur-lex/lex/
  JOHtml.do?uri = OJ:C:2004:310:SOM:EN:HTML.
Ulster-Scots Agency
  http://www.ulsterscotsagency.com.
Universal Declaration of Human Rights
  http://www.un.org/Overview/rights.html.
Universal Declaration of Linguistic Rights
  http://www.egt.ie/udhr/udlr-en.html.

Index